THINKING IN ART:

A Philosophical Approach to Art Education

CHARLES M. DORN
The Florida State University

1994

National Art Education Association
1916 Association Drive
Reston, VA 22091-1590

About NAEA

Founded in 1947, the National Art Education Association is the largest professional art education association in the world. Membership includes elementary and secondary teachers, artists, administrators, museum educators, arts council staff, and university professors from throughout the United States and 66 foreign countries. NAEA's mission is to advance art education through professional development, service, advancement of knowledge, and leadership.

About the Noted Scholar Series

Thinking in Art: A Philosophical Approach to Art Education by Charles Dorn is in the NAEA's noted scholar series. The series was designed to recognize and honor art education scholars. The other titles in the noted scholar series are *The World of Art Education* by Vincent Lanier, *Collaboration in Art Education* by Al Hurwitz, and *Revisitations: Ten Little Pieces on Art Education* by Harlan E. Hoffa.

About the Author

Dr. Charles M. Dorn is currently a Professor of Art Education and Arts Administration and Director of the Center for Arts Administration at Florida State University, Tallahassee, Florida. He is a former Chair of the F.S.U.'s Department of Art Education and prior to coming to F.S.U. was Head of Purdue University's Department of Creative Arts. His teaching and administrative contributions include appointments at California State University, Union University, and the National College of Education where he also was a teacher of art grades 1-8.

Professor Dorn served both as Executive Director and as President of the National Art Education Association and is an NAEA Fellow and Founding Fellow of the American Council for the Arts in Education.

© 1994 The National Art Education Association, 1916 Association Drive, Reston, VA 22091-1590.

ISBN 0-937652-69-5

To Jo, Jan and Chip who believed
in me and patiently waited, and to
Ralph Beelke whose professionalism
inspired me.

Table of Contents

Acknowledgments

I am indebted to a number of individuals and groups for the opportunity, the inspiration and the ideas expressed in this work. For the opportunity to publish my thoughts collected from over 40 years of teaching and administering art programs, I am indebted to the 1989-90 NAEA Board and to the 1993-94 Board for honoring that commitment.

I am also indebted to the 1961-62 NAEA Council who took the chance of hiring a relatively unknown college professor to assume the post of Executive Secretary, to the NAEA membership who elected me its president and the 1976-78 NAEA Boards who supported my efforts in that office. These opportunities made it possible to model my own professional goal after some of the art teaching professions most distinguished leaders including such professionals as Ralph Beelke, Edward Mattil, June McFee, Laura Chapman, Elliot Eisner, Arthur Efland, Ed Feldman, Guy Hubbard, Mary Rouse, Irving Kaufman, Jerry Hausman, Al Hurwitz, Manny Barkan, Reid Hastie, Ken Lansing, Stanley Madeja and Harlan Hoffa to mention only a few.

As to the text's content, I am particularly indebted to Professor David Wright for his ideas on 20th century thought, to Roger Scruton whose ideas on philosophy I have generously borrowed and to Andrew Harrison for his thoughts on making and thinking. And the greatest debt of all to my graduate students at Purdue and Florida State for their attention and late night efforts to help me make some sense out of these excursions into the ineffable.

Lastly, I am indebted to all those who read the manuscript, and helped improve it including Jerry Hausman who read it all in draft form and tried his best to keep me honest. To Pam and Sharon, who did the grueling work of deciphering my hieroglyphics and to Mary Fitzsimmons and Carol May who took on the major task of editing the final draft for publication. To these individuals and many others, I am especially thankful.

Foreword

At almost every point in its history, art education seems to be moved by the educational fashion of the times to embrace a singular view of how schools can best educate children and youth in art. When, as a field, we focus on a single view of what we should achieve, we fail to realize the much greater potential that exists for expanding our vision about educating children's artistic thinking and creating. Presently, we are focused on the potential to enhance student cognitive development through art learning, which narrows our vision and limits both what teachers can teach and what children can learn in school art. What is needed, rather, is a philosophical approach to art curriculum conception that offers newer ways to think about the questions of whom to teach, what to teach and how to teach it. Such an approach is offered in this text, and it provides the possibility of more than one curriculum model being used in the pursuit of effective art teaching and learning in schools.

Adoption of a more inclusive view, first requires a look at the philosophical premises which fund these differing modes of thought and which, in turn, inspire differing conceptions of art. Because the method is philosophical, it requires an understanding of the philosophical assumptions that drive these conceptions. This is necessary to inform both how philosophical thought relates to artistic thinking and creating and also how different modes of thinking relate to the individual reader's personal frame of reference for thinking about and making art.

When teaching is approached through examining differing philosophical positions, the reader can begin to see how concepts in art and education relate to 20th century thought and how the conceptions held by artists, art historians, art critics, and even scholars in other fields are shaped more by their frame of mind than by the art disciplines they work in. Breaking down these art disciplinary barriers also leads to a greater awareness of the notion that artistic thinking and making can be a unified conception rather than separate and fractious ways for thinking about and making art and, by extension, for educating.

Because teachers are concerned about art as an educational process, readers who are teachers should view these conceptions as paradigms or philosophically funded frames of mind that can be used to think about art and education and that offer multiple rather than singular solutions to curriculum practice. More importantly, these paradigms suggest that the disciplinary distinctions currently made between artists, art historians, and art critics are no longer viable, that we no longer need to see ourselves as a field of competing disciplines and that we now have more cohesive ways to think about art and its role in education.

When 20th century artistic paradigms are compared to the claims of art curriculum theorists, readers will find that these paradigms cohere with the curricular paradigms many art educators advocate, and ones which provide us with many different but practically tested curricular plans to be used by teachers as curriculum makers in relating their personal conceptions of art to the curriculum they use in the art classroom. Teachers thus have paradigms to use as guides in thinking about the who, what and how questions' paradigms that are consistent with their own values and that can be tested in curricular practice.

Charles M. Dorn

Introduction

Philosophy, Art and Education

Developing art curricula in today's schools requires those responsible to provide thoughtful answers to the curriculum questions of *whom* to teach, *what* to teach, and *when* and *how* to teach it. The answers to these questions rest heavily on responses to the even more important question of what should be the goals of art education in American schools. Since art was first introduced into American schools in 1842, goals and programs have undergone almost continuous change, without, however, providing answers on which emphases are most worthy of support. This monograph is, then, about schools deciding upon the proper goals for the art program and about helping teachers to understand and wisely select goals that reflect both doing the right thing and doing it right.

Knowing where art education has been in the past can assist in making wiser claims for the future. And American art educators over the past 170 years have responded in many different ways to curricular issues. However, the continuous change that has historically characterized this field has been driven not so much by any new knowledge of children, art or education, but rather by shifts in the social beliefs and educational priorities of the times. Art education curricula in American schools have reflected at least nine major thrusts since 1821:

1. Training in eye, hand, and perceptual faculties.

2. Training for artists and designers.

3. Teaching drawing.

4. Teaching picture study, art appreciation and the study of taste and beauty.

5. Teaching art in everyday life.

6. Teaching art as instrumental learning.

7. Teaching art as disciplinary study.

8. Fostering creativity and

9. Improving self-image.

Art Education for the Training of Eye/Hand and Perceptual Faculties

When art was first introduced into the public schools in Boston by William Bentley Fowle, its purpose was its supposed disciplinary value in training the eye, hand, and perceptual faculties. Between 1821-1851 the chief emphasis in art education was on form. Instruction was highly formal and mechanical in all grades; for example, first grade children dealt with such concepts as the axis of symmetry, the tangential union of lines, semi-diagonals, and concentric squares. Object drawing frequently was done with the aid of mechanical instruments; linear drawing and the study of perspective were common parts of the program in all grades; and courses in drawing and art, which were never clearly separated, bore such titles as "isometric projection and shadows," "size," " form," "geometric design," "orthographic projection and shadows," and "linear drawing and measuring."

Art Education for Training Artists and Designers

Growth of the New England textile industry during the period 1851-1870 created a demand for artists and textile designers and for the public schools to supply them. Because New England industries at the time were striving to compete with European products of skilled design, the commercial possibilities of art were discovered. Public schools in industrial centers came to be looked upon as a place to train technical designers. Tedious drawings from cast or still life and mechanical teaching of drawing were prevalent in the period.

Art Education to Teach Drawing

In 1872 Walter Smith was brought from England to become State Director of Art Education, Scholastic and Industrial, for the State of Massachusetts and principal of the Massachusetts Normal Art School. Smith's drawing manual, *Teacher's Manual of Freehand Drawing and Designing*, had an important influence on the teaching of art from 1872-1900. Logan gives a description of Smith's Manual with its emphasis on great detail and skill:

> After the squares filled with line patterns came drawings of triangles and polygons. On the next page is the Greek cross, the Maltese cross, and a silver cup; then simple and compound curves. In order followed flat molding, wave scrolls; vases; historical ornaments, rosettes; objects based on simple division of the central vertical line (vase, hourglass); conventional ornament; conventionalized leaves; letters and figures; designs from natural foliage; horizontal, vertical, central repetition; ornament

from medieval manuscript; drawing from nature (tomato leaf); designing, horizontal molding, maple leaf; symmetry, botanical analysis; monograms and rosettes; a page of snow crystals; a design for a lace curtain. (Logan, 1942, p. 67)

Art as Child Centered and As Education in Taste and Beauty

At the beginning of the twentieth century, progressive education, the child-centered movement, and art as education in taste and beauty all began to influence art teaching in the schools. The aims of art in the public schools shifted to emphasize creative expression, originality, and the appreciation and study of taste and beauty. In the child-centered approach, students were urged to express their ideas freely on any subject and with any material they wished to select. During the period 1901-1920, programs favoring those areas of learning related to the promotion of drives, urges, and interests were stressed. Emphasis was placed upon broad, creative experience. It was believed that the individual needed technique only to make the presentation of meanings clearer, and therefore technique was only a part of the natural process of expression.

In stark contrast with the progressives were the efforts in the popular journal, *Applied Arts Book*, to promote by every legitimate means the progress of sound art instruction and the development of public taste. To achieve taste and beauty the journal recommended the drawing of flowers in order to gain an understanding of the principles of variety, rhythm and balance. By 1915, the journal had expanded to include projects in bookbinding, leather tooling, lettering, blackboard drawing and birdhouse construction for the expressed purpose of helping students improve their taste and create beauty.

Art in Everyday Life Movement

The introduction of art for useful and everyday purposes was the distinct contribution of the period, 1927-1947. Emphasis in this period was given to both the development of good taste and the selection of items for daily use. The Owatonna Art Education Project and the Harriet and Vetta Goldstein book (1947), *Art in Everyday Life*, greatly influenced art educators. The consensus was that art in the school should not be conceived as something distinct from life, but rather as experiencing life, as participating in life, as life itself. Art as a school subject was supposed to grow logically out of the child's experience taken as a whole, and the art education program should be planned with reference to the needs of boys and girls (Goldstein, 1939, p. 115). Good taste was important in the study of art because of the experts' view at the time that we are all consumers and every time we make a purchase, however humble, we are consciously or unconsciously using our power to choose. Since art exists in most of the objects seen and used every-

3

day, one of the great needs of the consumer was a knowledge of the principles fundamental to good taste.

Art as Instrumental Learning

Strongly influenced by the philosophy of John Dewey, art education from 1948-1962 moved strongly in the direction of art as a means to an end rather than an end in itself (Dewey, 1947). Dewey believed that when an activity is productive of an object which affords continuously renewed delight it requires that the object be, with its successive consequences, indefinitely instrumental to new satisfying events. In his view the quality of great art was its renewed instrumentality for further consummatory experiences.

During this period, art education strongly emphasized the importance of social interaction. Supporters of this view held that

1. To be a member of the arts is to join a community of individuals (Read, 1953).

2. The art program provides opportunities for children to become a part of the total human picture while working to express ideas in group projects (Keiler, 1951).

3. The group is also a creative force in art and

4. Individual creativity is not destroyed by group action because an art work is essentially creative (Shultz & Shores, 1952). The art experience in this context was considered to be an inextricable part of the social experience where the quality and value of an activity must be considered in relation to life in a community as well as in relation to the development of the child.

The writings of Viktor Lowenfeld especially his book *Creative and Mental Growth* were particularly important in establishing the psychological value of art education during this period. Lowenfeld believed that art plays an important part in the integration of the personality and in the forms of growth responsible for a well-balanced human being. He believed that the child by identifying himself or herself with art media, through experiencing them in their living quality, would gain appreciation and insight into the meaningfulness of art and social culture.

Art Education as Disciplinary Study

The current period of American art education is said to have begun in 1962 when Manuel Barkan predicted a renewed energy would become apparent in the creative development of teaching materials and courses in art history and criticism. Barkan's view was not simple speculation, but was developed in

4

the form of a carefully constructed position using Bruner's arguments on the primacy of the discipline as a basis for new curricular conceptions. Barkan's "prophecy" was essentially a new curricular conception of the field in which he, unlike Lowenfeld, proposed, "that artistic activity is anywhere the same, whether at the frontier of art or in the third grade classroom" (Barkan, 1962, p. 14). His 1962 prediction about the growth of courses in history and criticism challenged the then popular notions of creativity and classroom approaches using a variety of art media. Barkan challenged his readers to accept the notion that the student learning art is an artist. But it was his stress on art education's new cognitive mode which attracted the attention of his contemporaries.

Barkan made essentially three claims in support of art cognitive studies in general and of the study of art history and criticism in particular. First, he proposed that there is a subject matter of the field of art; secondly, he likened the creating of art to creating with verbal language; and thirdly, he supported the need for students to develop artistic judgment through acquaintance with and careful study of great works of art.

In the 1970's and 1980's, Barkan's prophesy provided one of the bases for what we now know as discipline-based art education or DBAE. This particular effort supported by the J. Paul Getty Trust has been described by a number of different art education scholars. For example, Ralph Smith (1987), viewed formal art study as important grounding for the concept of art as a school subject with distinct goals, content, and methods. In his view, the purpose of the new content is to develop an educated understanding of art itself, through helping students gain an understanding of mature arts and developing those qualities of mind necessary to engage in perceptual finesse. With respect to the new academics he concludes, "In this respect, one can say that the principle purpose of art education is the fashioning of worthwhile disposition in the artistic realm" (Smith, 1987, p. 27).

Not all U.S. art educators, of course, agree with the DBAE approach, and some are challenging the concept of art as specified general studies. Hausman, (1988) for example, although believing in accountability, views the world of art as one in which individuals confront diverse situations requiring different orientations and modification in response. He questions the DBAE approach of a top-down, district-wide curriculum that can be evaluated like other subjects and/or make an entire school district accountable. More to the point, Hausman notes "there's no academic super structure or verbal facade that explains or analyzes the nature of art" (Hausman, 1988, p. 112).

Hausman, along with other rationalists in the field, values the notion that art teachers should be treated like professionals and given the authority to design programs for their students and themselves. London, (1988) like Hausman, is fearful of art teachers being given a perspective of art education that precludes to any other contending view. Burton, in a similar vein, is concerned that efforts to help children know about the art of others could mute the children's voices in the process (Burton, Lederman, & London, 1988) while Brigham warns that we cannot capture the meanings of fine art objects through words just as the need to convey and represent in art cannot be expressed linguistically (Brigham, 1988, p. 69). What these varying views do affirm is that matters relating to making and thinking about art are ones about which reasonable people reasonably disagree. Such disagreements do not necessarily signify that any one point of view is either right or wrong, but rather imply that like colleagues in other school subject disciplines, art educators hold diverse opinions, values and judgments about which course of action to pursue in educating children and youth in art.

This diversity of opinion does not, in itself, make art education a discipline; it is also incumbent that opinions and judgments be based on coherent resources, or evidence, and that rational systems of logic be used to analyze and compare alternative courses of action. Unfortunately in applied fields such as education, there is always a gap between those who perform as scholars or theorists and those whose job it is to apply theory in practice. Although those who theorize may have at one time been practitioners and practitioners fresh from their graduate programs may have, at one time, been theorists, both the educational climate of today's schools and the recollections of theories once learned are changed over time.

For the last three decades, the art teaching profession has sought a discipline-based conception upon which to base a unified curriculum sequence and scope in the school art program. This search has accelerated in recent times, partly because many in the profession feel they need a publicly acceptable rationale that gives the arts academic parity with the "three R's." Examples of such efforts include the CEMREL Aesthetic Education Project of the 1960's and the Getty Discipline Based Art Education Project of the 1980's, both of which have focused on increasing scholarly art study and on shifting the art program emphasis from the studio to the study of art history, art criticism and aesthetics.

The struggle of the art teaching profession to agree on a single conceptual basis for determining the curriculum is well documented in the literature of the field. Lanier (1972) identified four historically different objectives in his review of the art education literature: (1) those benefits which promote the training of the professional artist, (2) exposure to genteel accomplishments such as embroidery and painting on china for the daughters of the wealthy, (3) inculcating standards of good taste among potential consumers of manufactured goods, and (4) promoting art skills among those who might later use those art skills in industry. Carlisle (1982) also pointed out the existence of such goals as an appreciation of the beautiful, creative power as a divine gift, art as a way of life, art as visual problem solving, art as inventive and

metaphysical truth, art as transcendental moral principles, art as visual literacy, art as environmental design, and art as human relationships.

Others, including Efland and Harris, also have identified the field's
emphases over time in differing aesthetic and psychological orientations.
Efland (1979) identified four curriculum orientations: (1) mimetic aesthetics
as psychological behaviorism, (2) pragmatic aesthetics with cognitive psychology, (3) expressive aesthetics with psychoanalytic psychology, and (4)
objective aesthetics with Gestalt psychology. Harris (1963) outlined, in great
detail, three historical drawing theories for children, and one of his own: (1)
gestalt theory, (2) organismic theory, (3) theories assuming that organization in drawings is given by experience and (4) (his own) neuro-psychologic
theory of perception.

The views of these authors as well as those supporting the differing historical emphases mentioned earlier suggest that art educators not only have
traditionally embraced various ideas, but also, on today's and future answers
to what to teach, how to teach it and to whom remain divided. Art educators
frequently associated with the Getty disciplined based art education
approach, (DBAE) include Smith, Eisner, Clark, Day, Greer and Broudy.
They support the notion that there is an agreed-upon body of scholarly content which must be learned and manipulated. Others including London,
Burton, Hausman, and Gardner that art education should have both unity and
diversity in its approach.

This split puts pressure on art teachers to incorporate the disciplines of art
history, art criticism, and aesthetics into their teaching while retaining traditional emphases such as the creative, personal, and social goals of the art
education program. This text examines both the problem of incorporating
the content of the disciplines of art, history, and aesthetics into the current
school art curriculum and suggests ways these contents can be linked to each
other in the curricular domains of art production, art criticism and art history.

The links are based on the premise that the study of art like the study of
science and other disciplines should be approached from what Perry (1981)
calls a "relativist position." Relativism, in Perry's view, suggests that a discipline involves diversity of opinion, values and judgment from coherent
sources, evidence, and logic systems and includes patterns allowing for
analysis and comparison. In such pursuits according to Perry, some opinions
may be found worthless and there will remain matters about which reasonable people will reasonably disagree. In this context, Perry views disciplinary
knowledge as qualitative and dependent upon context.

For Perry context is more than adapting content to immediate classroom
restraints; it is also taking into account the teacher's own values, choices and
commitment to his or her career, teaching discipline, and lifestyle. Areas
such as social responsibility and human interaction should be included not
because they, in and of themselves, are teaching content, but because they

reflect what teachers value about themselves, about art, and about the approaches they use in teaching it. This view assumes further that effective art teachers know that they must be whole-hearted while tentative, fight for their own values, yet respect others, and believe in their deepest values and yet be ready to learn and grow.

Most critically needed are alternative paradigms for aesthetic conception that interrelate artistic activity in what Langer (1953) refers to as the impressive and expressive realms, that is, looking at and making art. Such paradigms unfortunately may not come from either the art studio or the scholarly art disciplines because as disciplines both tend to view themselves as mutually exclusive. The alternative of bending the goals of art making to the goals of educational theory or the goals of art to history or criticism will not remove the barriers to effective practice. Only when the differing philosophical assumptions and the aesthetic values of competing conceptions are addressed can the true parameters of the problem be understood.

This text attempts to bridge the gap between theory and practice and supports a modest proposal for the integration of the domains of art production, art history, art criticism and aesthetics into the current school art program. But first a variety of approaches to making and thinking about art are examined as well as several possible connections between these approaches and the various concepts and modes of teaching art in the schools. The views of a variety of scholars, artists and teachers on both making and thinking about art are presented and several pathways toward closing the gap between theory and practice in art teaching are suggested.

Any effort to examine the processes used in making art and those used in thinking about it raises important questions about their relationship to each other and also about whether one process or the other comes first. To examine one through the other or assume that one precedes the other both suggests that a causal relationship may exist between them or that either discipline can go beyond its own mode of inquiry. A major problem in organizing this text, therefore, was to avoid both the inference of a cause-and-effect relationship between thinking and making and the limitations imposed by analyzing one discipline in terms of the other. Because, for organizational reasons, one had to come first thinking was placed before making while still attempting to treat them as separate and self-sufficient concepts. For the reader with a preference it should be possible to make sense of the text by reading either in whichever order appeals. To provide some order and also to suggest that there are fecund relationships between disciplinary conceptions of thinking and making the text is organized around common or similar concepts in thinking and modes of making are also grouped together.

The linking of concepts in thinking about art with modes of making art is essential, if the art teacher is to conceive of a curriculum that is consistent in both the ends it seeks and the means it uses to achieve them. Thinking is involved in both the contemplation and the making of art: this seemingly obvious claim becomes much more problematical when the scope of those who disagree with it is realized. For centuries, philosophers and aestheticians have argued over such issues as (1) the relationship between thinking about art and thinking about making art, (2) the role of thinking in both the planning and execution of art and (3) the use of thought when thinking about art in general. Until the reader has a clear understanding of what is meant by artistic thinking, no true course for establishing the curricular goals of the school can emerge.

Some of the ways scholars think about thinking itself need to be addressed before an examination of thinking in art or education. It is, therefore, necessary to touch on at least some of the ways we think about the objects in our world and about the events that give these objects form and meaning. Such thoughts are epistemological that is, an inquiry into how we know what we know. Moreover, these determinations are foundational; they specify the a priori assumptions that lead to what is truthful, valuable and good and how it relates to the world and the role the individual wishes to play in it. What the individual decides in such matters also determines what objects and events he brings into being and what actions, if any, he needs to take in regard to them.

Organization of This Book

To pursue this inquiry in a logical manner, this text is organized into five chapters. Chapter I provides a brief review of 18th and 19th century philosophical thought ordered according to three differing epistemological concepts of the relations between objects and events. Chapter II explores these concepts as they are interpreted by 20th century aestheticians, art historians, critics and artists addressing concerns specifically in thinking about and making art. Chapter III examines three paradigms for artistic conception that reflect the differing philosophical and aesthetic concepts identified in Chapters I and II. Chapter IV identifies how these paradigms now function in the art curricula of schools and Chapter V how the paradigms relate to curriculum practice.

The purpose of Chapter I which analyzes pre-20th century thought from a meta-philosophical point of view is to identify the philosophical assumptions underlying differing epistemological conceptions on how we act and think about objects and events in practical life. Understanding these conceptions should assist readers in identifying those philosophical systems closest to their own beliefs and offering the most guidance in selecting art teaching goals that express their own philosophical and psychological values.

At least two conditions are implied in this approach: (1) any philosophical position, will generate a number of questions that lie beyond its own methods of inquiry and that it is, therefore, powerless to answer and (2) philosophy, like art, is not necessarily getting "better" over time, that is, accepting of a steady obsolescence of successive systems. This lends support to the notion that both ancient and modern philosophers need to be revisited as seriously now as they ever were and the study of both the newer and older philosophies is critical to any complete understanding of educational thought.

While it is beyond the scope of this text to offer a complete course in philosophy or try to examine all existing philosophies, it will attempt to identify and contrast the principle assumptions of the pre-20th century philosophies most especially as they apply to the historical, cultural, aesthetic and productive dimensions of the art object. The intent here, then, is not to make the reader a philosopher, but rather to achieve enough understanding to make intelligent and thoughtful decisions on matters affecting the goals of art education.

Chapter II will shift from pre-20th-century modes of thinking about general relations between objects and events to 20th century modes of thinking about art and culture in general. Various emphases and events shaping 20th century political, aesthetic, historical and cultural thought will be described especially as influenced by rationalist, neo-idealist and empirical ideologies. The text will also look at 20th century aesthetics, especially on the relations between form and matter—relations critical to determining the aesthetic premise underlying both the impressive and expressive dimensions of a work.

Chapter III attempts to link Chapter I's discussion of the ways of thinking about objects and events and Chapter II's discussion of and modes of thinking about art and life itself to three conceptual modes of art making and thinking basic to the education of artists and artist-teachers. These modes include three different conceptual paradigms entitled in this text (1) art as schema-motif, (2) art as form-gestalt, and (3) art as linguistic-metaphorical.

Art as schema will be explored through an examination of the studio strategies advocated by Kimon Nicholaides (1941) and as supported by art historian Heinrich Wolfflin, the psychologies of E. H. Gombrich and aesthetician E. G. Collingwood. They provide psychological, philosophical and historical arguments for artistic conception through reconstructing existing images and motifs. The art as schema idea is one borrowed from art historian E. H. Gombrich (1972) who argues that the images artists make start with the schematic conceptions in the artist's head and are later corrected to fit the expressive form of the work.

The second mode of making to be examined in Chapter III explores art making and thinking in terms of art coming from within the picture plane itself through the thinking processes advocated by expressionist artist Wassily Kandinsky, aesthetician Suzanne Langer, historian Erwin Panofsky and psychologists James Gibson and Rudolf Arnheim. The concept itself is borrowed from Kandinsky's book, *Point and Line to Plane* (1979). In Kandinsky's view, art is a spiritual object which is the outward expression of the artist's inner needs in abstract form. Kandinsky viewed abstraction as realism and realism as abstraction advocating that the quantitative decrease in the image can be equated as a qualitative increase in expression.

The third and final form of art making explored in Chapter III is termed in this text art as linguistic/metaphor. It comes from the structural approach to art advocated by Jack Burnham (1971) and is demonstrated through the drawing methods advanced in a number of texts including Claudia Betti and Teel Sale's *Drawing/A Contemporary Approach* (1986). Burnham's argument advanced in *The Structure of Art* is that if the essence of science, ethics, language and ceremony is conceptual relationships, the same might be true of art. Also analyzed are the views of cultural anthropologist Claude Levi Strauss (1976) who argues that artists paint pictures not because pictures are good to see, but rather because they are good to think about. Works of art, in his view, are totems which systematically define themselves by associations with other works. Artists make art using historical and formal transgressions which create a form of meta-art or art about art mostly in a post-modern mode of establishing either a non-uniqueness or a short circuiting of established norms of thinking and making in art.

Chapter IV addresses the applications of the three conceptual paradigms to the art teaching literature in the domains of art studio, art history and art education as they reflect the three paradigmatic modes identified in Chapter III. The chapter addresses several important aesthetic and philosophical premises as they relate to the problem of specifying curricular content, sequence, scope and evaluation.

The curriculum examples cited in the areas of art studio focus on the art production theories of Viktor Lowenfeld and Lambert Brittain, June McFee and Rogena Degge (1977), and Edmund Feldman (1970). These were selected on the basis of their philosophical and aesthetic relevance to the forms of making advanced in the third chapter. Historical curricular approaches presented include those of Gerald Brommer (1988), Guy Hubbard (1987), and Laura Chapman (1987). These examples present several different and successful approaches to teaching art studio and art history in the classroom. The analysis provided on these curricula is to assist the reader in understanding the philosophical, aesthetic and educational premises on which they are based.

Such an understanding can lead to intelligent choices among existing curricula or in the construction of newer curricula which reflects the reader's own values or the values of the school art program. This analysis can also provide teachers with a conceptual basis for making and defending their curricular decisions with the school administration, their colleagues, and the community. The need to address the curriculum construction process from a philosophical viewpoint is necessary to establish a basis for determining the consistency of curricular means and ends, or put another way, between the goals the curriculum seeks to achieve and the curricular structure used to achieve them. The aim here is to avoid, for example, trying to achieve democratic goals through authoritarian means or aesthetic goals through non-aesthetic means.

Chapter V presents a plan for curriculum practice that examines the teacher's philosophy; suggests ways to analyze existing curricula; and discusses how to structure a curricula including educational aims, scope, sequence, content, organization and evaluation. It also covers how to implement it in a classroom setting. This process is accepting of the notion that several different curricular conceptions are possible and that any one of these conceptions has potential in curriculum practice. The reason for examining varied curricula in terms of their claims is not to develop a single curriculum for all students to pursue, but rather to offer alternative modes for curriculum decision making, consistent in curricular means and ends and offering a choice among alternative modes for school art curriculum construction. The text concludes with possible solutions to the problem of establishing valid curricular goals. Using Ralph Thompson's (1975) term "curricular viability," six criteria for judging curricular viability are examined. These include psychological validity, social validity, philosophical validity, subject validity, political feasibility and technical adequacy.

This text attempts to provide some alternative curricular conceptions for thinking about and making art in schools. It was impossible to include all the philosophical, psychological and sociological theories needed to support the claim that there is more than one cultural paradigm useful in setting goals and constructing curricula in schools. The use of the term "paradigm" in Chapter III to describe different conceptual systems in art and education is borrowed from the philosopher Thomas S. Kuhn (1970) as he used it in his text entitled, *The Structure of Scientific Revolutions.* Kuhn surprised the scientific world through claiming that the history of science is not an objective progression toward truth but rather a structure heavily influenced by what he calls nonrational procedures (Kuhn 1970). By adopting Kuhn's paradigmatic model this text, in effect, proposes that newer theories of art like newer theories in science do not come any closer to the truth but rather reflect peaceful interludes punctuated by intellectually violent revolutions in which one conceptual world is replaced by another.

Moreover, the basis of this text also accepts the claim that the history of art like the history of science has experienced over time various revolutions where its professional community could no longer evade the anomalies which subverted existing traditions or artistic practices, thus requiring a new set of commitments as a basis for future practice. As in the scientific community the art community also had to invent new theories for thinking about and making art which also required changes in the rules governing practices. These new theories, based as they were on newer artistic discoveries and newer conceptions of art, were also never just an addition to what was already known but rather a reconstruction of prior theory and a reevaluation of prior practice which was never as Kuhn (1970) notes completed by a single person or, for that matter, overnight. The cultural revolutions presented are those revealed by the artistic community through its literature and through its educational and artistic practices. It is through such study and practice that members of the art community learn their trade and find it possible to construct paradigms.

Kuhn's (1970) claim is that a paradigm has at least two characteristics:

1. Its achievement was sufficiently represented to attract an enduring group of adherents away from competing paradigms.

2. It was sufficiently open-ended to leave all sorts of problems for the new practitioner to resolve. Just as in science, a paradigm for art must also prepare the art student for membership in a particular movement which he or she will later practice. As Kuhn also notes, it is through this process that the novice learns the basis of the field which form the same concrete models used by those who practice in it. This suggests that individuals who are committed to shared paradigms are committed to the same rules and behaviors for thinking about and making art, rarely disagreeing at least about fundamentals.

The cultural paradigms presented in this text were drawn from the literature in the philosophy of art and aesthetics, the psychology of art, art history, art criticism and the texts used to educate (both mature and younger) students in art. These sources reveal over time thinking about art and about educating people in it. Like science, art also involves matters of form and content uniting the ideas held about art with what is learned in the laboratory (studio). Such sources, both elementary and secondary advance the body of accepted theory and demonstrate many or all of its successful applications.

Finally, to those who say that the literature of art is not the same as the creation of art I can only hope my methods will suggest a salt and pepper connection. These connections first occurred to me when I moved away from my preoccupation with making art to what I thought was a new world of ideas about art only to discover that what I learned there was not radically different from what I had learned in the studio. It was in fact, through my discovery that art itself had a scientific paradigm that I first realized it was only through the existence of the cultural paradigm that Kuhn's scientific paradigms became possible.

13

References

Barkan, M. (1962). Transition in art education: Changing conceptions of curriculum and teaching. *Art Education, 15*(7), 12-18.

Betti, C. & Sale T. (1986). *Drawing a contemporary approach*. New York: CBS College Publishing.

Brigham, C. (1988). Doing DBAE differently to achieve its primary goal. In *Beyond DBAE: The case for multiple visions of art education*. North Dartmouth, MA: University Council on Art Education, 64-75.

Brommer, G. (1988). *Discovering art history*. Worcester: Davis Publications, Inc.

Burnham, J. (1971). *The structure of art*. New York: George Braziller.

Burton, J. Lederman, A., London P. (Eds.) (1988). *Beyond DBAE: The case for multiple visions in art education*, Southeastern Massachusetts University, North Dartmouth, MA: University Council on Art Education.

Carlisle, B. (1982). Towards an iconography of arts education. *New York University, Education Quarterly*, Winter, 23-28.

Chapman, L. (1987). *Discover art*. Worcester: Davis Publications, Inc.

Dewey, J. (1947). *Art and education*. New York: Barnes Foundation Press.

Efland, A. (1981). The schools arts style: A functional analysis. In G. Hardiman and T. Zernich, (Eds.) *Foundations of curriculum development in art education*. Champaign: Stipes Publishing Co., 453-462.

Efland, A. (1979). Conceptions of teaching in art education. *Art Education, 26* (6), 21-33.

Eisner, E. (1986). *Beyond creating: The place of art in America's schools*. Los Angeles: J. Paul Getty Trust.

Feldman, E. (1970). *Becoming human through art*. Englewood Cliffs, NJ: Prentice Hall, Inc.

Goldstein, H. & Goldstein V. (1947). *Art in everyday life*. New York: The Macmillan Co.

Gombrich, E. H. (1972). *Art and illusion*. Princeton: Princeton University Press.

Harris, D. (1963). *Children's drawings as measures of intellectual maturity*. New York: Harcourt, Brace and World, Inc.

Hausman, J. (1988). Unity and diversity in art education. In J. Burton, A. Lederman & P.London (Eds.), *Beyond DBAE: The case for multiple visions of art education.*, North Dartmouth, MA: University Council on Art Education.

Hubbard, G. (1987). *Art in action*. San Diego: Coronado Publishers.

Kandinsky, W. (1979). *Point and line to plane*. New York: Dover Publications.

Kaufman, I. (1989). The subject is art. *Studies in Art Education, 30* (2), 84-92.

Keiler, M. (1951). *Art in the schoolroom*. Lincoln: University of Nebraska Press.

Kuhn, T. (1970). *The structure of scientific revolutions*. Chicago: University of Chicago Press.

Langer, S. K. (1953). *Feeling and form*. New York: Charles Scribner's Sons.

Lanier, V. (1972). Objectives of teaching art. *Art Education, 25* (3), 15-19.

Levi Strauss C., (1976). *Structural anthropology (Vol 2)*. Chicago: University of Chicago Press.

Logan, F.M. (1955). *Growth of art in American schools*. New York: Harper and Brothers.

London, P. (1988). To gaze again at the stars. In J. Burton, A. Lederman & P. London (Eds.), *Beyond DBAE: The case for multiple visions of art education*. North Dartmouth, MA: University Council on Art Education.

Lowenfeld, V. & Brittain, L. (1975). *Creative and mental growth*. (6th ed.). New York: MacMillan Co.

McFee, J. & Degge, R. (1977). *Art, culture and environment*. Belmont, CA: Wadsworth Publishing Co.

Nicolaides, K. (1941). *The natural way to draw*. Boston: Houghton Mifflin Company.

Perry, W. G. (1981) Cognitive and ethical growth: The making of meaning. In A. Chickering, et. al. (eds). *The Modern American College*. San Francisco: Jossey Bass, 76-116.

Read, H. (1950). *Art Education Today 1949-1950*. New York: Teachers College Columbia University.

Smith, R. (1987), The changing image of art education: Theoretical antecedents of discipline based art education. *Journal of Aesthetic Education, 21* (2) 3-34.

Thompson, R. (1975), General criteria for curriculum analysis. *Peabody Journal of Education, 52,* 247-251.

Weitz, M. (1959). *Problems in aesthetics*. New York: The Macmillan Co.

Kandinsky, Wassily. *Improvisation 31 (Sea Battle),* Ailsa Mellon Bruce Fund, © 1993 National Gallery of Art, Washington, 1913, oil on linen, 1.451 x 1.197 (55 3/8 x 47 1/8).

Chapter 1

Objects and Events

Questions of whom to teach, what to teach, and when and how to teach it require more than casual answers, especially if they are to reflect the reader's true beliefs and also be responsive to the public trust given to the educators of the nation's children and youth. Although the answers will be based on the individual's own experience, reasoning and intuition, that individual can never be certain that his or her particular vision of reality is not a reflection of personal bias unless that reality is tested against the other realities supported in human thought. To know whether your answers and consequently your programs are truly effective will happen only after you test your own beliefs and thoughts about art and education against the thoughts others have in addressing such issues.

The search for answers must, therefore, begin with thinking about thinking itself. More than simply acquiring information, this thinking is both a process and a product that reveals the character of the mind. That is to say not only do we think thoughts but we also *think*. What we think is shaped both by our experiences with objects and events in the real world and by the state of mind we have at the time we experience them. To think about the ways we can think about such things requires that we become concerned about both the objects and events we experience and the state of mind we have when we experience them. Thinking about objects and events and about the ways which we may perceive them is foundational to knowing what a work of art is, what it means and what processes are most likely to bring it into being. One's state of mind in deciding such issues affects the answers given in regard to art and also in response to those important ones of whom to teach, what to teach, and when and how to teach it.

An excellent starting point is the examination of several visual, verbal and inactive systems of thought from the viewpoint of how these systems have sustained themselves over time and also how they have changed. The examination begins with the first or foundational principles of these systems, and then looks at how these first principles have been expanded to address newer concerns raised in contemporary art and life. Thus, the discussion begins with ancient Greek systems of thought including how they were later expanded in 18th and 19th century philosophical writing. To do otherwise would be to immerse the reader into 20th century systems of thought far too complex for most beginning philosophers to grasp. For the sake of clarity, the philosophies are approached both logically and systematically and complex issues are reduced as much as possible to comprehensible units that can be understood and manipulated. Even when simplified, however, these matters are not easy to deal with, especially if the reader truly wants to understand what is behind the decisions he or she and others make about art and the art educational process.

The discussion begins with the foundational assumptions of philosophers because all systems of thought begin with *assumptions* about such issues as what it means to be human, the nature of the universe, the purpose of life, and so forth. Because answers to these assumptions cannot be verified with any certainty, there are only competing systems of thought rather than some objective and certain truth obtainable if one tries hard enough. Even scientific truth which appears to many as irrefutable is decided by experiments validated by mathematical systems that specify the conditions of their own proof.

These foundational questions are outlined in the domains of metaphysics, epistemology, logic and axiology, all of which attempt to resolve the basic questions about the meaning of life that human beings have wondered about since the beginning of recorded history. The questions include: How did this planet evolve? How did we as human beings come to exist? Is there a God or spirit, not of this world, which guides our destiny? These and others are real questions which so many people think about privately but rarely publicly except in the church, synagogue, or philosophy class.

To make these systems of thought more understandable, the discussion will frame them in three dominant 20th century philosophical systems that fundamentally have remained the same throughout the history of the Western world. These systems, here called Rationalism, Empiricism, and Neo-idealism, while in most ways remaining the same over time also show the capability of being expanded on to account for new forms of knowledge and to meet new challenges of 20th century life. This discussion will focus on how these systems have approached thinking about objects and events, a focus germane not only to exploring these systems but also to the next chapter's view of the problems posed in modern aesthetics, art history, art criticism and the psychology of art. This chapter's discussion should lead to a realization that knowing generally how to think about objects and events is fundamental to knowing what a work of art is and how it relates to the forces that bring it into being. In this text, these systems will be presented as the rationalist position of objects existing mainly in the mind, the empiricist position of objects as demonstrated in fact and the neo-idealist position of objects being something found in human experience. Looking at thought-about objects and

events from these perspectives leads, by extension, to a view of the artist, his or her education, and the impact of that educational process on the individual.

Claims in art education are grounded mainly on individual beliefs about art, about teaching children, and about the learning conditions necessary for children to learn and grow. To believe that art is creativity is to believe every child can develop new, individual and, personally unique ideas. This infers philosophically that one supports a belief system that accepts human nature as (1) instinctful, (2) change oriented, (3) good, (4) responsive and (5) exercising of free will. It may, in addition, infer any or none of the following: we believe in creationism; the self is a social-vocal phenomenon; purposeful activity imposes purpose; reality is a changing thing; existence is only flux and change; knowledge is fractional and *a posteriori*; what has value is related to interest; we are optimistic about the worth of living; and the highest good is self-realization.

Although, at any given moment, the premises which fund an individual's beliefs do not pass before the mind like arguments in a judicial trial, they do, none the less, influence his or her professional claims. This book was written with the idea that while we may not always be conscious of every belief influencing our day to day judgments, they do require our attention, that is, if we are to achieve effective thinking in our profession. To function in the real world we must, of course, have beliefs even though we are not always sure what our beliefs imply. What we decide professionally does reflect the beliefs we hold about life in general. Although we cannot analyze all our decisions imply in every instance, we are not relieved of the responsibility for understanding what our professional claims mean, especially if we wish to feel confident about the decisions we make in our classrooms and in our profession as a whole.

There is much to be said for Suzanne Langer's (1953) claim that philosophy does not treat things in general but rather constructs notions useful in forming special and particularized knowledge, that is, practical, scientific, social, or purely intuitive knowledge. Its work, she notes, is a constant process of generalization that requires logic, technical imagination, and ingenuity. It cannot, she claims, begin with generalities such as art is expression or beauty is harmony but rather with such ideas occurring at the end of a philosophical inquiry.

Langer also viewed philosophy as a living venture with its questions not being by their nature insolvable. She thought that philosophical questions differed from scientific questions in that they were interpretations rather than factual reports and that philosophy's goal was not to increase our knowledge of nature but our understanding of what we know. She believed that through a philosophical analysis of basic concepts knowledge about subject matter becomes more systematic and that by focusing on actual problems and mak-

ing them clear similar ideas can emerge to aid the construction of a whole Cosmology, Axiology or Epistemology.

In accepting Langer's course of action, we need to first identify the practical, that is, what it is we do in the classroom, then move to construct philosophically consistent goals which communicate to others the belief systems guiding what we do. While this course of action may appear to put the cart before the horse, it does recognize that our philosophy, or why we do what we do, most often determines our personal and professional behaviors. To take an opposite course, that is, to deal first with all the philosophical belief systems which are possible, takes us too far from what we started out to do. Furthermore, it increases the risk of arriving at logically deduced constructs that cannot be implemented. When Langer speaks about subject matter ending in the construction of a whole Cosmology, Axiology or Epistemology, she is talking about the domains of Metaphysics, (a study of the nature of reality) and Epistemology (a study of the nature of knowledge). Philosophers formally construct their philosophy on the basic assumptions they make in these and at least two other philosophical domains: Logic and Axiology.

The Metaphysical Domain

In the domain of metaphysics, philosophers determine basic premises in such areas as: (1) Cosmology, which explains the origin and development of the universe, (2) the nature of man, (3) mind/body relationships, (4) problems of freedom, (5) conceptions of and about God, (6) purpose in the universe, (7) constancy and quantity, and (8) the ontological concerns of what it means to exist and have being. What each individual decides on such matters reflects how close his or her personal philosophy comes to the beliefs held by the various schools of philosophical thought. Today these schools are conceptually represented in at least three relatively distinct philosophical positions: Rationalism, Empiricism and Neo-idealism. These positions differ most on how we know what we know: Rationalists believe in the idea of the self as the primary source of knowledge, empiricists in knowledge coming from the discovery of relations between objects and events, and the neo-idealists in the self as it functions in a world of objects and events.

If one's philosophy of life reflects a rationalist view of self, the self is a soul and a spiritual being. If it reflects an empiricist view, the self is essentially the same as the body, and from a neo-idealist view the self is a social-vocal phenomenon. Each position uses different assumptions to determine the nature of self and has different ways of deciding matters affecting ourselves and others. Among the three schools three different views of self merge: We can believe (1) man is not free to choose, as all actions are determined by outside forces; (2) free will exists which means we have the power of choice and are capable of genuine initiative; or (3) our choices are neither

free nor determined but can be only acted on as a basis for deciding new directions for subsequent activity.

What we believe metaphysically about the nature of the universe, the nature of man, freedom, and the meaning of existence affects our social philosophy of education, which in turn affects how we view the purposes of schooling. If one is a rationalist and believes, for example, that human beings are not free, then the rationalist as educator needs to decide who is worth educating and in what they should be educated. If another is an empiricist who believes individuals should play a part in deciding what they want out of life, then the empiricist's students should decide what is worth learning and who is worth educating. Or, again, a neo-idealist may decide that both conceptions of self are equally viable and that both educators and learners should decide on who should be educated and what they should learn.

The Epistemological Domain

A second domain philosophers wrestle with is epistemology, which deals with theories about the nature of knowledge. If one is an empiricist, conclusive knowledge of ultimate reality is an impossibility; for a rationalist, true knowledge of ultimate reality is possible; and to a neo-idealist, knowledge is always fractional, never total, and functions in a given situation where it is needed. These differing views of how we know what we know determine whether we believe that (1) knowledge is based on experience and observation; (2) it is self-evident and can be learned from principles not requiring proof, or (3) it is experimental and functions as a means to carry knowledge forward in a satisfactory or rewarding way.

What we believe epistemologically determines what the education process should emphasize: (1) the acquisition of subject matter knowledge, (2) the training of students in the requirements of a discipline, (3) fulfilling a cultural (re-capitulationist) destiny, (4) the growth needs of children and youth, or (5) a planned program of real-life experiences. If one supports a rationalist view in art education, students would study the elements and principles of design; if one is an empiricist, the disciplines of art production, art history, art criticism and aesthetics; and if a neo-idealist, creative performing and a study of the different ways to think about and make art.

The Domain of Logic

A third philosophical area is the domain of logic, which can be defined as a system of reasoning. Philosophers ground the validity of their arguments using three different systems of logic: (1) *induction*, reasoning from particulars to a general conclusion, (2) *deduction*, reasoning from a general principle to particulars included within the scope of that principle and (3) *experi-*

mental, or practical reason which uses both inductive and deductive reasoning to reach a workable solution to a problem as applied to an area of concern. Rationalists tend to view art content as something relatively fixed, empiricists as continually new and changing in its meaning, and neo-idealists as a consequence of expressive behavior.

The system of logic adopted by an individual influences the teaching methods he or she uses and the content and scope of the curriculum offered. Rationalists, for example, tend to use individualized content historically organized, while empiricists emphasize disciplinary study of topical content, and neo-idealists a mixture of both. Rationalists would encourage students to develop their intuitive powers, empiricists their social powers, and neo-idealists whatever powers are needed to solve practical problems. For learning to take place in the arts, rationalists believe in subject matter historically sequenced and broad in scope, empiricists in subject matter inductively sequenced, and neo-idealists in whatever content is needed at whatever time it is needed to solve a particular human problem.

The Domain of Axiology

The last of the domains addressed here is axiology or the nature of value. Depending on which system of philosophy is used, "valuable" can mean: (1) what interests us (2) what we know to be worth doing or (3) what will yield the greatest personal gain. Values are usually established on the nature of good or evil, the worth of living, the highest good and criteria of conduct. Determining what has value is based on one's individual view of life, that is, whether life is worth living, whether existence is evil and we need to escape it, or whether we can even know such things although through intelligent effort we can, at least, improve our situation.

The values teachers hold affect mostly how they teach students how to learn. What they decide affects both which values shape their instruction and which values they hope the students will learn. Rationalists value that which will achieve the highest perfection of self, empiricists that which brings the greatest good to the greatest number, and neo-idealists what helps us most to lead an effective life.

Students who learn the values transmitted in the classrooms are affected by what philosophers call the criteria of conduct. Students educated to believe they should be guided by certain principles, or by the need for self-preservation, or by discovery of the probable consequences of a particular action will feel differently about what it is they need to know and what they should value. Both the rationalists and neo-idealists value the interests of self which can be best achieved through individual actions. The empiricists value the interests of others and the group as a whole—fullest selfhood, in their view, is achieved through seeking the best interests of others.

There may be general agreement that such matters just described need to be studied and understood for their possible impact on teaching art, but few have the luxury of dedicating a lifetime of study to such matters. But while it may not be possible to know about everything, teachers, administrators or curriculum builders in the arts can expand their knowledge of those matters that are of practical use in their professional lives.

Thinking and Making: Goals and Limitations

What is covered here has to do eventually with deciding on goals for thinking about and making art in schools. Therefore the most useful philosophical knowledge may be achieved through addressing the epistemological problem of how do we know what we know, especially as it relates to the text's more central problem of thinking about and making art. As the reader may already suspect, what is decided upon in such matters depends upon which epistemological premises are used. That thinking occurs in both thinking about art and in making or creating art is a matter on which there is agreement; as to whether the thinking done in thinking about art and making it is one and the same is a matter on which few agree.

A recent book well worth reading on the topic of thinking and making art is one written by Andrew Harrison (1978) entitled *Making and Thinking: A Study of Intelligent Activities.* Harrison's view is that works of art are both a vehicle of thought and formed by thought and that artists make something which did not exist before through the thinking processes they use in both forming the materials (matter) and conceptualizing the thing (form). Harrison believes further that the making of a work of art is the construction of an artifact which is a vehicle of thought because it demands the viewer's understanding and interpretation of it and of the person who makes it. The problem, as he sees it, is to answer the question of what went into the making of this rather than what is this.

Harrison is concerned about the place of thought in the activities of making something new, something that goes beyond pre-established aims, principles or rules for action. He claims that historically the maker of things plays as central a role as the talker or writer. He also criticizes overdrawn distinctions between what is practical and what is theoretical. He biasedly believes that practical people make and do with things, running the risk of getting their hands dirty, while theoretically minded people do not and, therefore, run no risks.

The tendency is, he believes, to think of reason as suggesting a world of thought more readily than one of messing around with materials. Such thinking exists because the context of reason is one of reasoning, giving and having reasons, thinking and concluding. In rebuttal, Harrison argues that making things is, or at least can be seen as, a rational activity, is informed by

23

where thought reflection, knowledge and speculation have their outcome in doing. Making, in his view, is a philosophy of action which changes the world by bringing into existence objects that did not exist before. The ways in which thought may be exercised or expressed in making things, according to Harrison, is through how the maker relates his thoughts and actions to his materials and to the object he or she is making. The form and matter problem is resolved by the object being both a thing made and an object of the artist's activity, which makes the material of which the thing is made the object of his attention in the activity of making.

While Harrison's arguments are rationally supported, his effort to exclude the possibility of thinking and making being related to one another suggests more of a philosophical bias than a recognition of making and thinking about art as an open concept. He does in fact, end with the classical E. G. Collingwood argument on the difference between art and craft wherein he notes in his comparison between the sculptor and the carpenter that the logical gap between acting on materials and doing something to what is made is only sharp and clear when the specification of what is to be made more or less precedes the making of it. Harrison's philosophical bias is not unique among philosophers who explore the epistemological problems of objects and the events which bring them into being. Such bias is not the fault of Harrison or any other writer, but rather it occurs because no philosophy can go beyond its own methods of inquiry.

For this reason, it is useful to look at the claims made about objects and events in light of the varying positions taken by the three schools of philosophical thought: Rationalism, Empiricism and Neo-idealism. Before we look at the differences in these positions, however, it would be useful to review some of the major figures and different conceptual beliefs which account for these schools adopting different methods of inquiry.

The Greek Philosophers

Differences in philosophical viewpoints became evident in the thoughts of the early Greek philosophers some 600 years before the first century A.D. The earliest cited differences were in those laid out in the writings of Plato (428-348 B.C.) and Aristotle (385-322 B.C.). Their views differed mostly about how we know what we know, which essentially marks the differences between so called idealist and empirical modes of thought. Plato in the *Republic* 373 B.C. dealt with what Durant calls the psychological problem by defining the goals of philosophy as first to think clearly, which is metaphysics, and second to rule wisely, which is politics (Durant, 1961). To think clearly, Plato believed that the student should study the doctrine of ideas found according to Plato behind the surface phenomena and particulars which greet the senses and which are the generalizations, regularities and directions of development not perceived but conceived by reason and thought.

According to Plato, these laws and ideals are permanent and therefore more real than the senses through which we perceive particular things and through which we conceive and deduce them. Plato thus laid out the concept that it was the ideas we hold about things not the things themselves which revealed the most important truths. It was also Plato who is credited with defining art as appearance and claiming art as being an imitation of an imitation. Weitz (1965) in supporting this argument cites Plato's dialogue from the *Republic* in which he claims that both beds and tables are ideas and that although the carpenter makes them in accordance with the idea he does not create the idea itself. Plato views the artist who makes a painting of the bed as being even further removed from the idea by becoming what he calls the maker of all the works of all other workmen. There are three beds according to Plato: one by god (idea), one by the maker, and one by the painter. In his dialogue, Plato notes that it is god who is the real maker of the real bed, the carpenter the maker of a bed and the artist a mere imitator of what others have made. Objects are therefore according to Plato not what they appear to be but rather the ideas we hold about them. Thus, the cup or painting appearing before us does not cease to exist simply because we remove it from our view, as we can know the cup and the painting exist even though we can not see or touch them in a strictly physical sense.

While it is true that Aristotle, Plato's student, also believed that art was an imitative process, he differed from Plato mostly through his scientific tendency to demand definitions for almost everything and his efforts to create a science of logic. Aristotle believed that the definition of an object or term had two parts: (1) assigning the object to a class or group and (2) indicating how the object differs from all other members of its class. Durant (1961) claims that it was on the question of universals where Plato and Aristotle most disagreed and which started the war between the "realists" and the "nominalists". In Aristotle's mind, common nouns such as man, book or tree are universals, but universals that are subjective notions are not tangible objective realities. His view was that these universals are names, not things, and that all that exists outside of us is a world of individual and specific objects, not generic and universal things. Men, trees and animals exist, but man, in general, or universal man does not exist, except in thought.

The debate about how we know what an object is, what causes it to exist and what its relationship is to the events associated with it began with Aristotle's criticism of Plato and continues today in the claims and counterclaims of Rationalist, Empiricist and Neo-idealist philosophers. In many ways the arguments involve issues substantially the same as those argued by Plato and Aristotle, though over time they have broadened and deepened. What has changed are the claims offered by the earlier idealists and realists and those offered by 20th century philosophers. They have been influenced by the more modern concerns first introduced by the 16th and 17th century philosophers who found the epistemological issues argued by Plato and Aristotle no longer germaine to the changing views of society and the new knowledge of the physical world which occurred over the intervening 2000 years.

Rationalist Philosophical Thought

Philosophical literature generally indicates that the roots of rationalist philosophy are contained in the writings of Rene Descartes (1596-1650), Benedict de (Barach) Spinosa (1632-1677), and Gottfried Wilhelm von Leibniz (1646-1716). All three worked in context of the powerful traditions of church, the conception of a necessary being, and a knowledge of the efforts of St. Thomas Aquinas to fit human nature into a coherent theology by describing the relations between God and man.

In one form or another, all three philosophers provided arguments for the existence of a God (spirit) but departed the strict doctrine of the Church to argue that all understanding is in the last analysis one of personal reason. Descartes is credited with the phase "I think, therefore I am" (*cogito ergo sum*) which is self-verifying in that it cannot be entertained without at the same time and for that very reason being true. Spinosa suppressed the first-person emphasis of Descartes by inventing a kind of third-person level of knowing sometimes characterized as "sublime impersonality "Liebniz advanced Spinoza's notions of reasoning as matters of fact and relations between ideas to advance the notion of fundamental laws or principles of thought. Since all three were mathematicians, notions such as principles and axioms of thought were consistent with the intuitional structure of mathematics which provides its own system of proof reflecting both *a priori* truth and experimental verification in practice. In the world of the mathematician, "2 + 2 = 4" is not validated through experience but rather through its relation to the premises set by the mathematical concept that brings it into being.

Descartes' epistemological view of objects and events contributed at least three basic constructs to rationalist thought: (1) Things or objects exist in the mind, (2) knowledge of objects comes about through reason or rational reflection, and (3) knowledge is personal or self-knowledge. The argument that objects are mental rather than physical things was illustrated through Descartes' analogy of the lump of wax: Perceived in its original form as having a certain size, color or perfume, though melted, it remains, in effect the same piece of wax.

Descartes' view that one's knowledge of objects is a matter of reasoned or rational reflections came from his reliance on geometry, again a mathematical science where validity is dependent not upon empirical verification but rather on the proofs provided by the theroms and axioms of geometry itself.

Descartes' willingness to accept the possibility of our knowledge of things as being self-verifying comes from his first-person privilege of noting that we are able to know what we think, feel, and experience with an authority different from any other authority that attaches to our knowledge of any other person or thing. This first person privilege case is generally considered to provide the paradigm of certainty the rationalists used to develop a systematic view of the world.

Spinosa's concepts of objects (substance) and events were an extension of Descartes' "I think" notion to the more objective stance that objects themselves were self-verifying through the ideas we hold about them. Substance, in Spinosa's view, is that which is in itself and conceived through itself and does not depend upon the conception of another thing from which it must be formed. Substance could not, in his view, be conceived of in insolation, nor caused, and therefore must be its own cause.

The so-called sublime impersonality notion attributed to Spinosa can be seen in his transference of the mental construct of idea to ideas existing in things. He claimed that in every physical event in the body there is a mental event that constitutes its idea and that in every modification of the mind there is some modification of matter which is identical and vice versa. Spinosa's conception of mind-body relationships is reflected in his three-level concept of the value of the mind, which later evolved into art as the expressive paradigm embraced by 20th century rationalist philosophers. Spinosa's three levels of mind are: (1) sense perception or imagination (2) reasoned reflection leading to principles and (3) the highest level of thought, called intuition. It is likely that the thinking of Spinosa led to the twentieth century rationalist aesthetic concept of the objectification of form, which advances the idea that feelings can exist in objects which are in themselves non-feeling.

Leibnitz, generally regarded as a rationalist and best known for his fundamental laws of thought or first principles of thought, also contributed to the empiricist notion that everything which is true is also expressible in language and to Kant's neo-idealism that the physical world is a system of appearances. Concerning objects and events Leibnitz felt that one's ideas about objects could not depend on other objects and that there could not be any interaction or genuine relations between objects. According to Leibniz, what one perceives as relations are simply differences suggested by the object's relation to some event in time and space. This idea contributes heavily to the rationalist aesthetic notion of the incomparability of objects or the events which bring them into being. This suggests that two works by the same artist or by different artists painted under the same or different circumstances can not be compared except with respect to the particular circumstances surrounding their creation.

Empiricist Philosophical Thought

The foundation of modern empiricist thought is generally attributed to Thomas Hobbs (1588-1679), John Locke (1632-1704), George Berkeley (1685-1753), and David Hume (1711-1776). Hobbs contributed through his philosophy of language in which words acquire meaning through representing thoughts; Locke, through his idea that all communication depends on the common significance of words; Berkeley, through the concept that everything we say derives its sense from experience; and Hume, through arguing that nature is governed by immutable and universal laws.

All four made conceptual contributions to what today is called Empiricist philosophy, and all four held general notions that sensory experience gives us knowledge of particulars and that words (names) which express our thoughts must ultimately have reference to particulars. It was Hobbs, however, who laid the groundwork for the later philosophies of Locke, Berkeley and Hume.

John Locke, credited with developing the theory of ideas, noted that words get their meaning by standing for ideas and that ideas only enter the mind through experience. He is best known for his conception of the mind as a *tabula rasa* or blank slate which waits the inception of experience. Locke's key contribution was his theory that all communication depends on the common significance of words referring to the experience whose significance is being explained.

Berkeley attacked Locke's doctrine of abstraction by arguing that since everything that exists is a particular thing there can be no such thing as an abstract idea. Berkeley's greatest contribution was to make experience and ideas one and the same, making the object, the image of that object, and the idea of that object all examples of the same thing. This led to the concept that everything denoted by a word becomes, in effect, an experience or an idea which should leave no doubt as to what is meant by the words uttered. This notion was later interpreted by positivist aestheticians as meaning that pictures are propositional statements of truth such as "all dogs have four legs."

Hume is said to present his philosophy as though it began as a natural science of the human mind (Scruton, 1981). His most famous dictum known as "Hume's Fork" dispenses with rationalist methodology by asserting that reason or enquiry may be divided into two kinds, relations of ideas and matters of fact. Hume classified the first as coming from the sciences of geometry, algebra and arithmetic which are intuitively or demonstratively certain, and the second as matters of fact which never imply a contradiction. Matters of fact in Hume's view are derived from experience and are ideas expressed as factual propositions which we accept. Moreover, the evidence attained from them cannot be obtained deductively, thus denying the possibility of applying deductive logic to propositions regarding what things ought to be (ideals) and what things are (fact).

The philosophers Hobbs, Locke, Berkeley and Hume made it possible for objects or works of art to be considered as means for the communication of ideas, concepts or propositional statements of fact. Locke attempted to distinguish ideas from qualities which he defined as primary and secondary by defining these qualities as the powers of objects to produce ideas in us. Primary qualities in Locke's view are inseparable from the objects in which they exist. Secondary qualities are simply powers that produce ideas or things conveying certain impressions of things. According to Locke, secondary qualities in an object merely need someone to perceive them; only primary qualities link the object to the person who perceives it permitting us to explain how that object appears to the one who perceives it.

Berkeley went even further than Locke to dispute the rationalist view of intuitive forms of knowing by claiming that no one can refer to a world other than what they know and therefore cannot speak of objects having some kind of reality beyond the powers of observation. He believed that objects are what we can observe from an objective point of view. For Berkeley it is meaningless to speak of a world which transcends the world as it appears. What seems to be, according to Berkeley, reveals the mental state of the observer not the existence of things which are not mental (fact). The philosophical claims of these early empiricists about understanding objects and events thus differ dramatically from the rationalists who conceived of the possibility of things existing as mental constructs which supported the idea of impression as a detachment from reality or experiencing a state of "otherness" in imagination.

Locke, Berkeley and Hume as empiricist philosophers made at least three broad claims about objects and events: (1) ideas exist in objects (2) objects are only what we can observe factually about them and (3) observations (objects) change over time. Locke's efforts to distinguish between primary and secondary qualities advanced the proposition that objects have the power either to produce ideas in us or only to produce ideas (responses). Objects with primary qualities thus resemble the ideas that they express (communication), and secondary qualities (such things as the taste of salt, smell, or a particular shade of blue) do not. By establishing the concept that objects containing primary qualities have that quality within them it became possible for empiricist aestheticians to think of art objects as presenting truth (idea) through accurately representing the truth (idea) which inspired it. This was later interpreted by empiricist aestheticians to mean works of art function through their capacity to communicate specific ideas in unambiguous ways. More importantly from the interpretive mode, Locke's ideas make it possible to know what a work of art communicates, what the value is to the person who encounters it, and what that work communicates.

Others—Berkeley, in particular—challenged the view that objects could have another reality (spirit) that could not be seen. To Berkeley, it was meaningless and unverifiable to speak of the world of appearances or the manner in which things affect our mental state. This rejection of the rationalist view of objects as mental things reinforced Locke's idea that ideas exist (communicate) in things (works) and provided additional arguments to support expressive ideas as being factual and anchored in a real rather than in an imaginary world.

Hume's ideas that the relationships between things at different times is contingent and that there could be no necessary inference from past to future supported the empiricist notion of physical objects changing identity through time. Hume's concept, in all probability, influenced empiricist aestheticians and historians to conceive the meanings of art works as also changing over time. In particular, it probably suggested to the postmodernists that (a) the meanings of art works can only be interpreted from the prospective of contemporary life and (b) rather than one single history of art, many histories exist including those reflecting various gender, race, or sexual orientations.

Neo-Idealist Philosophical Thought

Neo-idealist philosophy sometimes referred to as German or post-Kantian philosophy appears to have originated in the writings of the philosopher, Immanuel Kant (1729-1804), and further adumbrated by philosophers, G.W.F. Hegel (1770-1831), Arthur Schopenhauer (1788-1860), Soren Kierkegaard (1813-1855), and Friedrich Wilhelm Nietzsche (1844-1900). Kant's principal idea was that neither the philosophy of empiricism nor rationalism was adequate and that the only realistic metaphysics was one constructed from both empiricist and rationalist concepts.

Kant claimed that for any viable philosophy both knowledge of the self and knowledge one's external world existing outside of our personal knowledge must be considered. Kant's view of the self was articulated in his transcendental unity of apperception, a form of self-consciousness existing both as a pre-supposition of self-knowledge and as a self discovered through experience. Self, according to Kant, is both a subject which has unity through awareness of its own existence and as an object in the process of its discovery. Thus an individual, in Kant's view, becomes a self as a subject which presupposes itself as an object. This conception of the self as being both aware of what it is and what it is becoming, that is, being at the same time both the subject and the object, powerfully challenged the prior definitions of subject and object offered by the rationalists and the empiricists. It is also this feature which makes neo-idealist thought the most difficult to understand, most particularly in Dewey's pragmatism and Heidegger's existentialism. When art cannot be understood either through the thoughts we have about it or through its physical appearance, one has to wonder if it is even possible to know what a work of art actually is.

Kant's disciple, G.W.F. Hegel, was, the neo-idealist philosopher who had the most influence on 20th century philosophy, specifically on the views of John Dewey, Martin Heidegger and Jean-Paul Sartre. Hegel's philosophy of being survives in the writings of Heidegger's dialectical process and in the pragmatism of William James and John Dewey. It is Hegel's dialectical process of thesis and antithesis which most influenced Dewey's (1934) ideas in *Art as Experience*. This work outlined the struggle between the known and the unknown that moves the individual to a higher state of knowing rather than to any form of absolute knowledge. Hegel's ideas also helped bring into existence the impersonal thinker associated with philosophical pragmatism and the existential concept of being which contains within itself its own negation—nothing, which was central to the duality expressed in Jean-Paul Sartre's *Being and Nothingness*. Hegelian epistemology, according to Scruton (1981), melts metaphysics into a philosophy of mind and theoretical understanding into practical reason.

Schopenhauer, a contemporary of Hegel, portrayed by some philosophical historians as having a love-hate relationship with the Hegelian system, put his faith in the Kantian value of practical knowledge which he believed found existence in knowledge of the will. Schopenhauer argued that it was impossible to assert that there is any aim to human activity, thus making life intrinsically meaningless. Satisfaction, in his view, was the fulfillment of one's desire in the form of the will which he felt continues even after death. The will according to Schopenhauer is not known through intellect but rather immediately through the actions we take, implying that what we are is what we do and what we are can only be known through the will which causes it.

Soren Kierkegaard like Schopenhauer put his faith in the inscrutable and in the challenge to refute the ideas of Hegelian rationalism, where the real is rational and the rational real. Like Schopenhauer, he also sought to find the spirit of life in the individual except that his particular interest in supporting the Christian faith was accomplished through the creation of a new philosophy called Existentialism. Critical of Hegel's logic envisioning a so-called universal subject, Kierkegaard claimed that the only legitimate subject is concrete and individual and only found outside of the laws of thought and in individuals who find their existence in the life activities which give them their subjectivity.

The philosophy of Friedrich Wilhelm Nietzsche, like that of Schopenhauer and Kierkegaard, also began with an emphasis on the individual but departed through his doubts about the ability of the individual to overcome his or her so-called common nature. Nietzsche sought a doctrine that allowed the individual to overcome human instincts in order to achieve mastery over, rather than slavery to, experience. Nietzsche's most important and also perhaps his most maligned contribution to philosophy was his goal of self-mastery through the development of courage, pride and firmness, a goal sometimes interpreted as mastery over others. This aspect of Nietzschian thought is most often characterized through references to his concept of the individual as a superman, capable of pride and self-confidence, rejecting the trivial and ineffectual, learning to control rather than be beholden to others.

While it is true that Nietzsche's ideas are most noted for their tough-mindedness, he is also recognized for his ideas of the individual taking responsibility for living through practical reason. It is Nietzsche's practical view of the individual which had the most influence on William James' and John Dewey's commitment to pragmatism. Unfortunately, Nietzsche's views which reject good and evil, see man as a law unto himself and define pity as a morbid fascination with failure are discussed more frequently than his arguments for the individual accepting responsibility for leading a more effective and responsible life.

As previously noted, neo-idealist thought on the individual's relations to objects and events can border on the unfathomable. Compared to rationalist and empiricist ideas they seem needlessly complex and confused. Where the rationalist views objects and events as things existing in the self and empiricists view them as things in themselves, the neo-idealists think neither concept is possible as nothing can ever be a result of self-knowledge or a matter of fact. In the neo-idealist view, objects and events are known both through self-knowledge and observation. When applied to art objects and the events in which they are created or observed, neo-idealists claim not to know about them either subjectively or objectively but rather through a state of objectified subjectivity.

The neo-idealist paradox of something being at one and the same time both objective and subjective comes mainly from Kant's claims that: (1) knowledge of an object is achieved through a synthesis of what we know *a priori* to seeing the object and what we learn from our more immediate experience with it, (2) the self is both the subject and the object of experience, and (3) objects and events are not real but only appearances which we perceive or are casually related to our perception. Objectified subjectivity as a concept also is supported by Hegel's notions that: (1) objects while not being two things at the same time can be two different things in succession, (2) knowledge of the self is also knowledge of objects, and (3) knowledge of objects constitutes a concept which may be objectified through individuals reflecting the universal.

The objectified subjectivity concept of objects and events laid out in the ideas of Kant and Hegel were later answered in a kind of "so what" response by philosophers Schopenhauer, Kierkegaard and Nietzsche who sought to apply the epistemological concerns of Kant and Hegel to real individuals functioning in a real world. Of the three philosophers Schopenhauer was perhaps the most pessimistic, believing that objects and events are only temporary representations which we must renounce as worthless and temporal pursuits. This has come to mean in 20th century art a rejection of the artist's intent as necessary to the aesthetic act. (Kierkegaard was somewhat more hopeful than Schopenhauer by concluding that the way we come to know the truth *is* the truth.) It is also according to Schopenhauer not what we believe as we can not know except through the process of knowing, which, at least proposes the possibility that we can learn *how to learn*. It was not until the 19th century when Nietzsche more practically noted that while we may not fully know what an object or event really is we can assess the possibility of these objects or events having a positive affect on our growth, pride and confidence in our self-hood. In the 20th century, the views of Schopenhauer and Kierkegaard came to be used as grounding for the values of creative expression and art as emotional release and the views of Nietzsche as central to the instrumental value of education through art.

The preceding analysis of selected and conceptually related philosophers on people's relations to objects and events was designed to suggest not only that differing philosophical conceptions are possible but that they are the cumulative result of over more than two thousand years of human thought about such issues. While admittedly both the number of philosophers and philosophical positions reviewed are not exhaustive, they are, at least, representative of the principal philosophical ideas advanced in 18th and 19th century thought. Also while these concepts may not always seem directly related to concerns about art and education, they are pivotal to answering the time honored problems still before us: What is our nature? What does it mean to exist and have being? How do we come to know what we know? How do we reason about what concerns us? How do we know what is valuable and worth doing?

In choosing to explore these philosophical issues this text supports the concept that when all things are not of equal value choices have to be made and a basis is needed for making informed decisions about what we can and should do in schools. Thus, having a philosophy regardless of which one you choose is essentially a practical matter and is central to the formulation of intelligent thought and expression in life itself. Again, this is not to say that intellect and aesthetic expression are one and the same thing but like the salt and pepper shaker, where there is one you are likely to find the other.

The next chapter describes the philosophical positions taken about objects and events laid out in this chapter as seminal to the development of 20th century thought and to the cultural paradigms most influencing our attitudes and behaviors in the process of setting goals and develop-ing curricula in today's schools. While this text cannot establish any causual relationship between the world of ideas and the world of aesthet-ic expression, it can demonstrate enough similarities to support the notions that important connections do exist and that they can provide sev-eral different intelligent courses of action for the conduct of art education in American schools.

References

Dewey, J. (1924). *Art as experience*. New York: G.P. Putnam's Sons.

Durant, W. (1961). *The story of philosophy*. New York: Washington Square Press.

Harrison, A. (1978). *Making and thinking: A study of intelligent activities*. Indianapolis: Hackett Publishing Co.

Langer, S. (1953). *Feeling and form*. New York: Charles Scribner's Sons.

Scruton, R. (1981). *From Descartes to Wittgenstein*. New York: Colophon Books.

Weitz, M. (1965). *Problems in aesthetics*. New York: The Macmillan Co.

Chapter 2

20th Century Thought

Chapter I, which addressed how the Greek and some 18th and 19th century philosophers thought about objects and events, suggests that whatever conclusions reached such matters are as a much a product of the individual's thoughts, as they are a result of the phenomena observed. The mode of thought used, in effect, determines the meaning of the object and event which will, in turn, vary according to the kind of attention one pays to it. Every mode of thought provides a different schema for attending to the world, and because we can attend to objects in different ways, different individuals can come up with different conclusions about the object's form, meaning and evolution. The mode of thinking used can also be construed, in a general way, to help make sense of our world both cognitively and affectively.

Thought is not just related to how we view objects but also to our feelings about life in general. This is due to the fact that our thoughts and feelings are related in both our physical and mental activities. In thought-feeling relationships we can, then, find ourselves mentally searching for a classification system which gives our search a sense of order and at the same time view ourselves as human beings who hold definite feelings about who we are and what we want to do in life. This suggests, moreover, that our thoughts about life and art are not processed in the mind differently from the thoughts we hold in the physical act of forming or creating art.

That thinking about life and art involve the same kinds of mental activity is amply demonstrated in the thinking and creative activity of important 20th century scholars, artists, and scientists. That the work of artists, scientists, and philosophers are shaped at different times by similar modes of thinking and feeling about life in general can be demonstrated through examining the common influences that have shaped this century's ways of thinking. These commonalities or similarities in thinking between different scholarly fields can also be said to exist within the field of art, especially through the common modes of thought artists, art historians, art critics, educators and aestheticians have used in writing about, teaching, and forming art in this century.

Interdisciplinary Influences

While it can be noted that most 20th century disciplines were influenced by the new science; in the arts, the effort to achieve, if not science, at least a new objectivity is particularly evident. Inspired by both the new science and the need for objectivity, newer interpretations and newer combinations of rationalist and empirical thought were developed and articulated by various 20th century philosophers. These newer interpretations were required to meet the challenges of the new science and technology and the demands for a new social order urged by an intelligentsia disillusioned by a revived sense of nationalism and by the human suffering experienced in two world wars.

In the first half of the century the rationalist ideas of Descartes, Spinosa and Leibniz were transformed by G.E. Moore, Clive Bell, and others into a more systematic and individually centered system for understanding and evaluating art. Einstein and others offering the new discoveries in relativity and physics inspired the rationalists to search for a new objectivity in expressive form and caused the empiricist ideas of Locke, Berkeley and Hume to be redefined into a language of art criticism. Changed also were the neo-idealist philosophies of Kant and Hegel which were reinterpreted through newer combinations of rationalist and empirical thought in order to meet the newer 20th century discoveries in sociology, psychology, and economics.

While these newer modes of thought were rooted in premises laid down by the Greeks, they were also aimed at finding different ways to meet the rapidly changing scientific, artistic, political and social challenges of the time. In art, the twentieth century was a time when

- Einstein's discoveries of relativity and of the time-space continuum affected the way space was ordered in painting.

- Marx's political thought and Freudian psychology radically influenced its form and content.

- The positivist ideas of Wittgenstein and the anthropological views of Levi Strauss inspired new uses of language and ritual now seen as the basis for the revisionist and the deconstructivist art of today.

Because the way we think about things is influenced by significant events such as new discoveries and inventions, wars, and revolutions, this chapter is organized chronologically beginning with Moore's new objectivity and continuing on with the discoveries of science, the influences of two world wars, and the effects of the communist revolution. This order is to suggest that patterns of thought are linked to significant events but should not be interpreted to mean that a clear cause and effect relationship exists between modes of thought and the events that inspire them. As previously noted patterns of thought do not invent themselves instantaneously, occur in sequence, replace one another, nor become obsolescent. They do, in fact, evolve slowly and from time to time come to the surface and are recognized while at other times they submerge into obscurity.

There are, in this century, essentially three central themes or modes of artistic thought which have developed and continue to reappear from time to time:

• The concept of objective art form.

• The role of the subconscious and irrational in artistic forming.

• Art as language and criticism.

This chapter attempts to show how these different modes of thought reveal themselves in the common patterns of thought used by philosophers, aestheticians, art historians, art critics, and artists at a given time. The sequence begins in each period by first discovering the philosophical, socio-logical, or psychological concepts influencing the period, secondly identify-ing the aestheticians who have used the concepts in defining art and thirdly, offering the views of various artists, art critics, and art historians who have attempted to use the concept in either thinking about or making art.

In characterizing the 20th century, it might help to begin by noting that in the first decade Max Planck published his quantum theory, Sigmund Freud his *Interpretations of Dreams* and Edmund Husserl his phenomonological doctrine entitled *Logical Investigation*. R. A. Fessenden transmitted the first wireless speech over one mile, sound recordings on wax discs were invented, Wilber and Orville Wright flew the first airplane; and Albert Einstein announced his special theory of relativity. By the close of the first decade, Lenin had published his *Two Tactics for Social Democracy in a Democratic Revolution* and Henry Ford introduced the Model T.

Probably no direct parallels will ever be found in the simultaneous emer-gence of Ford's Model T and Frank Lloyd Wright's Robie House or in Einstein and Paul Klee being born in the same year (1879) or in the Fauve painters' uses of color at the time Edwin S. Porter developed the art of film editing in *The Great Train Robbery*. Some events may be connected only because they occurred at the same time, others possibly, because modern artists, thinkers, inventors and politicians unconsciously influenced one another's ideas or works. In still other cases actual structural and metaphori-cal parallels do exist to establish the connections. McMullen in his book, *Art Influence and Alienation*, feels that real parallels do exist mainly because different groups were seeking solutions to similar technical problems, responding to similar intellectual challenges, and trying to solve similar emo-tional difficulties (McMullen, 1968).

McMullen also believed what made the modern period unprecedented is that in nearly every category, the old reality was not replaced by something equally substantial, accessible and satisfying. The old, in his view, was replaced in some cases with a question and in other cases, a negation. He cites, as examples, that 20th century religious figures defined Hell as mental rather than physical, scientists had to deal with the decline of positivism, mathematicians with the discovery that internal consistency is not provable mathematically, and aestheticians with no longer being able to define art.

These changes in the century's political, religious, social and cultural values were evident in at least four 20th century movements or events: (1) the rationalist challenge to traditional modes of ethical and aesthetic inquiry; (2) the new objectivity in science and art; (3) the new science, politics, the subconscious and irrational; and (4) the atomic age forms of feeling fostered by existentialism and alienation.

Analytical Philosophy Early in the Century

Philosophical historians, especially those seeking early events that influenced change in 20th century art, generally see some change beginning with the analytical philosophy of George Edward Moore (1873-1958), an important British empiricist. The analytical approach used by Moore is best known through his work entitled *Principia Ethica* published by Cambridge University in 1903. Moore's method challenged the existing idealist notions of ethics and beauty as being determined by canons of inquiry external to the viewer's experience. Moore's analytical methods (unlike the methods used to determine ideal beauty) required that the process of inquiry consider at least four important steps: (1) to establish clear concepts, (2) to use unambiguous terms and definitions, (3) to find discernable elements as descriptors, and (4) to arrive at appropriate conclusions. Most novel was the concept that the viewer was central to the critical process.

Applying this process in the *Principia Ethica*, Moore first distinguishes between two kinds of questions: (1) what kinds of things ought to exist for their own sake? and (2) what kinds of actions ought we to perform? Secondly, Moore decides on the nature of evidence in answering the question deducing that there can be no answer to question one but there can be proof or disproof of question two (Moore, 1903). Moore's approach to the ethical problem is both personal and informal. Evidence exists in two forms according to Moore: truth with regards to the action in question, and causal and ethical truths.

In the *Principia Ethica*, Moore lays out at least three conceptual notions undoubtedly influenced by rationalist thought and later enlarged upon by other rationalist aestheticians. These were (1) a concept of relations between subject and object, (2) a morphology of feeling in aesthetic response, and (3) a conceptual base for aesthetic judgment. Moore's object-subject relationship belief suggests that objects are, in effect, mental things in which no distinction can be drawn between real or imaginary sense. Moore defined a morphology of feeling in aesthetic response as involving three stages: (1) recognition, (2) awareness of emotion, and (3) response to that emotion. On matters of aesthetic judgment he believed that the value is in the response rather than in the object and that art had no causal relationship with ordinary life. Moore also believed that aesthetic judgment is the highest of all value judgments that form and content are inseparable, and that what is ugly is a conception of truth which ultimately is a corruption of the self.

Some 10 years after Moore's *Principia,* the prominent critic Clive Bell

- Incorporated Moore's elements and principles in Bell's idea of significant form.

- Introduced the element of aesthetic emotion in the form of Moore's recognition, awareness, response categories.

- Reaffirmed Moore's criteria for aesthetic judgment by rejecting the separation of form and content (though noting the ethical character of aesthetic judgments) and in separating artistic response from ordinary life.

Bell, like Moore, viewed art from an egoist viewpoint believing that art was an end in itself. This view is evident in his two most important concepts, aesthetic emotion and significant form: He felt that all systems of aesthetics are based on the personal experience of a peculiar emotion and that the quality shared by all objects which provokes that emotion is "significant form." Bell's definition of aesthetic emotion borders on being mystical. It is, in his view, something which one does or does not have, a peculiar emotion provoked by works of art and a felt emotional response which signifies the object's status as a work of art. Bell attacks the possibility of any criticism outside of one's own personal aesthetic response by rejecting the idea of an objective aesthetics being possible and by noting the uselessness of critics telling us whether something is a work of art or by interpreting the work for us. In Bell's view recognizing an object as a work of art is possible only through our feelings; any critic can only help us to see; and an object cannot be considered a work of art until we react emotionally and validate it through our feelings.

Because Bell believed that not all persons can have an aesthetic emotion, some view Bell as supporting an "Art is caught not taught" educational view. Bell even states that "art is not learned, at any rate it is not to be taught" (Bell, 1958, p. 253). He also believed that art schools do nothing but harm; that drawing masters teach only the craft of imitation and that art is not something to study but rather a thing to enjoy. With regard to museum education, Bell notes, "An artisan of exceptional sensitivity may get something from the masterpieces of the National Gallery provided there is no cultivated person at hand to tell him what to feel or to prevent him feeling anything by telling him to think" (Bell, 1958, p. 285).

Bell's iconoclastic educational stance is somewhat refuted, however, in his recommendations for the art education of the young when he notes,

> Do not tamper with that direct emotional reaction to things which is the genius of children. Do not destroy their sense of reality by teaching them to manipulate labels. Do not imagine that adults must be the best judges of what is good and what matters. (Bell, 1958, p. 286)

Bell believed that we should not educate children to feel anything, but rather put them in the way of finding out what they want and what they are. His educational view, generally, was that we should encourage everyone to create artistic form at least up to an amateur level status.

Bell is, of course, most widely known for his concept of "significant form" which he believed exists in all objects which provoke aesthetic emotions. Bell defines significant form as the particular way certain forms and relations of form stir our aesthetic emotions. These are sensed, he believed, in combination of lines and colors, and recognized through perceiving intellectually the rightness and necessity of the particular combination of forms. Why these forms move us, according to Bell, is because they express the emotion of the creator. The artist-viewer relationship, in Bell's view, centers on the artist's aesthetic emotion in the work evoking an emotion of the same kind in the mind of the viewer. Summarizing Bell's views, the artist experiences material beauty through forms, lines and colors, form relationships, and principles, all of which invoke emotions expressed by the artist as form relationships and when experienced by the viewer, evoke similar emotions which are not visual. Aesthetic judgment of the work is thus found in a rightness of form due to the rightness of emotion.

The form the artists creates, according to Bell, is for the objectification of emotions and is not a literal thing, but rather one in which the emotion conveyed from the artist to the viewer is an emotion of the same kind. Bell believed the object of the artist's emotion while unknown is expressible. The artist is not bound to vision, but to an emotion and an expressive form free of anything seen or found in the ideas of life. "We cannot know what the artist feels but only what he creates" states Bell (1958, p. 58). What is right form, according to Bell, is the rightness of the emotion in the first place, that is, the right state of mind in the artist which provokes an aesthetic emotion in others—a thing in itself.

The Objective Challenge in Science and in Art

In all probability one of the greatest influences on this century was the work of Albert Einstein (1879-1955). He advanced his (best known) special theory of Relativity in 1905, when he was only 26 and is today considered to be one of the fathers of the atomic age. Einstein contributed three important papers that year, which are now acknowledged as the century's most important contributions to science. One paper argued that light could be thought of as a stream of small particles called quantum which is now part of the *quantum theory*. A second paper titled, *"The Electrodynamics of Moving Bodies,"* presented his special theory of relativity and a third paper was on the Brownian involvement concerning the irregular motion of microscopic particles suspended in a liquid or gas which confirmed the atomic theory of matter.

Einstein's quantum theory paper made possible the invention of the photoelectric cell and the development of motion pictures and television. The second and perhaps Einstein's most important paper demonstrated the equivalent of mass and energy expressed in the equation $E = MC^2$. In the formula, E stands for energy, M stands for mass and the C^2 is a constant factor equal to the speed of light squared. This formula laid out the basis for atomic energy, which helped scientists determine in the process of splitting atoms how to calculate the amount of mass that was changed into energy.

Einstein actually proposed two theories of relativity, one called the special theory in 1905 and a second known as the general theory in 1915. The special theory refers to motion and is used to describe natural happenings. These have to do with time, space, mass, motion and gravitation. This theory deduced several important physical notions including: (1) no material can move with a greater velocity than light, (2) the rhythm of a clock on a fast moving train is faster than the rhythm of clocks on the ground, (3) two events judged at the same time by an observer on a train are not simultaneous for the observer on the ground, (4) the length of objects on a fast moving train are shortened in the direction the train is moving and (5) a particle of matter accelerated to 86% of the speed of light has twice as much mass as when at rest. For example, a car battery with its energy used weighs less than one fully charged and a compressed spring weighs more than the one which is uncompressed.

Einstein's theory made answering when and where an event took place much more complex as his theory of relativity demonstrated that rods can change their lengths, and clocks their rhythms depending on the speed of the object which propels them. As a result, when and where an event occurs is modified, especially the "when" which has no meaning unless we know the special factors characterizing the event.

Alfred North Whitehead (1861-1947), the 20th century philosopher most frequently noted for his efforts to define scientific relativity in terms of philosophical relativity, argued that observational knowledge is perception through duration rather than only in the present. Whitehead was an English philosopher and mathematician who was especially noted for his work to narrow the gap between philosophy and science. His main contribution was to recognize that scientific knowledge, though precise, was incomplete and needed both philosophical principles and the insights of the artist.

Whitehead (1982) in his book entitled, *An Enquiry Concerning the Principles of Natural Knowledge*, attempted to inquire into the problem of how space is rooted in human experience which he felt might be answered in a new way through the new modern theory of relativity. He acknowledged the contributions of Larmor, Lorentz, Einstein and Minkovske toward establishing a physical basis for explaining relativity, but felt also that the philosophical ideas of Berkeley, Hume, Kant, Mill, Huxley, Bertrand Russell and Bergson were equally important. His concern was not only to address the object as perceptual knowledge, but also the synthesis of what he called the knower and the known.

In his inquiry, Whitehead reasoned that a conception of location in space is distinct from that of being situated in an event, therefore, hypothesizing that an object is located in an element of instantaneous space which is always an ideal of thought. Using music as an example, Whitehead argued that a tune cannot be situated in any event comprised of a duration too short for the successive notes to be sounded, thus requiring a minimum quantum of time. A tune, he observed, is not a uniform object in the sense a chair is recognized as an object. A musical note he argued cannot exist in a period of time shorter than a period of vibration too short for anyone to hear it (Whitehead, 1982).

Whitehead argued also that past conceptions of objects and events led to the idea that space is related to objects not to events. This concept, he felt, led to notions of different kinds of space, (for example, tactile space, and visual space), which was in his view due to the error of deducing space from the relations between forms. Whitehead concluded that with the newer notions of relativity, we must reject notions of different kinds of space.

In rejecting the notion of space being tied to objects and by accepting the notion that an object is a characteristic or product of an event, Whitehead, in effect, challenged Bell's ideas of significant form as relations between forms. Instead Whitehead suggested "that objects are known only through a full knowledge of the parts as situations of objects, and the parts by a full knowledge of the whole" (Whitehead, 1982, p. 195). This, Whitehead argued, is because objects express life but do not live as in the individual life of a human being.

Whitehead's ideas on objects and events if applied to art objects suggest we must consider them as having duration, being relational, having continuity and extension, and needing verification. He supports the notions that

- An object must be studied over time, from varied viewpoints and with no preconceptions.

- Objects are relational and make sense only over time and in relation to other objects.

- An object represents a continuity of events being both an event and part of other events.

- Our perceptions of objects must be relative and require interpretation which must be verified.

A number of important artists, critics and historians share Whitehead's belief that 20th century art has been influenced by science. Maurice Raynal in 1912 noted its influence in cubist art through their analytical separation of objects, all bodies owing their form to mathematical means, objects being amplified by movement and diminished through repose, and the dynamics of one body influencing the status of another. Raynal noted also, that the futurists sought to render movement in various objects and accepted the importance of relativity in human experience by endorsing the Kantian aesthetic which supports painting as both science in search of absolute truth and as pure sensuous pleasure. Painting, he believed, should be art derived from the disinterested study of forms, noting Juan Gris's practice of numbering rather than giving titles to his paintings.

Guillaume Apollinaire, like Raynal, also noted the new artist's use of geometry by noting like the scientists of that time, painters also, by intuition, were led to pre-occupy themselves with the new possibilities of spatial measurement designated as the fourth dimension. Cubist painting, he felt, needed a dimension greater than the third in order to express a synthetic of views and feelings toward the object. Apollinaire saw the source of the fourth dimension in plastic terms as springing from the three dimensions by representing space eternalizing itself in all directions at any given moment—a dimension of the infinite.

Paul M. Laporte (1944) some years later tried to make the case that it was Picasso who was most involved in using the space/time concept in art. Laporte noted that up until the time of Picasso the viewer was outside the space depicted in the work. Picasso, he believed, really established the principles of an entirely new space concept through striving for simultaneity of several points of view. Citing as an example Picasso's "Les Demoiselles d' Avignon," he argued that it was Picasso who wanted to re-create nature, the essence of which was a variety of bodies moving through space with different speeds in different directions. He also thought that it was more than coincidental that Einstein's special theory of relativity was published in 1905 just two years before Picasso finished his painting.

Laporte believed that both the scientist and the artist were faced with the problem of explaining the relations between space and time at about the same time in history. The problem faced by the artist was, in his view, the need to integrate kinesthetic sensations with visual perceptions in such a manner as to make the four dimensions of space and time equivalent to each other. Laporte describes Picasso's space invention by comparing it with Renaissance space by noting,

> The "Renaissance" picture is observed through an infinite number of lines issuing from the picture and meeting in one point in front of it. There is a definite reference of the extension of the picture to the sense limitations of the observer. A "conic view" is established, the observer taking the position of the point of the cone. The manner of observation needed for the Renaissance painting is connected with the naively egocentric method of the natural sciences of this period, and with the psychologizing tendencies of the Reformation. (Laporte, 1949, p. 32)

In 1951 Felix Marti-Ibanez, a medical historian, delivered an extremely detailed paper on the "Psychological Impact of Atomic Science on Modern Art" at the 13th International Congress of Psychology in Sweden. Marti-Ibanez believed that the scientific changes of early 1900's were due less to scientific discovery than to a conception of new relationships among various ideas. This is supported through his claims that people needed to develop their own ideas about the atomic structure of matter because "the conception of the atom was from the beginning in apparent contradiction with the testimony of his [man's] own senses" (Marti-Ibanez, 1958, p. 513).

Marti-Ibanez also believed that historically scientific and artistic thought influence each other even though the artist does not deliberately reflect scientific truth in his or her art. Moreover, he believed that the modern artist is both a businessman in transactions and a scientist in techniques. Behind the stroke of every brush, he notes, there is a hand directed by a person whose brain is permeated by the ideas of the century in which he or she lives. Marti-Ibanez saw this influence beginning in 1907 in all forms of modern art including Surrealism, Cubism and abstract art. He found evidence of this influence in the cubists' efforts to create new combinations of known forms, the futurists glorifying the dynamism of the machine, the surrealists' violations of custom and convention, and the abstract artists' representing only geometric form which is pure and abstract. Abstract art in particular, he believed, accepts the fact that form can be an end, a basis of function, or function itself preceding structure.

The Objective Challenge of the Spirit in Art

At the same time the arts were being influenced by the empiricism of the space/time concepts and the new science, they were also being influenced by another view coming from the experiential side of empirical thought. This view was first introduced by Kant (1963) in his Transcendental Unity of apperception later referred to as both Transcendental Idealism and the

Transcendental Analytic. Kant's notion was that the self has an identity over time and, as a presupposition of self-knowledge, contributes to the transcendental deduction which presents the possibility of thought as if it were objective. This notion is funded also in Kant's view of the self as both subject and object in the experience of becoming, which accepts experience as both an *a priori* concept of substance and an idea of substance which is a reflection of being in experience.

Kant in dismissing Berkeley's "empirical idealism" asserted that his philosophy of "transcendental idealism" was a form of "empirical realism." By this Kant meant that the world of which we have knowledge really exists independently and is a world of appearance only in the sense that it exists in time consisting of objects and processes which are either perceived by us or else causally related to our perception.

Kant's Transcendental Analytic is essentially a discussion of the logical foundations of human thought and is defended on the basis that certain basic and fundamental assumptions are necessary for thinking to take place. This is supported by the notion that experience implies a concept which can be stated as the synthetic-apriori proposition that makes thought possible. The objective-subjective arguments in Kant's theory assume that ideas conceived by the mind are independent of experience and applicable to all minds in a nonsubjective way. This becomes possible through developing conceptual categories or pigeon holes which become prior mental concepts for organizing sensations in order to think about them.

Hegel, like Kant, also saw the ideas of both the empiricists and the rationalists as problematic, wanting to keep the best features of both philosophies through constructing a thought hierarchy beginning at the lowest level with sensations, moving to memory and then imagination, reaching the highest level in reason. Hegel argued that art resolved the antithesis of mind and senses through representing particular insights into the "world spirit" which was a record of the mental state of insight. The sensuous in art, he felt, was spiritualized, appearing in sensuous space (Gray, 1970). The method used in art production was characterized by Hegel as a subjective activity with the same properties found objectively in the work. He argued also that this was a form of spiritual activity which in itself contained both the elements of sensuousness and immediateness.

Hegel undoubtedly found his spiritual premise in Kant's notion of "objective purpose" described by Kant as "purposiveness without purpose" (1963, p. 32) and believed by Hegel to be essential in judging what was beautiful. Kant felt, furthermore, to judge objective purposiveness one must understand that this purposiveness is an internal perfection and not an external usefulness and that things of qualitative perfection are judged through the conformity of the thing with the concept of what sort of thing it should be. Hegel further advanced Kant's idea by stipulating art in the same category as science yet exempt from scientific rules, arguing that while beauty and art are part of the business of life they also adorn our surroundings, sooth the sadness of our condition, cover the embarrassments of life and in doing so fall outside the real purposes of life.

In the 20th century, Hegel's notions of art as a spirit and Kant's purposiveness without purpose are contained in what we refer today as the philosophy of the spirit or the spiritual in art. The concept has been written about by a number of aestheticians and, artists, in particular the Italian aesthetitian Benedetto Croce and the Russian artist, Wassily Kandinsky, both of whom were born in 1866.

Benedetto Croce's notions about the spiritual in art and about purposeness were primarily addressed in his book entitled *Aesthetic* published in 1909 (reissued in 1983). To Croce the spirit which wills itself, its true self, the universal which is the empirical and finite spirit: This formula defines the essence of morality with the least impropriety—the will for the true self as *absolute freedom*. In his *Aesthetic*, Croce includes art, religion and philosophy among the disciplines he calls the "mystical aesthetic" a term most closely associated with his concept of artistic intuition.

Croce, while accepting generally the ideas of Hegel and Kant, is critical of some of their views. He accepts Hegel's notion of intuitive knowledge but criticizes Hegel's distinctions between art and science which he felt made art the lesser domain of the two. He also criticized Hegel's concept of art as being too abstract and too cognitive. His criticism of Kant's aesthetic was that Kant, too, was tied to the intellect and was directed more to aesthetic judgment than to art.

Croce's aesthetic is primarily associated with his idea on intuition and emotion, noting that intuitive knowledge needed no further proof, that it was linked to perception and objectified impressions. In this regard Croce states:

> Intuition is the undifferentiated unity of the perception of the real and the simple image of the possible. In our intuitions we do not oppose ourselves as empirical beings to external reality, but we simply objectify our impressions whatever they be. (Croce, 1983, p. 4)

Croce felt that intuition functions in art because art is an expression of impressions rather than an expression of expression. There is, in his view, only one aesthetic, and that one is the science of intuitive or expressive knowledge which is an aesthetic or artistic *fact*. Aesthetic intuition is thus knowledge, truth, and theory, but distinct from intellectual knowledge and from perceptions of what is real. Art is knowledge of form, a knowledge separate from the world of feeling or from psychic matter. This is possible, he believes, through elaborating the artist's impressions, thus freeing the artist from them, objectifying them and making the artist superior to them.

What makes art factual, according to Croce, is the activity of externalization, which satisfies aesthetic vision through the will to preserve and communicate it to others. Expression, in his view, is theoretical activity and precedes practical and intellectual knowledge. Expression does not, Croce notes, possess means, because it is not an end, making art independent of utility, morality and practice and thus becoming in the process pure theoretic contemplation.

The artist most closely associated with the spirit movement in art was the Russian painter, Wassily Kandinsky (1866-1944). Kandinsky studied law and political economy and played the piano and cello, all of which he gave up at the age of thirty in order to pursue a career in painting. His connection with the spiritual is described mainly in his book, *Concerning the Spiritual in Art* (1977). Kandinsky became well known as both a painter and a writer, and particularly for his writings on behalf of the *Blaue Reiter*, for a biography in 1913 and for his 1912 book *Uber das Sastigein Gestige in der Kunst (Concerning the Spiritual in Art)*. In 1919 he became Director of the Museum of Pictorial Culture in Moscow, and in 1920 was named Professor of Art at the University of Moscow. He later taught at both the Weimar and Dessau Bauhaus, moving to Paris in 1933.

Kandinsky in his *Concerning the Spiritual in Art* argued that a work of art was born in the artist in a mysterious and secret way which assumed a life of its own. Art, in his view, had the power to create a spiritual atmosphere and only when its form was poor did it become too weak to call forth a "spiritual vibration." A painting is well painted, noted Kandinsky, when its spiritual value is completed and is satisfying to him. Painting is an art which is directed to the development and refinement of the human soul, raising it to what he calls "the triangle of the Spirit" (Kandinsky, 1977, p. 10). Kandinsky also felt that the painter had at least three responsibilities: (1) to return to the talent he has, (2) to create a spiritual atmosphere, and (3) to adopt those thoughts and actions which are the materials of his creations into a positive influence of the spiritual atmosphere. The artist was, in his view, the guardian of a beauty produced by internal necessity which sprang from the soul moving the "spiritual triangle" upwards and forwards.

In order to grasp the meaning of Kandinsky's ideas on the spiritual, the reader needs to accept both Kant's categorical imperatives and Hegel's dialectical. Kant's imperative has three properties: It makes no reference to desires, is restrained by reason, and contains a motive to act or to persuade obedience. The imperative supports the notion of a thing having objective necessity which is achieved through the individual reflecting both needs and desires and empirical determinations bound only to rational nature alone. Hegel's dialectic on the other hand is an attempt to apply the Socratic method in an effort to find a philosophical truth through disputation. Hegel's dialectic functions through the concept of thesis and antithesis which begins with *thesis* as a potential description of what is real but containing its own negation as *antitheses* which is resolved through the struggle between them. Through repeating this process the conflict is resolved through reaching a higher plane which can finally be comprehended and reconciled through *synthesis* which generates another new concept which, in turn, generates its own negation continuing the process until the reality of it becomes apparent (Kandinsky, 1977, p. 36).

In Hegel's dialectic in art the goal is to move from the *physical level* of material to the *idea level* which forms the *spiritual*. Although Kandinsky does not mention either Kant or Hegel in his text, he views the painting process as a visual dialectic applying a visual *thesis, antithesis* and *synthesis* which finally comes to be the form of the work. Form in this sense is the total effect or the "gestalt" of work. This view denies the possibility of form and content being separated from the expressive import of the work. The work, in this aesthetic, is thus a synthesis of what is expressed and the means used to express it, and the victory is when the push-pull of thesis and antithesis makes the spirit become the victor over matter.

Between the Wars: Art, Science, Politics, The Subconscious and the Irrational

Interestingly, Surrealism is probably the only art epoch to begin at the end of one war, World War I, and conclude just before the start of another, World War II. Describing surrealism in the context of the effects of World War I, Maurice Nadeau notes:

> Moralities aesthetics have been created to make you respect fragile things, What is fragile should be broken. Our heroes are the parricide Violette Nozore the anonymous criminal of common law, the conscious and refined perpetrator of sacrilege. 'The traditional opposition of 'bourgeois' and 'artist' is replaced by the violent antinomy of the revolutionary and the property-owner, the slave and his master. Having started from a rather mystical idealism of the omnipotence of spirit over matter, the surrealists arrive, at least, in theory, at a materialism of revolution in things themselves. (Nadeau, 1965, p. 5)

As to the events shaping the period, Nadeau points out in particular, that following the armistice neither the victors nor the vanquished found their destitution less severe. After four years of slaughter and destruction of every kind, he notes both sides faced a material destitution and impoverishment severe enough to shake confidence in their respective regimes. The loss of confidence, he felt, was due to the government's gigantic efforts to rectify borders and conquer new ports, creating a disproportion between means and ends that bordered on madness. The feeling of the times, he believed, was that the elites applauded the massacre in every country and the intellectual disciplines including the sciences, philosophy, art and literature were bankrupt and unable to prevent civilization from turning against and devouring itself. The major disillusionment, he felt, was in having a war to inaugurate a new stability everyone knew could not happen and in finding reason, logic, time, and space turning people into cerebral monsters with hypertrophied rational faculties useless in changing the real world.

The period reflected, for Nadeau, the cynicism of people torn between reason, discredited but arrogant, finding solace only in dreams—the true source of their acts, thoughts, and life—and separating private life from public life, the unconscious from the conscious, and dream from logic only to reduce the leaning tower of bourgeois respectability to rubble. It is time, he notes, for no more knowledge as "knowledge dispenses with reason, action transcends it. Beauty, Art have been the conquests of logic; they must be destroyed. Poetry must be 'soul' speaking to 'soul', dreams must be substituted for directed thought" (Nadeau, 1965, p. 49).

Nadeau's references to the "Dream" and to the "bourgeois" and to the decline of logic reflect at least three important influences of this period: (1) Sigmund Freud's (1856-1939) contributions to the field of Psychoanalysis, (2) Karl Marx's (1818-1883) Dialectical Materialism and the development of Communism and (3) the influence of Ludwig Wittgenstein (1889-1951) and Rudolph Carnap in the development of Logical Positivisim.

The link between these three separate influences can be found mainly in the new science and the emergence of the new political philosophy of Hegel and the Post-Hegelian philosophies of Schopenhauer and Nietzsche. It was mainly the spirit of empiricism which helped form the basis for modern political philosophy. Thomas Hobbs in the 18th century was the first to propose that men are not obligated to the state unless they are part of the consent process. The sovereign, in his view, acts with the authority of all who seek his protection. Marx's historical materialism borrowed both from Plato's ideas on rights and powers and from Hobb's notion that sovereign power creates the possibility of a just order. Marx rejected John Locke's idea of the "natural rights" to life and limb, freedom of choice and property but accepted his idea of labor generating ownership and the criterion of legitimacy in the mutual consent of individuals to reject their rights and freedoms.

Hegel's notions of human rights were influenced by the doctrine of the "social contract" associated with Jean-Jacques Rousseau's idea that conflicts with the general will must be constrained by the general will which, in effect, ensures that people will be "forced" to be free. Hegel's politics have roots in the conception of the individual self which could be realized through a dialectical interaction with others bringing recognition of the existence of a social being and a moral law which recognizes the selfhood of others as ends not means. Hegel's argument makes it clear that a political philosophy cannot be conceived independently of a philosophy of mind which replaces the doctrine of "natural right" with the intrinsic obligation to be ruled by a government which provides for individual autonomy. The idea that a concept of mind could account for the fact that individuals create themselves and their own institutions undoubtedly influenced both Karl Marx and Sigmund Freud. This influence can be seen in Marx's attempt to synthesize Hegel's philosophy of mind with empiricist economics and in Freud through the definition of intuitive and expressive knowledge espoused by Hegel's student, Benedetto Croce. That Freud valued this definition and built upon it can be seen in his citation of Hildebrant's definition of the Dream

> 'A dream is something severed from the reality experienced in waking life, something as one might say, with a hermetically sealed existence of its own and separated from real life by an impossible gulf. It sets us free from reality, extinguishes our normal memory of it and places us in another world and in quite another life story which in essentials has nothing to do with the real one' (Freud, 1965, p. 43)

Sigmund Freud

Sigmund Freud (1856-1939) in his *Interpretation of Dreams* (1965) challenged the concept of reason through the irrational. In this work, Freud explored all that could be known about neurotic behavior from the viewpoints of both Darwinian rationalism and Nietzchean irrationalism. His most important discovery was the duality of the unconscious rational mind and of an irrational existence driven by the instinctive force defined in Darwin's construct of instinct. Freud believed what was unconscious was only observable in neurotic behaviors, slips of the tongue, and the analysis of dream content. He viewed all behavior not in the Hegelian sense of being goal-directed but rather as determined by the sex drive and the death wish. He is, of course, best known for his conception of human behavior existing on three distinct levels: the *id* as instinct which is both sexual and death directed, the *ego* which is the conscious preservation of instinct, and the *super ego* which he views as the conscience or parent stimulus. Life was, in Freud's terms, a Hegelian dialectic between these three instincts,—the *id, ego* and *super ego*—in search of an equilibrium or synthesis through the rechanneling of repression and sublimation.

According to sociologist C.D. Axelrod, Freud also accepted Hegel's notions with regard to human rights as evidenced in Freud's words that "the patient's relationship to the norm (and the law) tends to subvert his authorship and that his membership in the community interferes with authenticity." (Axelrod, 1979, p. 18) Axelrod also viewed Freud's concept of ego as a form of political-social identity in which ordinary conversation is both organizational metaphor for party doctrine and the method by which ego defines its membership in political-social life.

Axelrod also observed that Freud used science as a metaphor for authenticity which in the therapeutic encounter progresses toward authenticating the patient's speech. This did, however, create a curious problem for Freud because science like the law is yet another one of society's institutions with a set of rules ordering and restricting speech. He suggests further that this was a problem Freud himself recognized and that in the final analysis Freud felt that science itself must be disregarded in order to begin to speak authentically.

Axelrod viewed Freud's text, *The Interpretation of Dreams*, as making it an occasion to contest and interpret human speech and more specifically deal with the problem of human expressiveness. Axelrod notes that

> dream reports are used to chart an area of double-meaning expression. Speech possesses both manifest and hidden meanings. For Freud, while any speech functions to allow ego to maneuver within its concrete world, this same speech is also a disguised version of human expressiveness. (Axelrod, 1979, p. 29)

Freud did apply his psychoanalytic concepts beyond the practical concerns of therapy. He included psychoanalysis in discussions of literature, politics, law, religion and the arts. In art, one of his most famous works was a book on Leonardo entitled, *Eine Kindheitserinneruny des Leonardo da Vinci*, (A Childhood Reminiscence of Leonardo da Vinci, 1947).

In this book Freud suggested that Leonardo was motivated by homosexual feelings—feelings apparent in Vasari's claim that Leonardo felt he had not done his duty to his art. Freud finds proof of this in da Vinci's late-in-life abandonment of painting, leaving much work unfinished, and in his lack of concern for the future fate of his works. Freud's psychoanalysis of Leonardo was performed through an examination of early 20th century writings about da Vinci's life and of Leonardo's notebooks.

Through this paleopsychological material Freud attempted to show the psychosexual evolution of the child Leonardo, noting that the psychic experiences of his childhood could have led to a neurosis, perversion, or abnormality. He used these writings about Leonardo's life (and age) and grouped them around the story of Leonardo's phantasy of a vulture which visited him in the cradle and forcefully opened his mouth to manipulate it with his tail. This action was interpreted by Freud as corresponding with the idea of *fellatio* which displaced Leonardo's memories of being nursed by his mother. In Freud's analysis, Leonardo's early vision which Leonardo transformed into a phantasy replacement of a mother suggests that he missed his father and felt alone with the mother. This event along with other observations led Freud to conclude that Leonardo was homosexual. Freud views the forces of Leonardo's psyche as being responsible for his art productions which Freud believed served as an outlet for his sexual desire. Freud notes,

There is now hardly any doubt that the productions of the artist also gives an outlet to his sexual desire. In the case of Leonardo we can refer to the information imported by Vasari that heads of laughing women and pretty boys, that is representations of his sexual objects attracted attention among his first artistic efforts. (Freud, 1947, p. 113)

Freud's conclusion from the study of Leonardo was that artistic talent is intimately connected with sublimation.

Freud's Hegelian concept of the dream and his view of the therapeutic encounter closely parallel the views held by the principal idealogue and originator of the term "Surrealism," Andre Breton. An important artist of his time sometimes referred to as the surrealist 'pope', Breton embraced the Marxist tenet of a dialectical program leading from thought to action. He is best known in the literature of the times for his *Manifesto of Surrealism*, (1924, reissued in 1969), for his periodical *Surrealism au service de la Revolution* (1930-1933) and his manifesto *Towards a Free Revolutionary Art* jointly authored with Leon Trotsky. Philosophically, Breton became the principal conduit for the ideas of Freud in Surrealism and of Marx through his efforts with other artists of his time to create a new social order (Seltz, 1968, p. 457).

Breton's 1924 *Manifesto of Surrealism* is probably the best known work dealing with the belief system undergirding Surrealism. Indeed, it is hard to separate Surrealism from Andre Breton for as Chipp notes,

Surrealism may be described in two quite different ways: in the broadest philosophic sense, as one of the important poles toward which art and the thought have always been drawn and specifically, as the ideology of an organized group of artists and writers who from about 1924 on gathered about Andre Breton in Paris. It is to this latter group that we owe the term Surrealism itself, and to a large extent the recognition of its earlier manifestations. (Chipp, 1968, p. 366)

In the Manifesto, Breton credits Freud as his inspiration for the Surrealist movement. He gives thanks to Freud for his discoveries, makes numerous references to Freudian dream states, and in what he describes as his resolution of the two states, dream and reality, he coins the phrase "surreality" (Breton, 1969, p. 14). Breton also refers to the Nietzschean notions of mastery over self and others and to Marxian socialist ideals as he notes,

The time is coming when it decrees the end of money and by itself will break the bread of heaven for the earth. There will still be gatherings on public squares and *movements* you never dared hope participate in. Farewell to absurd choices, the dreams of dark abyss, rivalries, the prolonged patience, the flight of the seasons, the artificial order of ideas, the ramp of danger, time for everything! (Breton, 1969, p. 18)

The method Breton advocates and describes as true surrealist expression is what he calls, automatic writing. Like the automatic drawing practiced by the Dadists, it relies on the cutting and pasting together of statements, images or ideas randomly thought and presented as a stream of consciousness. The method, according to Breton, made it possible to discover in a dream-like context phrases, images and thoughts which were beautiful—flowing, as he notes, so abundantly that he felt pregnant with his subject.

Surrealism according to Breton is based on the superior reality of certain forms of previously neglected associations in a dream-like atmosphere through the Kantian notion of the "disinterested" play of thought. His definition of Surrealism is as he notes once and for all,

> Surrealism n. Psychic automatism in its pure state by which one proposes to express - verbally, by means of the written word, or in any other manner - the actual functioning of thought, in the absence of any control exercised by reason from any aesthetic or moral concern (Breton, 1969, p. 26).

Karl Marx

Karl Marx (1818-1883) like Sigmund Freud also had a profound influence on 20th century thought and politics. A philosopher, scientist, and professional revolutionary, Marx was known for his influence on two of the most powerful mass movements in history: democratic socialism and revolutionary communism. Marx, as a free-lance journalist, helped create and manage several radical journals in his native Prussia. In 1843 he moved to Paris, where he met Friedrich Engels. They became best friends and worked together on several articles and books.

Marx is considered the founding father of the communist movement. He also is recognized by 20th century scholars for his important contributions to the fields of economics and sociology. Friedreich Engels (1820-1895), Marx's most important collaborator, also made important contributions to Marxist thought including writing the first draft of the manifesto and editing the second and third volumes of *Das Kapital*. Engels outlived Marx by 12 years and developed some of their common ideas into works which essentially reflected his own point of view. It was V.I. Lenin (1870-1924) however, who put Marx's ideas into practice through his founding of the communist party in Russia.

Neither Marx nor Engels wrote a formal thesis about aesthetics, nor did either apparently work out a theory of the functions of Art. Two Marxian conceptions on art and literature however have been identified by the aesthetician Harold Osborne from official Marxist doctrine. One is the conception of art and literature as a socially conditioned reflection of society, and the second is a conception of art as a social force for the furtherance of revolutionary ideas (Osborne, 1970, p. 282). Osborne believed, also, that Mexican mural painting was the only Marxist and nationalist inspiration to achieve general recognition on aesthetic grounds.

Art historian Seltz suggests that while Marx, Engels and Trotsky influenced the period between the wars, which he refers to as the period of "The Artist and the Social Order," the period already had a start in the paintings of David about the French revolution and by the end of the 19th century through many artists and writers including William Morris, Leo Tolstoy and Vincent Van Gogh (Seltz, 1968, p. 456). Seltz believed these artists and others in the Expressionist movement were disappointed with the indifference and rejection of the bourgeoisie or were troubled by the constantly increasing gulf between the artist and society. The Expressionists in particular, he notes, hoped for a societal renewal in which art could take the place once held by religion.

Seltz does see Trotsy's revolutionary concerns being forwarded both through Andre Breton and the Mexican artist, Diego Rivera, who signed the *Manifesto Toward a Free Revolutionary Art* co-authored by Breton and Trotsky in 1938. While there were also Marxist influences evident in the ideas of Stuart Davis, as President of the Artist Union, and in the Federal Art Project, the most visible effect was in the ideas and work of Picasso who admired the achievements of the Communist resistance to Fascism and Nazism in Spain, France and Russia. Selz felt, however, that Picasso's statements in support of and his membership in the Communist Party were much more convincing politically than the political effect of his most famous painting of the period, *Guernica*.

The critic Anthony Blount in his book *Picasso's Guernica* agrees, in principle, with Seltz's view noting Picasso's eclecticism and his incorporation of past images as suggesting a painting which was maturing slowly in the artist's mind over several years and not one invented suddenly as a response to the German air force's destruction of the city of Guernica. To reinforce this view, Blount cites the fact that while the painting included political symbolism and suggested support for the communist party, Picasso did not join the communist party until the end of the Second World War. Picasso, in his view, painted the picture mainly for the glory of the Republican side of the war.

Whether the *Guernica* is or is not in support of the Communist cause will probably be debated for a long time to come. There is general agreement, however, that Picasso saw the possibility of art as a means to show his abhorrence of evil and to inform the world around him that humankind needs to adopt better ways. In support, Blount quotes Picasso as saying, 'I have always believed and still believe that artists who live and work with spiritual values cannot and should not remain indifferent to a conflict in which the highest values and civilization are at stake' (Blount, 1969, p. 56).

Logical Positivism

Logical Positivism like surrealism also had a limited existence largely bracketed between the wars. Rudolph Carnap is considered one of its most productive and distinguished representatives. The logical positive movement influenced by the ideas of both Bertrand Russell and G.E. Moore was formally organized in 1923 by a group of three scientists commonly referred to as the Vienna Circle. The circle grew out of a seminar conducted by Moritz Schlick, a professor of philosophy, in Vienna. Its original members were mainly exscientists who had become philosophers and practicing scientists with a concern for philosophy and the group was primarily directed toward empiricism. The Vienna Circle became the culmination of a movement starting in the 19th century, continuing into the 20th and supported by mathematical logicians Pierce, Ernest Schroeder, Whitehead and Frege. In the beginning, the movement was referred to as Logical Positivism though later renamed "Logical Empiricism."

Rudolph Carnap was the most influential member of the Vienna Circle, but the philosopher Ludwig Wittgenstein whose *Tractatus Logico Philosophicus* appeared in 1921 was probably the greatest positivist influence at least on the international scene. The movement essentially ended when Hitler came to power with Wittgenstein settling in Cambridge, England (in 1929) and Carnap becoming a professor at the University of Chicago in 1936. After its move from Germany to England and America, positivism broadened and accepted a number of new ideas from the English philosophers and from the Americans Pierce, Royce, James, Dewey, and others.

Philosophically the logical positivists moved beyond the *a priori* truths of a mathematical system independent of experience to adopt Wittgenstein's view that mathematics was simply a system of logic. Carnap extended Wittgenstein's model by claiming that much of traditional metaphysics and ethical discourse is meaningless and that philosophy is really the logical analysis of science, an analysis whose function is to look at all knowledge and, all assertions of science and of everyday life in order to make clear the assertions and the connections between them.

The method of verification proposed was both directly through perception or indirectly through propositions reduced from the original assertions, propositions which thus could never be completely verified thus remaining only a hypothesis. Any assertion that could not be deduced from other verified propositions would be in the Logical Positivist view no assertion at all—

only empty words without sense. In applying these concepts, the positivist would reject the a reality of the physical world not because it is false but because it makes no sense in either asserting or denying the thesis, thus rejecting the whole question.

Ethics are in the positivist's view a philosophy of moral values or moral norms which are not an investigation of the facts, only a "false" investigation of what is good or evil or right or wrong. A value statement for them thus becomes a command in a misleading grammatical form that is neither true nor false, does not assert anything and cannot be proved wrong nor disproved through reductive means. The positivist's conceptions moved first from mathematics to logic then to language which in their view had both an expressive and a representative function. The expressive function was as the carrier of feeling and the representative, as assertions about a certain state of affairs by which something can be judged. In this view, metaphysical statements about the arts are neither true nor false; therefore they are only expressive and exist completely outside the field of knowledge or theory. The positivists thus conclude that only propositions of mathematical and empirical science have sense and all others are without sense.

The notion of a moral science was also argued by philosophers aligned with an earlier movement called Utilitarianism, which rejected the criterion of legitimacy in the public realm unless it had utility. This movement was influenced by Jeremy Bentham (1748-1832) who argued for a form of psychological hedonism where people seek pleasure and avoid pain and by John Stewart Mill (1806-1873) who reaffirmed Bentham's so called "greatest happiness" principle. Mill also proposed a criterion of harm principle suggesting that individuals are at liberty to pursue whichever of their desires causes no harm to their fellow human beings. Some historians conclude that the Positivists were the successors of Utilitarianism.

As a movement, logical positivism has been looked at in a number of ways. As a philosophy it was considered mainly as a house-cleaning effort to get rid of unnecessary philosophic frills. It emphasized the facts; became, at least for some, a sort of romantic view of science; pushed the scientific method to be applied to philosophy; and sought a science of morality. It viewed art primarily as a social function in which art provides social cohesion. This view is evident aesthetically in the ideas of John Ruskin and William Morris in the arts and crafts movement, in the architecture of Frank Lloyd Wright, and in the Bauhaus and DeStyl art movements.

Conceptually, positivism's roots are to be found in the philosophy of Gottlob Frege (1848-1925). Frege, a mathematician, made his greatest contribution to philosophy in his philosophy of mathematical logic. While relatively unknown in his time, his ideas later had a profound influence on such notables as Edmund Husserl, Bertrand Russell and Ludwig Wittgenstein. He is credited with leading a realist revolt against Hegelian idealism.

Frege's investigations led him to propose a philosophy of language based on mathematics with three fundamental theses: (1) the mental images which a word arouses in the mind are irrelevant to its meaning, (2) only in the context of a sentence does a word have meaning, and (3) only proper names can be used to talk about an object. Frege believed that language is not governed by logical laws and, that adherence to grammar would not guarantee the correctness of thought. He thought a system of symbols was needed from which every ambiguity was banned, having, as it were, a logical form from which content cannot escape (Bynum, 1972, p. 85). This was to be found, he believed, in the arithmetic language of formulas which express the facts without the intervention of speech. He sought to do this through blending a few of his own symbols with ones already available in mathematics to form a single formula language—a formula language of pure thought. This, he thought, could be done by replacing the concepts of subject and predicate with the actions of argument and function.

Ludwig Wittgenstein (1889-1951) is best known for his theory of descriptions which is devoted to an explanation of the meaning of the word "the." Scruton lays this out in the following manner

> Consider the sentence, the King of France is bald. For this to be true, there must be a king of France and he must be bald. Moreover to capture the distinctive sense of the word 'the' we have to add that there is only one king in France. The conditions which make the sentence true give us its meaning; hence we can say that 'the King of France is bald' is equivalent to the conjunction of three propositions: there exists a King of France: everything which is a king of France is bald, and there is only one King of France (Scruton, 1982, p. 273).

Scruton goes on to analyze the statement concluding that if there is not a King of France then the original sentence is false. The phrase "the King of France" which seems to be a denoting phrase or name becomes a predicate attached to a concealed existential claim which is in effect a logical fiction. More importantly he quotes Wittgenstein as saying 'that where of we cannot speak we must consign to silence' (Scruton, 1982, p. 277).

Wittgenstein in his *The Proposition and its sense* explains what he believes about meaning in language. His discourse though satisfying to the linguist may hold little for the artist except for his frequent references to language as a "picture." Wittgenstein notes, for example, that understanding a sentence can be compared to understanding a picture, noting when he sees a picture first one way then another it is comparable to the experience of first reading a sentence with and then without understanding (Rhees, 1974, p. 42). Understanding a description he believes means making a picture of what is described with the process more or less similar to making a drawing to match a description.

For Wittgenstein, language, in order to achieve status as propositional truth, requires both accuracy in description and knowing the context within which the descriptions are used. Context is most frequently illustrated by Wittgenstein as a game metaphor. In one such metaphor he notes,

> When a man who knows the game watches a game of chess, the experience he has when a move is made usually differs from that of someone else watching without understanding the game. It differs too from that of a man who does not even know that it's a game. (Rhees, 1974, p. 49)

Wittgenstein's critical observation of the use of "is" in a sentence had a profound influence on those 20th century aestheticians seeking to apply linguistic analysis to definitions of art. In this regard, Wittgenstein notes,

> What does it mean to say the 'is' in the 'Rose is red' has a different meaning from the 'is' in 'twice two is four?' (Rhees, 1974, p. 49)

The analysis Wittgenstein uses to explain the differing meanings of the word "is" suggests that in different statements it has different meaning bodies behind it. Using Wittgenstein's argument, the 20th century aesthetician Morris Weitz argued that in art the word "is" can be used in one way as valuative such as "This *is* a work of art" and in another way as descriptive, such as "The painting *is* an arrangement of red squares on a blue background." Rejecting the valuative use of "is" as unsupportable, Weitz thus claims there can be no verifiable definition of art.

Because Wittgenstein's influence on 20th century aesthetics was mainly through his approach to language, it permitted aestheticians to talk about art in a propositional way. Paintings for Wittgenstein were matters of observable facts identified through the kind of factual statements or claims usable to verify their existence. Wittgenstein was not interested in any empirical facts about language as empirical facts but rather with the form of descriptions we might use. The description is, for Wittgenstein, only a game as he believes describing language is not explaining anything. In effect, his view reductively moves any evaluative discussion of art to rather discussing the meanings of the discussions we can have about it. This does of course reduce art to talk about art.

The Atomic Age, Existentialism and Alienation

Historians have characterized the period following World War II in different ways. Many feel that it was a turning away from science to embrace more humanistic concerns. This was the result, it is thought, of a society embracing a new sense of fatalism and despair in a world which was out of control and perhaps even facing its final destruction. Under such circumstances the only recourse appeared to be in providing a greater openness to the human spirit, becoming more accepting of the needs of minorities and the poor, pushing for a desystemization of thought, and demanding a new accountability from government and from big business with perhaps even an abandonment of the so-called "me" generation.

Philosophically at least three newer movements emerged: (1) Phenomenology influenced by the psychology of Bretano (1838-1917) and his student, Edmund Husserl (1859-1938), (2) Existentialism supported in the writings of the philosopher, Martin Heidegger (1889-1976) and Jean-Paul Sartre (1905-1980), and Structuralism associated with the writings of Claude Levi-Strauss, Roland Barthes, and Noam Chomsky.

The three philosophies had in common that they all were grounded in one or more of the older philosophical systems already mentioned. The term phenomenology had been used by Hegel in his work on the nature of moral life, existentialism also found its beginnings in Hegel, and structuralism in the ideas of Leibnitz.

Phenomenology is said to have started with Franz Bretano (1838-1917) who began an investigation of the mind that rejected the premises of idealism and that postulated the true subject matter of psychology was a universal, abstract "Geist." Edmund Husserl (1859-1938), Bretano's pupil, expanded on Bretano by advancing two major notions: (1) a reaffirmation that we have knowledge of our own conscious status and (2) a belief that the intentionality of the mental makes meaning or reference essential to every mental act. Husserl also proposed a method to isolate statements of consciousness from matter because matter inhibits our understanding of these statements. He called this process phenomenological reduction or bracketing.

Martin Heidegger (1889-1976) added even more confusion by claiming that philosophy is the study of phenomena and thus is a fundamental form of ontology or a study of what is. Heidegger, most of all, attempts to answer the question of what is the meaning of being, which he sees as a lack of reason for existence in that we are simply here. This is what he calls the phenomenon of fear or what others have called alienation. Heidegger describes this alienation as "inauthenticity," a term also used by Freud in which we flee from ourselves, lose ourselves in anxiety and frustration, and become objects which deny ourselves through assuming impersonal roles.

Existentialism, another modern philosophy, is said to have begun with the writings of Jean-Paul Sartre (1905-1980) a pupil of both Husserl and Heidegger. Sartre believed that existence precedes essence with man making his own essence through achievement in his existence. In Sartre's view, an individual exists fully only when he or she is what he or she proposes to be. Sartre has also been recognized for his defense of ethical values in which he has argued that any system of objective values transfers a person's freedom into a world of objects where he or she can lose it. Sartre claims that all love and all human relations are grounded in a contradiction and that we must see all human relations in terms of that struggle.

Structuralism, as a new 20th century philosophy, was founded on the ideas of three individuals: Claude Levi-Strauss, Roland Barthes, and Noam Chomsky. Claude Levi-Strauss's view of structuralism is found in his concept of Structural Anthropology which argues that unconscious mental processes remain fixed for all cultures, primitive and literate alike. All customs in a society, according to Levi-Strauss, fill specific functions and act as supplementary languages. In developing his theories, Levi-Strauss draws from several sources including communication theory, Hegelian dialectics and structural linguistics.

Levi-Strauss, not unlike Hegel, held the view that science and art are societal myths having divergent logical methods. Like Hegel he also was criticized for putting art in a lesser category than science by suggesting that both art and myth are only our responses to scientific truth. He, indeed, suggests that art or myth dies when it tries to explain more than itself. Levi-Strauss's system begins with the notion that for primitive people totemism expresses the totality of the relationships between culture and nature. Art is for Levi-Strauss a form of totemism in which it (1) assumes the status of the things it requires; (2) defines the rules of behavior reflected in totemic relationships; and (3) has no set rules, intrinsic characteristics, or prescribed materials. The function of art in this context is to make certain the convertability of ideas held at different levels of the social system.

Not unlike the positivists, Levi-Strauss believed that works of art are devoid of meaning and exist only in such referential systems as the History of Art. Jack Burnham adopting Levi-Strauss' view believes,

> Art's unifying order exists in how the artist reassembles signs within a structure which produces a sense of mediation (art) for him. Linguistically art's effectiveness depends on its surface "vagueness" which is not meant in the lack of a focus but rather in the artist's success in shifting our minds from an empirical level of comprehension to the Mythic. (Burnham, 1971, p. 13)

Roland Barthes, another contributor to structuralism, is best known for his idea that organized social relationships are in themselves complete language forms. Barthes insisted that language must remain the focus of analysis for any social code; thus all iconic messages have their social equivalents in the language in verbal form, especially those used in art criticism, scholarly analysis, and art history. Barthes also felt that interpretive language provides clues to hidden social meanings in all forms of communication. He viewed Semiology as a segment of linguistics through its accepting of the terms, phrases and concepts missed in structural linguistics. He also viewed mass produced goods as evidence of a sign system which, unlike speech, is thoroughly regulated. Burnham in analyzing Barthes's view suggests that the study of mass produced goods offers a system defined by common usage, unlike today's individual art which demands recognition of the innovator and is controlled by groups such as the artists' peers, critics, galleries, museum curators, art historians and collectors (Burnham, 1971). Burnham suggests that by depersonalizing art through focusing on mass produced products we are helping to identify the forms of totemism most supportive of Barthes's theory.

A third major contributor to structuralist thought was Noam Chomsky, whose contribution to semiology includes his theory of generative grammar and a new substructure for the discipline of structuralism. In clinical psychology Chomsky is recognized for his attacks on behaviorism which he alleged did not recognize that learning and mental behavior are too important and varied to be explained in mere stimulus-response terms. Chomsky insisted that any useful psychology must include a notation of competence or other theory to account for new learning and potential capabilities. His major question to the psychologists was how to use speech creatively and how to adapt it to new experiences.

Osborne in his examination of the influence of 20th century thought on aesthetics, identifies two somewhat counter movements as representing the two most characteristic influences of the new. One is the influence of analytical philosophy and linguistics and the other the return to what he calls the "autonomy of the art object" (Osborne, 1970, p. 262).

The contributions of linguistic and analytical schools of thought are in Osborne's view directed toward the repudiation of systematic aesthetics through the futility of defining "what is Art." Wittgenstein's writings were seminal in answering this important question, but it was Morris Weitz, while at The Ohio State University, who directly posed the question as to whether art can be defined. In his article "The Role of Theory on Aesthetics," republished in *Problems in Aesthetics*, Weitz claims that art has no set of necessary and sufficient properties thus making a theory of it logically impossible (Weitz, 1959, p. 147). His argument is based on the claim that all the great theories of art, Formalism, Voluntarism, Emotionalism, Intellectualism, Intuitionism, and Organicism, fail because either they do not adequately define the nature of art or they have left out some necessary or sufficient property. Weitz paraphrasing Wittgenstein asks if it is even possible to employ a concept of art without having a logical description of the actual functioning of the concept, including a description of the conditions under which we can correctly use it.

Because such a concept of art is not forthcoming Weitz argues that art is therefore an "open" concept noting,

> The primary task of aesthetics is not to seek a theory but to elucidate the concept of art. Specifically, it is to describe the conditions under which we employ the concept correctly. Definition,

reconstruction, patterns of analysis are out of place here since they distort and add nothing to our understanding of art (Weitz, 1959, p. 153).

Osborne sees Weitz and others using these new linguistic approaches to find a new way of tackling the aesthetics of Croce's followers and the idealism of Bradley and Bosanquet. Positivism was a system, according to Osborne, that was symptomatic, cautious, empirical, analytical, and more keenly alert than other systems to the special characteristics of the individual arts of music, painting, poetry and the theatre. Positivism, in his view, centered on the logic of clarifying the concepts of criticism in each of the arts and making explicit the different criteria of valuation that were employed. Aesthetics for Weitz and others using the linguistic approach, in Osborne's view, was a kind of metacriticism or language about language restricting art to the useful functions of analyzing and giving coherence to the things sensitive people might say about it.

Osborne, while noting that 20th century aestheticians dropped their romantic references by using such terms as "emotion" and "expression", also saw the period as one returning to art as a thing in its own right. Such a concept brings attention to art as a distinct artifact with standards and functions of its own. While not denying that works of art may legitimately reflect a reality other than themselves or that they embody and promote social, religious and other values, these notions, according to Osborne, are not essential to their character and indeed may even be irrelevant in determining their quality as works of art. Under such a concept Osborne notes,

> A work of art, as it is now held is in concept an artifact made for the purpose of being appreciated in a special mode of aesthetic contemplation and although particular works of art may be intended to do other things and may in fact serve other purposes as well as this, the excellence of any work of art *as art* is assessed in terms of its suitability for such contemplation. (Osborne, 1970, p. 263)

The phenomenologist Heidegger, in his essay "The Origin of Art", probably had more to say than any other philosopher about the work of art as a thing in its own right. In Heidegger's view, "the Artist is the origin of the work and the work is the origin of the artist" (Heidegger, 1977, p. 149). Heidegger believed that to discover the essence of art one needs to go to the actual work and ask what and how it is. Works of art, in his view, have a thingly character which cannot be ignored. As things they have properties displayed directly in what we know as "formed matter." As such they are, in effect, thing-being and in order to understand this artistic reality one needs to find the art prevailing in it.

Heidegger believed further that to gain access to the work an individual needs to remove it from all relations to something other than itself in order to let it stand on its own. The temple, in Heidegger's view, in its standing there gives things their look and people their outlook on themselves (Heidegger, 1977, p. 167). For Heidegger a work is a work which means something is effected and what distinguishes the work as a work is that a work has been created. Works of art are for Heidegger a truth happening as revealed through the work itself. It is first and foremost a work involving "craftsmanship" and "technique" which in themselves do not signify only the action of making. Truth thus establishes itself in the work, and art is the creative preserving of truth in the work.

Summary

This chapter's journey through 20th century thought about art and life itself began with the analytical philosophy of George Edward Moore and Clive Bell and concluded with the linguistic methods of Wittgenstein and the thing-being of Heidegger. It should be apparent that no new or more definitive system of thought has replaced the previous views of life and art at least since the times of the Greeks. It can be said, however, that this century has witnessed a broader variety of approaches than ever before on ways to think about art and about the conditions which bring it into being. While not all of the possible ways of thinking about such matters have been discussed here, it is hoped that a representative sample of some of the more influential ideas of the century have been examined and their intents made clear. These include the analytical philosophy of George Edward Moore and the critic Clive Bell; the natural philosophy of Alfred North Whitehead; the spiritualism of Kant, Hegel and Croce; the social ideas of art in the claims of Freud and Marx; and the new Linguistic approaches of Wittgenstein, Claude Levi-Strauss, Roland Barthes and Noam Chomsky.

Some of this century's newer philosophies include analytical philosophy, Phenomenology, Existentialism, Sociological Aesthetics, Positivism and Marxism. All have had an effect on expanding our understanding of the art object and the events that bring it into being. Unfortunately for those who may have hoped for a resolution of such issues through finding an objective standard of correct taste based on empirical evidence, no such thing has been forthcoming, at least, as a replacement for the ideas of those who have dealt with such issues in the past. Put another way, these newer theories do not necessarily support that a steady improvement in aesthetic quality of artistic works is likely to be achieved in this century or the ones which follow.

Since 1920, as Osborne notes, evolutionary theories of art and culture generally have suffered a recession in popularity for, as Wolfflen noted, not everything is possible at all times. When art works are seen in isolation from the cultures which shape them and are contemplated mostly in galleries and in books, their impact is primarily visual and their emotional appeal is direct. Artists have since the time of impressionism been more interested in making pictures than in representing some outside reality. The thing created thus exists as paint and not as having another potential or ideal existence.

What is really new may be the artistic conception of the "Gestalt" idea that the whole is greater than the sum of its parts and that we cannot know the parts unless we know the whole. While some works may require the attitude of "disinterested attention", others, Osborne notes, are not served through it. These newer assumptions may, however, be more operative in our encounters with art than in our philosophical theories.

An examination of 20th century theory also suggests that no theory should require a look at only one set of features in a work of art, as art may still be valued for other reasons and may be said even to be good or bad. The aesthetic of any object is, in the last analysis, its capacity to reward us in its own way, for as Osborne notes

> When we attribute aesthetic value to anything at all we judge about its suitability to sustain the self rewarding activity of aesthetic contemplation. To ascribe this value is not to deny that the object may have other values or that these other values may be fairly intimately linked with the aesthetic values it has. (Osborne, 1970, p. 296)

All of this points to the fact that in order to proceed on our course of determining the proper goals of the art program, we must start by examining the art work itself as central to the development of any viable art instructional goal. This chapter ends with a concern for the work itself to reject the view that the art object and its creation are no longer central to the problem of education in art. To rightfully place art making as central in the process of establishing the goals of the art program, the following chapter will introduce three alternative paradigms for artistic forming sustained by selected literature in art, aesthetics, philosophy and education. These modes of making are organized in such a way as to suggest that they are more than casually related to the main philosophical issues posed in this and the preceding chapter.

References

Axelrod, C. D. (1979). *Studies in international breakthrough.* Amherst: University of Massachusetts Press.

Bell, C. (1958). *Art.* New York: Capricorn Books.

Bloom, A. (1987). *Closing of the American mind.* New York: Simon and Schuster.

Blount, A. (1969). *Picasso's Guernica.* New York: Oxford University Press.

Breton, A. (1969). *Manifesto of surrealism.* New York: Vintage Books.

Burnham, J. (1971). *The structure of art.* New York: George Braziller Inc.

Bynum, T. W. (1972). *Conceptual notation and related articles Gottlob Frege.* Oxford: Clarendon Press.

Chipp, H.B. (1968). *Theories of modern art.* Berkeley: University of California Press.

Croce, B. (1983). *Aesthetic*. Boston: Nonpareil Books.

Freud, S. (1947). *Leonardo da Vinci: A study in psychosexuality*. New York: Vintage Books.

Freud, S. (1965). *The interpretation of dreams*. New York: Avon Books.

Gray, J. G. (1970). *G.W.F. Hegel on art, religion, philosophy*. New York: Harper and Row.

Heidegger, M. (1977). *Basic writings*. New York: Harper and Row.

Kandinsky, W. (1977). *Concerning the spiritual in art*. New York: Dover Publications, Inc.

Kant, I. (1963). *Analytic of the beautiful from the critique of judgement*. New York: Library of Liberal Arts Bobbs Merrill.

Laporte, P. (1949). The space-time concept in the work of Picasso. *Magazine of art, 1*, 243-246.

Marti-Ibanez, F. (1958). *Essays in the history of medicine, the history of Michael's ideas*, (pp. 511-540), New York: Centaur.

McMullen, R. (1968). *Art, affluence and alienation*. New York: Frederick A. Praeger.

Moore, G. E. (1903). *Principia ethica*. Cambridge: Trinity College Cambridge University.

Nadeau, M. (1965). *The history of surrealism*. New York: The Macmillan Co.

Osborne, H. (1970). *Aesthetics and art theory*. New York: E.P. Dutton.

Perry, W. G., Jr. (1981). Cognitive and ethical growth: The making of meaning. In A. Chickering, et al. (Eds). *The modern American college*, San Francisco: Jossey-Bass, 76-116.

Rhees, R. (ed 1974). *Philosophical Grammar Ludwig Wittgenstein*. Oxford: Basil Blackwell.

Schapiro, M. (1956). Leonardo and Freud an art historical study. *Journal of the history of ideas, XVII*, (9), 250-280.

Scruton, R. (1982). *From Descartes to Wittgenstein*. New York: Harper Colophon Books.

Seltz, P. (1968). Art and politics: The artist and the social order. In B. Herschel, Chipp (Eds). *Theories of modern art*. Berkeley: University of California Press.

Seltz, P. (1969). The aesthetic theories of Kandinsky. In Harold Spencer (Ed), *Readings in Art History*, New York: Scribners.

Weitz, M. (1959). *Problems in aesthetics*. New York: The Macmillan Co.

Whitehead, A. N. (1982). *An enquiry concerning the principles of natural knowledge*. New York: Dover Publications, Inc.

Braque, Georges. *Still Life: Le Jour*, Chester Dale Collection, © 1993 National Gallery of Art, Washington, 1929, canvas, 1.150 x 1.467 (45 1/4 x 57 3/4); framed: 1.464 x 1.784 (57 5/8 x 70 1/4)

Chapter 3

Paradigms for Thinking and Making

Chapter II identified different modes of thought and differing philosophical conceptions about objects and events. The goal of this chapter is to show how these different patterns of thought impact on what art professionals do, specifically how the common patterns of thought used by 20th century artists, philosophers, art historians, educators, and scholars in the psychology of art provide cohesive conceptions for professional practice. This fusion of ideas within the discipline of art suggests that professionals with different biases in their thinking can adopt different cognitive structures that contribute to the process of deciding which actions are to be taken in the discipline of art.

The discussion that follows supports the notion that integrated patterns of artistic thought are necessary for any viable conception of the field of art education to exist. That such commonly held patterns of thought among artists, art historians, art critics and artist educators exist can be demonstrated through a review of selected art literature reflecting these various points of view. The existence of these common patterns also suggests that conceptions of the field of art and education transcend the functions performed by individual members of the artistic community—a transcendence that is also necessary for developing any cohesive conception of the field.

The existence of these integrated concepts of art suggests also that the content of art study need not be restricted to what art historians, art critics, artists and artist educators do, but rather only to what unified conceptions of art thinking and making are possible. This challenges present notions not only that art education content is determined by the functions these individuals perform but also that these points of view are necessarily mutually exclusive. Because such conceptions exist also makes it possible to view students' thinking about and making art as being engaged in intelligent activity. This refutes the idea that distinctions need to be made between the kinds of artistic activity students engage in and/or in what kind of, or how much of, a given activity is needed for quality art study in schools. As long as educational goals require students to be engaged in intelligent art activity, no fur-

ther justification in needed to include art study as part of the general education program of the school. Programs which inspire thinking about and provide opportunities for expressing art as intelligent activity do not require a view of art as separate from life or thought. Nor do we need to demonstrate further that art contributes to thought, when art not only contributes, but is thought itself.

In order to organize the various patterns of thought used by art professionals into cohesive artistic concepts, this chapter is structured around three conceptual paradigms of art modeled after the scientific paradigm concepts developed by Thomas Kuhn (1970). Kuhn's work was selected because his paradigm model reveals both the use of thought in determining disciplinary products and the way paradigms function in determining the policies of professional communities. For a paradigm to be useful, it should have a key role in determining the systems of disciplinary practice and education supported by a given paradigm community.

Because the paradigms used must be inclusive of the entire artistic community, they must also be philosophically catholic reflecting differing points of view. Therefore, the literature cited in this chapter presents three paradigms with different philosophical points of view. The terms used in this text to represent these paradigms are *schema-motif, form-gestalt, and linguistic-metaphorical*. The schema-motif paradigm basically reflects a mostly rationalistic philosophical position, the form-gestalt a neo-idealist position and the linguistic-metaphorical an empirical position. These paradigms are supported by the writings of various art historians, artists, art critics, philosophers of art and artist-educators who share common modes of thought in thinking about and creating art. Citations of their statements in support of the paradigms demonstrates that common patterns of thought are used by professionals in thinking about and creating art. Moreover, their views are cited in language as close as possible to the language the individuals would actually use rather than restate them. Though perhaps cumbersome, this method does, it is hoped, more accurately reflect their views.

Hyphenated paradigm descriptions were used so as to be as clear as possible about the meanings of these descriptions since they have not been commonly used by others in the field to describe the character of the field of art or art education. The schema-motif designation is used to describe conceptions using art schema or motifs coming from both conscious and unconscious thought; that is, art either inspired by a motif or schema, seen in another art work, or one which exists in the mind of the artist as a result of some developmental state or mental stereotype. Because the literature suggests both conceptions of schema are possible, the hyphenated term, schema-motif, is used here.

The form-gestalt paradigm is meant to describe aesthetic activity that is primarily a response to aesthetic form (the object) in and of itself rather than

to things it refers to, which are outside itself. The term "form" is used in this context to mean the total import or the Gestalt of the work (the "wow" factor) rather than to mean shape. For this reason, again the hyphenated form-gestalt term was chosen to describe the paradigm.

The linguistic-metaphorical description refers to all modes of aesthetic thought which attempt to provide analogs for art objects or events rather than depend on personal reinterpretations of it. This paradigm thus refers to all forms of art which use language—concrete poetry, art as a statement of fact, or the use of visual metaphors as means for symbolizing social needs and behaviors. Essentially, all such forms involve a direct communication between artist and the viewer; however, some forms do this in more explicit ways than others.

This process has avoided the use of some of the more widely recognized paradigmatic terms such as mimetic, expressive, formalistic or objective (Mittler, 1980). These terms were deliberately not used because they are rooted philosophically in the so-called functions of art adumbrated in empirical philosophy. While there may be similarities between these descriptions and the paradigm descriptions used here, the more widely known descriptions are limited because of their philosophical bias and their lack of applicability to the tasks professionals need to perform in the art discipline. The term *mimetic*, for example, is meant to describe art which presents an accurate description of life or nature, the term *expressive* is art admired for its organization, and the term *objective* is art which communicates ideas, moods and feelings. The main difficulty in using such terms is that they fail to differentiate conceptually, as no art can be truthfully said to be an imitation of the real thing, and all art is, in one way or another, representative, expressive and communicative.

The Role of Art Making in Art Education

The philosopher, Suzanne Langer believed, "that a philosopher of art should begin in the studio not in the gallery, auditorium or library" (Langer, 1953, p. `lix). Her reasoning was that without any conception of the real problems and working concepts or without the artist to test the power of the concepts, we might never know the arts from the inside. To know the arts from the inside, she believes, we must adopt the language of the artist and not reject the artist's manner of speaking as some critics have done, thus giving only a limited examination to their ideas.

Such a critical view of art production appeared in U.S. art education in the 1970's with the "new eclecticism" which reflected a contextual view of the role of art in education. This view was inspired in part by the aesthetician, Morris Weitz (1959), who held that no definition of art was possible which would encompass all its aesthetic qualities. Weitz's claim about art not hav-

ing necessary or sufficient properties dominated scholarly thought in the field during the 1970's. Its effect on art curriculum development was in some cases to separate studio concerns from critical and historical concerns, thus leading a number of art educators to take a less than positive view of the importance of the studio in art education. Some like Broudy and Smith simply were not positive advocates of studio art education; others like Eisner decried what they perceived as an almost exclusive emphasis on studio, and still others such as Lanier saw studio activities as being of minor importance and suggested support of them, "avoids social and intellectual responsibility" (Lanier, 1972, p. 17).

Even Langer (1953), a philosopher inclined to view the studio in a positive light, may also have found some contradictions in her own efforts to explain the nondiscursive language of the studio within the constraints of a language system that could only provide a conceptual discourse about what was being articulated in paint, clay or stone. For, as she notes, more people are beholders of art than makers of it and even aestheticians find that they can treat the problem of artistic impression with more authority than they do expression. ↳ how the art looks.

It is no simple task to use language to describe images created for the first time out of things which are not words or sentences but rather things made of canvas, paper or wood. On the other hand, to deny that artistic forming is central to any serious discussion of art's role in education risks setting it apart from the individual creative function which makes it especially human. Art, as Langer notes, does not say anything, it displays and herein lies the central problem of discussing the act which brings art into being. Those who would have us believe that such a discussion is too mysterious, beyond reason, or beyond ordinary activity create an artificial division between thought in action and thought about action which Harrison reminds us, if we are concerned, we need to consider (Harrison, 1978).

To view thought as existing only in what we say and not in what we do is, in Harrison's view, to conceive of thoughts in action and thoughts about action (i.e. thinking and making), as two different acts and also two different ways of thinking. If, as educators, we accept the idea of separating thinking from practice, we may just as well move in our schools to educate some students to construct principles for understanding art and others to put them into practice. We must therefore, consider thoughts in action and thoughts about action as related, because as Harrison notes, while we could judge for others and tell others what to do, we can only perform our own actions. Using the right thing in the right way at the right time is, in Harrison's view, what constitutes the artist's thought in what he or she does. If we reach for words rather than materials, we are, he notes, teaching, explaining, instructing, rather than engaged in considering the expressive act (Harrison, 1978).

If we are to learn about art through the study of expressive activity, we cannot make distinctions among what the artist thinks, what is thought and done, and the thought in what is done. The connections between such thoughts are most evident in successful expression. Thus, a discussion of the expressive act itself must be the major focus of this chapter. In the process, it is hoped that the reader will recognize the connections in whatever is done between the various ideas of meaning in what the artist says and what he or she means to do. To see the connections, one must view the expressive act itself as offering the best evidence of what is thought or meant.

Connections Between Artistic Thinking and Making

This text attempts to make clear the connections between what artists, historians, educators and aestheticians say about the ways artists conceive of art forming and what artists actually do or advocate that other artists do in the act of forming. The three art paradigms for artistic conception are meant to suggest that a cohesiveness exists between conceptions of artistic thinking and making. This paradigmatic approach to understanding how the productive, historical and critical modes are related and how connections between thinking and making are possible is used because of the parallels evident between Thomas S. Kuhn's conceptions of the field of science and our own conceptions of art. In *The Structure of Scientific Revolutions* (1970), Kuhn argues that the texts with which each scientific generation learns its trade are no more descriptive of the science than a description of our national culture drawn from a tourist brochure or a language text.

It seems possible that the same may also be said for paradigms about the history of art, aesthetics, and art education. Kuhn claims that science texts are misleading because (these) authors view their task as chroniclers of incremental progress who are forced to admit that science does not develop through an accumulation of individual studies and inventions. Their predecessors' ideas which they have labeled as error and superstition were no less scientific nor more the product of human idiosyncrasy than scholars today. Given such a revolution, Kuhn notes, the historian of science must conclude that, "out of date theories are not unscientific simply because they have been discarded" (Kuhn, 1970, p. 3).

As a result, science scholars today who know what it is to be scientific legitimately may reach a number of incompatible conclusions on a given issue. This is due, Kuhn feels, to the scholar's prior experience in other fields and the beliefs learned from the schools of thought which prepared and licensed them for practice. Kuhn sees science as a discipline preparing students for membership in the particular scientific community where they will later practice. Because they join others who learned their field from the same models, there is, in his opinion, seldom an overt disagreement over fundamentals. This happens because scientists whose research is based on shared paradigms are committed to the same rules and standards for scientific practice.

Kuhn's paradigms in science in many ways parallel those in the discipline of art. It can be noted, for example, that both the history of Western art and the history of pictorial representation, like science, suggest models which inspire traditions in both historical and productive research. Such parallels may be even more germane to the art education discipline which for the past two decades has relied on the scientific method as its principal mode of investigation. To illustrate that parallels exist between the disciplines of art and the disciplines of science, I argue that it is possible to substitute the art historians, Semper, Wolfflin, and Panofsky and the artists, Rembrandt, Cezanne, and Picasso for the scientists, Copernicus, Newton and Einstein as individuals whose achievements were sufficiently unprecedented to attract a group of adherents away from competing modes of making and thinking in art. These and other makers and thinkers in art and others like them, I believe, provided differing conceptual models which attracted artists, historians, critics and educators to form communities and to build on shared paradigms to be revealed in their textbooks, lectures and laboratories.

Kuhn has characterized scientific schools as making significant contributions to scientific thought but as also excluding some of its most creative members, producing results which were less than scientific, and directing their dialogues as much to members of other schools as to science. Overall, these paradigms while attracting new adherents, also destroyed older paradigms, developed a closed society, and developed a literature understood only by its members. Further, he believes, these shared paradigms in the scientific community can be determined with relative ease, though he also notes shared paradigms do not always result in shared rules. The task, he claims, involves comparing community paradigms with each other and discovering what isolatable elements, explicit or implicit, the members have abstracted from their more global paradigms and deployed as their rules for research.

That existing paradigms or schools of thought in art are identifiable can, I believe, be demonstrated, although it is not possible within these pages to effectively describe paradigms meeting all the questions that could possibly be raised by the field. What I believe can be done, however, is to sketch the structure of at least three art paradigm communities which art scholars and artists can agree on and which have rules for practice clearly shared among its members.

Because in art as well as in science there are so many notable figures, intellectual triumphs and artistic breakthroughs, no attempt will be made to name any particular individual as the idealogue solely responsible for the development of a paradigm. And although paradigm community members do not always agree on all the shared rules of the paradigm, the focus will be on the coherence of their ideas relating to the process of making and creating art and the perceptual constructs undergirding it. The paradigms have been constructed primarily to show that a correspondence exists between what artists and scholars say about art making and what can be observed about what they do in the forming process. This investigation will focus on both the thought processes influencing form conception and on the actions taken in constructing the expressive image.

Schema-Motif Paradigm

Historical Definitions

The notion that pictures come from other pictures is one of the earliest beliefs as to the source of art image making in Western art. The term, schema, is borrowed from art historian E. H. Gombrich. His book, *Art as Illusion* (1972), is one of the field's classic studies of the psychology of pictorial representation. In it he uses the ambiguous rabbit/duck image to argue that we cannot see a shape apart from our preconceptions or anticipation of what it is we hope to find in it. According to Gombrich, while artists may learn by looking at nature it will not be sufficient because," looking alone has never sufficed to teach an artist his trade" (1972, p. 11). Artists are successful in the imitation of reality not because they see more but rather because they have acquired the skill of imitation. True to his discipline as art historian, Gombrich claims, "if art were only or mainly an expression of personal vision, there could be no history of art" (Gombrich, 1972, p. 4).

Perceptually, Gombrich believes that learning proceeds from the indefinite to the definite, not from sensation to perception, and that there are no rigid distinctions between perception and illusion as perception tends to weed out harmful illusions by our coming to an artist's works with an expectation of what we hope to see. All cognitive processes, in his view, take the form of perceived thinking or hypotheses we think up which later require answers that will either confirm or disprove them.

Also, according to Gombrich, what painters inquire into is not the physical world but rather our reactions to it. In understanding art, he believes, we come to it with our own expectations and with our perceptions already tuned into deciphering the artist's cryptograms. All culture relies on this interplay between expectation and observation and between the waves of fulfillment, disappointments, right guesses and wrong moves which make up daily life. In image making, he notes, style rules even if the artist wishes to faithfully reproduce nature and the artist begins with an impression, schema, stereotype or motif, not with an idea or concept. The familiar will always remain the starting point for rendering the unfamiliar and will exert its influence over the artist's image even if the artist strives to record an image of reality. All art, he feels, originates in the mind and our reactions to the world rather than in the world itself because all art is conceptual and is recognizable by its style.

In making images he also believes that the artist acquires a variety of schemata with which he or she can produce a schema for an animal, house or flower which is then modified until it corresponds with what the artist wills to express. Making, thus, comes before matching and creation before reference. More importantly he states, "the innocent eye is a myth. The blind man of Ruskin's who suddenly gains sight does not see the world as a painting by Turner or Monet" (Gombrich, 1972, p. 298).

Gombrich was not the first historian to develop a theory of schema but rather built on the ground work laid by earlier historians Gottfried Semper (1803-1929), Alois Riegel (1858-1905), Heinrich Wolfflin (1864-1945), and Aby Warburg (1866-1929). Podro who has written extensively on these early historians believes that it is essential that we explore art in light of our conceptions and go beyond interest in personal context or in individual history to draw on what he calls a general notion of art. It is our notion of art, he notes, "which suggests what it is relevant for us to look for: it is our notion of art which dictates that we should try to see a painting as drawing on traditions of usage" (Podro, 1983, p. XVI). Podro believes our conceptions of art help us to see how the products of art sustain purposes and interests which are both irreducible to the conditions which create them and are also inextricable from them. In his critical historical view, Podro sees Semper, Riegel, Wolfflin and Warburg as the art historians most wedded to the idea that motifs and patterns are basic to a conception of art history. In particular, he claims, Gottfried Semper was one of the first historians to construct a theory of art history based on motifs. Semper explored the way architects used the structural features of primitive buildings as patterns applied to different materials and adapted for reapplication in new structures. Semper's motif theory was, according to Podro, later combined with Herbart's psychology of simultaneous perceptions or ideas in the mind fusing by virtue of common features or conflicting because of the lack of them. Herbart's thinking suggested that patterns of past experience are reviewed and adjudicated in the mind in order to reconcile present experience from patterns learned in the past.

The art historian Heinrich Wolfflin later became heir to the ideas advanced by Semper which he adumbrated in his theory of empathy suggesting that we invest in inanimate objects inward states through analoging between their physical shape and our own bodily poise as a metaphorical force in architecture motifs. Wolfflin developed his theory of visual motifs in his book *Principles of Art History* where he expanded on the notion of the reciprocal adaptation of subject matter and the material of visual representation as a pattern of development in the progressive integration of architectural motifs.

74

Alois Riegl, a contemporary of Wolfflin, also adapted Semper's theory applying it to the acanthus motif which evolved from the lotus motif through an internal progression toward a more subjective form. He also was committed to a teleological (unfolding) schema which treated the visual arts as constant through reconceiving its goals and concepts of order to become more subjectively implicit. According to Podro, both Riegel and Wolfflin viewed the problem of accommodating the art of the past within the mental life of the present as a fundamental feature of the mind in pursuit of order.

Psychological Definitions

The notion of the visual schema as a structure for determining meaning in pictorial form was also investigated by the philosopher John Stuart Mill and the psychologist Helmholtz in the mid-17th century. In more recent times additional support has come from philosophers Wartofsky and Goodman, the art historian E.H. Gombrich and from psychologist Julian Hochberg. Hochberg, in particular, agrees with the ideas of E.H. Gombrich through claiming that eye movements are made when the viewer has visual questions to ask and that these glances are guided by and contribute to some anticipated and stored notion, schema, image or representation of the scene (Hochberg, 1988).

Hochberg also believed that we cannot understand the representation of the world by pictures unless we start to learn something about schemas. Schemas, in his view, are not copies of the physical world but are rather mental devices for dealing with the physical world and for anticipating what we will see if we try. Hochberg (1988) in particular notes,

> A schema, then is not merely a duplicate of the physical world. What I mean by schema is a particular mental device; what I mean by a mental device is some inferred function for which no plausible neural mechanisms are known. The functions that I group under the name schema comprise a mental device for predicting what we will see if we execute some perceptomotor act. (p. 379)

In supporting Gombrich's notion that the power of expectation rather than the power of conceptual knowledge molds what we see, Hochberg claims that eye movements occur when the viewer has visual questions to ask and ceases when there are none. The nature of these glimpses requires that the viewer asks questions about what will be found as answers for guiding subsequent visual inquiry. This, he concludes, means our glances are guided and contribute to some anticipated and stored notion of a schema or image which exists in the mind.

75

Educational Definitions

The use of schemata in the education of the artist has been examined by art historians Erwin Panofsky and E.H Gombrich. The role of schema in the education of the artist can be characterized as occurring in two periods, the earliest one in the study of the canons of schema for representation and, in more modern times in the overcoming of schema. In *Meaning in the Visual Arts* Panofsky (1955) devotes a good deal of attention to the history of the theory of human proportions as artistic schema. Panofsky traces its development through the canons used by the Egyptians, the Greeks, and the Medieval, Byzantine and Italian Renaissance artists and in modern times where the theory of human proportions is abandoned. Panofsky generally views art history theory as paralleling the general evolution of art itself where its importance diminishes as art seeks to emphasize the "subjective" conception of the affect rather than the object itself. He notes, for example, "in Egyptian art, the theory of proportions meant almost everything because the subject meant almost nothing; it was doomed to sink into insignificance as soon as this revelation was reversed" (Panofsky, 1955, p. 105).

Panofsky's view of the schema diminishing in importance is shaped by his idea that the artist's feelings are the primary influence in pictorial representation and shouldn't imply that the canons of schema did not continue even up until the present day. His view on the declining importance of schema differs from the ideas of Gombrich who also had a good deal to say about the historic and even contemporary influence of artistic education in picture making. Gombrich whose concerns are mostly with the development of pictorial representation believes artists learn more from looking at pictures than from looking, and artists see what they paint rather than paint what they see. It is, therefore, Gombrich's view that without a medium and without a schema no artist could represent reality.

Gombrich generally views the trained drawer as acquiring a mass of schemata with which he or she can produce a schema of a flower or a book on paper. Such schemata serve to support a storehouse of memory images to be modified until they match what the artist wishes to express. This notion principally serves as the foundation for his theory of schema and correction. Gombrich in *Art and Illusion* notes that trained drawers need to have a canon of appearances in order to know how to construct basic images: Even the apprentices of Michelangelo had to learn and practice how to draw objects before they were allowed to try their hand in their apprenticeship. In the academies, he notes, there was a carefully graded course starting with the copying of prints which students had to undergo for years before they were permitted to copy the master. It was this mastery, he believes, which established the continuity of art between the Middle Ages and the 18th century. Gombrich also notes that the sway of pattern remains unchallenged and eventually the use of prints was augmented by anatomy books on proportion and, later, by drawing books, 500 of which had come into print by 1888.

In the chapter "Formula and Experience", Gombrich describes the schematic patterns developed by Heinrich Vogtherr in 1538, Erhard Schons in 1558, Heinrich Hautensack in 1564, and Crispyn van de Passe in 1564. Gombrich concludes that although these books became vocabularies when applied by artists they rarely revealed the actual image from what the artist drew. We shall never know, he claims, what Ruben's children really looked like, that is, from the acquired patterns and schemata used to organize our perception. For the artist, Gombrich sees the schema as a form of short-hand notation from which the artist will expand, fill in and eventually modify in order to reach an effective portrayal.

Educational Programs

According to Logan, in the 19th century American institutions embraced the European Academy's concern for the faithful reproduction of the object as central in an artist's education. Logan mentions, in particular, a member of America's first academy, Charles Wilson Peale, who assisted Thomas Jefferson in improving a copying device called a polygraph; the 1807 formation of the Pennsylvania Academy of Art and its statues of classical antiquity; and the 1825 founding of the National Academy providing opportunities for art students to draw from casts after first drawing from whatever masters or near masters drawings the school possessed (Logan, 1955).

Later in the century, the practice of direct copy in the early American art academies began to decline particularly in schools inspired by the ideas of Emerson. Logan (1955) viewed this decline as a change in philosophy, noting,

> At a time when classes of school children were copying their teacher's blackboard drawings line by line Emerson was writing the following: Because the soul is progressive it never quite repeats itself, but in every act attempts the production of a new and fairer whole... Thus in our fine arts, not imitation but creation is the aim. (p.43)

Logan also noted the influence of Rousseau in this transition most especially through his efforts to elevate the development of the individual and to recognize the right of "natural growth." Recognizing also that the early academies and art schools paid little attention to student needs and that dissatisfaction among art students was growing, a change in artistic education was probably a change whose time had come. In the founding of the academies, Logan claims, any criticism of the academy as being artistically unimaginative was quite impossible. The first requirement of the academies, he notes, was to create an establishment and ensure the perpetuation of the proposed institution. Situations such as the cast gallery of the early New York Academy of the Fine Arts turning away students, and showing few courtesies or concerns for them seemed typical of the American art training institutions of the period. Considering also the requirements that students slavishly copy art prints, spend long hours drawing from casts by oil lamp light, and put up with inter-institutional squabbling over equipment and turf, a change in curricula and classroom practices must have been welcomed by students.

A shift from the copy of prints and drawing from casts as basic classroom practice actually began, according to Logan, in the post-Civil War years with the efforts of Thomas Eakins at the Pennsylvania Academy. Eakins, as its Director in 1879, introduced life drawing and the practice of alternating painting from the model with drawing. Eakins also began the practice of having the student "feel and represent the qualities of light, color and above all texture!!! and have a clear grasp of essential form." (Logan, 1955, p. 58) Other changes in art student education came from the establishment of the Arts Students League which was organized by students and included them on the Board of Directors. Logan points out that William Merritt Chase, the League's leading teacher, ended the duller and uninteresting practices of learning draftsmanship, encouraged drawing as an understanding of light and shade, and introduced the study of line quality. This new orientation, he notes, soon became associated with the idea that the artist, while in the world should not be too closely a part of it, in order to create paintings which were "grand or wistful and were inspiring in subject" (Logan, 1955, p. 63).

Today, when education in schema is taught in our schools and colleges, it generally occurs in the drawing class coming through what Wygant notes as change in drawing's original goal of uniform competence to accept aesthetic education as its more respected goal (Wygant, 1983). The drawing class today is the principle venue for the teaching of schemata in those institutions which prepare artists, teachers and artists/teachers. The goals of today's drawing class have, of course, changed over time as the institutions who educate the artists and art teachers expanded from the art academies and art schools, to include state normal schools, colleges and universities. In the 1870's both artists and teachers were educated in the normal/art school which by 1900 evolved into state normal schools. By the end of World War II they had dissolved or turned into present-day state colleges and universities. In the process, the European method of copy from drawings as practiced in the Early American academies shifted in the normal schools to the drawing, painting and compositional approaches of Arthur Wesley Dow and in the colleges and universities to the naturalist ideals of Ruskin and the design ideals of the Bauhaus.

Drawing was in 1870 and still is today considered foundational art study. In the 1870's, Wygant notes, drawing was considered an aid to the teaching of reading and writing and a means to promote concepts of form and desirable habits of work and learning. Although drawing as foundational study does vary among the institutions which train artists and educators, most arts institutions today consider beginning drawing and/or life drawing as basic in the education of the artist, teacher, and designer. Foundation courses today also vary in content among schools, becoming in some a beginning in painting, ceramics, or the like, in others a short-term encounter with a variety of art modes (e.g., painting, sculpture, crafts), but in most a requirement that students have at least two semesters of study in both beginning drawing and beginning design.

It is perhaps worthwhile at this point to examine how such drawing courses teach the means for both constructing and overcoming schema. The best example is found in the writings and studio drawing methods advocated by Kimon Nicolaides in his text, the *Natural Way to Draw* (1941). While Nicolaides's text may not be as popular as it once was, many of today's drawing teachers either studied from his text, had teachers who did so, or have used his approaches to drawing without knowing they originally came from his text. Almost every teacher who teaches gesture or contour drawing, whether they know it or not, owes a debt to Nicolaides.

Nicolaides's basic method involved the use of gesture and contour as a surrogate for the expressive idea underlying pictorial form in the drawing. This search for the expressive idea rather than for faithful appearances in figure drawing is similar to the strategies used by the so-called "method" actor who personalizes the feeling states of the character to be portrayed in order to express the emotion of the character rather than his or her own. The goal of the actor using the "method" is to create on stage that particular kind of dramatic moment which makes it possible for the audience to experience the feelings of the character portrayed but in the context of their own emotions.

The notion of art as idea was also a major focus in R.G. Collingwood's book, *The Principles of Art*. Collingwood, in addition to making distinctions between art and craft, lays out in a sometimes self-contradicting way the notion that art is not an object but rather the exercise of imagination and consciousness in thought. Art, in his view, has no real end in view even as an object but exists only as he would call it, as "a tune in the composer's head" (Collingwood, 1953).

The fundamental premise behind Collingwood's argument is to be found in the artist's pursuit of the universal thought though remaining faithful to perceived feelings that never err. Art, for him, is the pursuit of true imaginal thought neither uncorrupted by the need to motivate the behavior of others nor betrayed through a corruption of consciousness. To thine own feelings be true and to resist their corruption through verifying their correctness is, according to Collingwood, the route to achieving true artistic expression. In such a process, art becomes not the thing created but rather the idea which brought the thing into being. Nicoholaides's principal claim as an educator of artists was, like Collingwood, that the idea behind the model's action was more important than the process of recording the model's appearance. He differed from other artist educators of his time principally because his program connected the concept of the idea behind the drawing to the underlying physical structure of the drawing itself.

His approach is through what he calls a schedule of work designed to help the student arrive at the necessary relationship between thought and action. Each exercise, he notes, has its place and carries a certain momentum. If the student fails to fulfill a full three-hour time requirement, Nicoholaides feels he or she is in danger of disrupting that momentum. He also tells the student that his or her goal in drawing should be to think of one thing at a time in order to master it and through hard work become welded to the habits formed in the process. In learning to draw, Nicoholaides believed, students should not care what their drawing looks like as long as they spend the required time drawing. The efforts should not, he notes, be on the drawing but rather on the experience one is having, charted not on paper but on the new knowledge with which they should look at life around them (Nicoholaides, 1941).

The lessons prescribed in his text focus first on contour and gesture drawing, and secondly on their use in various media, then as applied to the whole figure and head, moving on to technique, light and shade, composition, structure and design in that order. As was common practice in the 1940's and 1950's the sequence was to approach drawing first in black and white pencil, ink and water color, then black and white oil and finally to exercises in color. Before work could be attempted in oil, however, the student was required to study and analyze composition and anatomy through the use of art reproductions.

Nicolaides was not alone in believing that the idea behind the gesture was seminal in learning how to draw. In all probability he learned both about the concept and the method for achieving it from Robert Henri's book, *The Art Spirit* (1958) which was first published in 1923. Henri who also was both an artist and a teacher is considered the first to spread the ideas of 19th century French art to students in the American academies and art schools. He was viewed by some as being an even more influential teacher than William Chase, for his influence both on the students enrolled in his school and later on students at schools where his text was required reading. Henri's lectures as recorded in *The Art Spirit* anticipated much of what Nicolaides incorporated into his method. Henri's ideas that the drawing should reveal the sense of the thing; and that the search was for the meaning in the model and the aim to capture the feeling the model expressed at the time were all notions adopted by Nicolaides. Even Henri's sequence of instruction parallels Nicolaides beginning with gestures of the head and face, moving next to the background, garment, value, and color and finally to the compositional models presented in the reproductions of Cezanne, Corot, Monet, Homer, Hogarth and Velasquez. More importantly both Henri and Nicolaides viewed gesture as the cement or unifying element for all the movements in the figure (Henri, 1958).

Several of today's texts in drawing also support the gestural schemata developed by Henri and Nicolaides. Some like Mendelowitz in *Drawing* (1967), support Nicolaides almost totally while others such as Purser in *The Drawing Handbook* (1973), Behrens in *Design in the Visual Arts* (1984), and Betty Edwards in *Drawing on the Right Side of the Brain* (1984) see the schemata as foundational but add other developments in order to achieve other important drawing venues.

Mendelowitz, in particular, adopted Henri's notion that, "if painting is painting, it is drawing." You do not stop drawing when you begin to paint, for painting is drawing (Henri, 1923, p. 243). In particular, Mendelowitz believed that drawings constituted fragments of thought in logical sequences which could aid the painter in formulating "intellectual concepts of the greatest complexity" (Mendelowitz, 1967, p. 11). He also claimed that through drawing the artist could come to know the nature of forms too complex to be comprehended at a single glance and that understanding of the visual character of the physical world could only be achieved through the patient accumulation of knowledge. As to the source of such knowledge, Mendelowitz (1967) believed that it came primarily from the cultural schema, noting,

> drawing constitutes a kind of visual exploration through which individuals and cultures become familiar with the various forms that make up the culture's artistic repertory. Such forms can be drawn with certainty, are accepted and understood by the cultivated populace and are part of the general cultural heritage. (p.12)

Purser and Behrens, as previously noted, while supportive of drawing as basic schema also recommend somewhat more expanded agendas for the student of drawing. Purser, who taught drawing at the University of Florida, basically saw the drawing of the figure as a foundational experience and believed strongly in traditional notions of symmetry, balance and proportion (Purser, 1973). He also believed in teaching drawing through gesture but added the necessity of the student to learn what he called "structure." Structure, for Purser, begins with the basic gesture which he calls "drawing from the inside out" but in the end achieving composition and/or placement. Falling somewhat short of the positioning approaches advocated by Hoyt Sherman who Purser may have studied under at Ohio State, he seemed more directly influenced by his colleagues, Hiram Williams and Kenneth Kerslake, to include the figure in compositional settings more in keeping with the aesthetic of the times.

Behrens in *Design in the Visual Arts* (1984) also departs from a strict adherence to schematic forms of understanding how to draw. Behrens does, however, in his chapter "Pictures and Patterns" lay out what he calls the priority of patterns as evidenced in such matters as balance and visual weight, broken continuity clues, compositional resemblances, structural features and representation. In particular, he sees historical references as necessary (a) for the artist to make pictorial meaning consistent with compositional features which he calls pattern meaning, and (b) for what he calls broken continuity clues and compositional resemblances. More specifically, Behrens (1984) notes,

> In terms of representing life (whether through patterns or pictures or both), the power of art is two-fold: in its similarity to the thing represented and its *difference*. The fact that it differs from 'real things' is precisely why its *art*. It is artifice or pretense which is not the same as life. (p. 82)

Drawing on the Right Side of the Brain by Betty Edwards is grounded in Nicolaides's methods, but Edwards departs from him to meet the goal of her text which is to teach drawing to amateurs. Her book, while not designed as a college drawing text, offers a number of approaches respected by drawing teachers. Edwards could be described as a "Nicolaides" only in a "What to do till the art teacher comes" context as the text was designed for home use and her lessons geared to locations where life models are not likely to be available.

Edwards, like Nicolaides, has students learn through copying of up-side down drawings and through tracings. Unlike him, she also tells her students to outline perspectives on transparent material and draw reflected images in the mirror (Edwards, 1978). Like Nicolaides she begins with contour drawing but, unlike him, also resorts to employing canons of proportion and using the facial oval schema for portrait drawings. Edwards seems to make two assumptions about teaching drawing: (1) that the student can learn to draw as traditional artists draw and (2) to do that they must overcome the stereotype schema they now use.

If space would permit, more could be said of these and other texts in support of historical schemata as foundational in the teaching of drawing. It is hoped that these claims taken from the literatures in the teaching of drawing, the theory and psychology of art, and art history and aesthetics suggest

- A concurrence among artists, scholars, and teachers for a possible concept of art using schema.
- Support for the concept used (as a model) by artists, scholars, and teachers in conducting historical and productive research.
- A community (with a system of shared beliefs) formed over time by important artists, historians, critics, and educators.

• Transmittal of these shared beliefs to prospective artists, teachers, and scholars in programs of study supporting drawing from life as foundational study.

Art as Form-Gestalt Paradigm

The Form-Gestalt notion of art making in the 20th century probably found its beginning in Clive Bell's notion of significant form. It also had roots in the notions of objectified form and intuitional form as adumbrated by Kant, Croce and Hegel. Critically, it has been referred to as Formalism though as an art concept it is broader than this. It includes conceptions found in Clive Bell, Suzanne Langer, John Dewey and Martin Heidegger, and reflects a range of both rationalist and neo-idealist philosophical positions.

These varied views share a common notion that the art work evolves from an intuitive encounter of the artist with the visual elements produced in the work. While Bell's view centers on art structure, Langer's on symbolic meaning, Dewey's on personal growth and Heidegger's on personal form, all four accept both the artist's private vision and the art object as paramount. The form/gestalt concept includes all approaches that center on the artist's using the marks generated in the process of making as the means for achieving an intuitively objectified form or Gestalt.

Suzanne Langer, a 20th century philosopher, is best known for her efforts to use the form concept to aesthetically define what constitutes a work of art. Langer makes a number of claims in support of this argument including:

1. Subjective feelings exist in individuals and objective feelings exist in things.

2. Works of art are the containers of feelings which can be experienced by others.

3. Significant form conveys experience that language is unable to convey.

4. Works of art are things in their own right and are independent of our prepared reactions (Langer, 1953).

Langer's notion that feelings can exist in objects that do not feel is not unlike Croce's notions of objectified form previously discussed. Objectified form according to Croce becomes a fact when mediated by thought and when articulated in an object of art. Works of art, according to Langer, are then objects in which feelings are embodied in such a way that anyone seeking them can experience them in a nonsensuous apperception of the feelings in question. Such objects she notes are called 'works of art' and by 'art' we designate the activity that produces them (Langer, 1953, p. 22).

Through her claims that works of art contain feelings but do not feel them and that the feelings experienced are those we have at the time, she supports the view that there are no direct connections between the feelings articulated in the work and those felt by the viewer. That objects can express feelings, she claims, is not peculiar to art and is consequently not what makes artistic value. What makes an object a work of art she notes, is when the feeling is given clearly and objectively for our contemplation and when its function is not the stimulation of feeling but rather the expression of it." (Langer, 1953, p. 26)

Langer is also critical of Bell's formalist definition of significant form and redefines it to mean, "a symbol contained in a highly articulated sensuous object which by virtue of its dynamic structure can express the forms of total experience which language is particularly unfit to convey" (Langer, 1953, p. 32). In defining art as a symbol, Langer hopes to make clear the distinction between the form or Gestalt of the work and the language, which is discourse, developed by discursive reason. Art, according to Langer, doesn't *say* anything, it *displays* it, which is different from the elements and propositions named and articulated in sentences. In noting this, Langer distances herself especially from the empiricists who believe that art is a means for conveying propositional truth.

The 20th-century philosopher, John Dewey, shares some of both Langer's rationalism and Weitz's empiricism but nevertheless comes down on the side of individuals making art as central to deciding what art is and what experiences have value. Like Langer, Dewey (1) separates art from the experiences of everyday life and (2) considers feelings as existing in objects. He does, on the other hand, also make distinctions between aesthetic and scientific activity by noting that the artist, unlike the scientist, cultivates resistance and tension for expressive potentialities, thinks as he or she works, and finds thought as something which is more immediately embodied in objects (Dewey, 1934, p. 15).

Dewey's notion of "doing" and "undergoing" in unison has much in common with Langer's commitment to the union of making and thinking as defining the activity which brings art into being and her belief in the relations between feeling and form. Dewey refers to this union by saying that "there is no such thing in perception as seeing or hearing plus emotion. The perceived object or scene is emotionally pervaded throughout" (Dewey, 1934, p. 53). In agreement with Langer, he also believed that to perceive a work, the beholder must create his or her own experiences.

Art History References

References to the form-Gestalt concept occurred in the art history literature as early as Heinrich Wolfflin in the late 19th century. Wolfflin first expressed his concern for the visual analysis of painting in his book entitled *Principles of Art History* (1950). In it he struggles with a number of ideas related to pictorial form including: (1) relations between the medium and the object, (2) the elusive property of painterliness and (3) the distinctions between closed and open form. Such concerns led Wolfflin to argue that a correspondence exists between the medium and the object portrayed; that our attention to the work could be through the impressions given by mere patches of light and shade; and that opposition in direction could be felt as implicit in the work itself.

According to Podro, however, the first major encounters with the concept occurred in the writings of Max Weber (in 1917) and Ernst Cassier (in 1918). He feels they offered a viewpoint that later engaged the full attention of the art historian, Erwin Panofsky. Panofsky, according to Podro, advanced at least two critical claims requiring an appeal to form: (1) that the critical understanding of art requires that we look for artistic intention and (2) that our judgment of art needs to be scientific. What Podro argues, however, is that Panofsky's claims need to be understood in terms of the Kantian conception of what makes a judgment scientific: Artistic intention is not a matter of looking nor of scientific judgement and is not discovered from experience. Rather it is discovered through the impressions we bring to experience in order to give it intelligibility. Explaining Panofsky's Kantian stance and also noting his debt to Cassier, Podro (1983) states,

> But what could correspond in our understanding of art, to the concept of cause in science? The answer put simply was a conception of the *coherence* of a *work of art*. And the conception of the coherence of a work of art was conceived as the resolution of two complimentary factors called subjectivity and objectivity. Panofsky's line of thought follows closely that of Cassier. (p. 181)

The interest expressed by both Suzanne Langer and Irwin Panofsky with the objective-subjective paradox is probably due to their mutual respect for the ideas of Ernst Cassier. Langer, indeed, dedicated her book *Feeling and Form* to Cassier and according to Podro, Panofsky was influenced by at least three of Cassier's claims: (1) a work of art aesthetically must be separated from accounts of how it came into being, (2) works of art reflect the science of natural law and (3) coherence is the total cast of mind which particular factors in the work follow.

Psychological Definitions

Theoreticians in the psychology of art and perception, particularly Rudolf Arnheim and James Gibson, have addressed the psychological implications of the artist's objectification of form in the articulated image. Arnheim laid out his concepts in at least two texts, *Towards a Psychology of Art*(1966) and *Visual Thinking*(1969) and James Gibson expanded on Arnheim's ideas in his "Theory of Pictorial Perception" (1966). Arnheim in *Towards a Psychology of Art* describes the Gestalt theory of expression as embodying at least four of Langer's aesthetic notions: (1) forms contain feelings, (2) expressive forms objectify those feelings, (3) visual patterns in expression exist as an organized whole and (4) the viewer's perception of the work is the perception of what is felt at the time the work is experienced (Arnheim, 1966).

Arnheim, also, believes that forms contain feelings because artistic expression is not limited to living organizations that possess consciousness (Arnheim, 1966, p. 64). Citing D.W. Gotshalk, he notes, something can be perceived as if it were actually present in the object of perception although literally it is only suggested. He further supports this by claiming that expression is a perceptual quality which is a means by which humans obtain information about friendly, hostile or other environmental forces. These are, he notes, physiognomic qualities or the body-language of forms which are more directly perceived than such things as qualities of size, shape or movement. Sensory data, Arnheim feels, carries self-evident expression becoming a concept in which all perceptions are dynamic, possessing directed tension in the components of a perceptual stimulus which recalls behavior forces elsewhere. Objectivity is possible he notes because "by endowing the object or event with a perceivable form of behavior, these tensions give it 'character' and recall the similar character of other objects or events" (Arnheim, 1966, p. 53).

Translating a Gestalt model of perception into picture making was one of principle tasks James Gibson (1966) undertook in his essay, a *Theory of Pictorial Perception*. This essay is probably one of the most complete and detailed descriptions of that process appearing in the literature of art. Although the essay contained more than can possibly be reported here, a summary of the main points might be useful in elucidating the thinking behind the form-Gestalt concept of art making.

Gibson essentially makes three claims: (1) a visual symbol functions as a surrogate for reality, (2) the most effective surrogates are abstractions reflecting the psychological activity of the producer and (3) the interpretations of surrogates are always within in the context of the picture's construction. Gibson's first claim—that words, pictures and models substitute for realities through becoming surrogates—stems from the ability of these words, pictures, and models to serve as a stimulus produced by another individual specific to some object, place or event not, at present, affecting the sense organs of the perceiving individual. Surrogates are thus created through the self-stimulation of the artist to construct stand-ins, which can serve as a projection, to be perceived by someone not in the presence of the artist. His second claim—that works of art are, as abstractions, the most powerful surrogates—rests on their potential for projection. The more nearly a surrogate is conventional, he notes, the more associative learning is needed to interpret it. Hence, the more arbitrary or abstract it is, the more it is free to specify anything, abstract or concrete. With symbolic responses, Gibson believes, we can make propositions and hence perform logical and mathematical thinking. Realistic pictures, in his view, cannot state a logical proposition and distortions, which exaggerates some unique characteristics, may actually improve our identification of it. More succinctly put, a drawing or a model can tell us more about a thing than the thing itself (Gibson, 1966).

Finally, Gibson claims a picture has a unique viewing point which affects the kind of perception it is intended to produce. A picture, he believes, is namely a surface, a substitute, or mediating object, which employs a graphic method presupposing the use of a room or a viewing device and thus limiting the illusion of reality. The picture presents a dilemma because it is intrinsically impossible to get into the space of the picture. This would cause, he believes, the perceiver to experience two spaces, one incompatible and incommensurable with the other.

Education as Form-Gestalt

The need to revise the education of the artist in light of the emerging new form concept was first identified by Gottfried Semper. In 1852 Semper criticized the academies for training the artist in the "high style" and for being little more than institutions for the "sustenance" of professors isolated from society. He urged a new relationship between master and journeyman be established (Semper, 1852, p. 18). Similar concerns were also addressed by William Morris in 1894 when he advocated a new public awareness of the role of art in the society, discouraged imitating older works, and encouraged only the most dedicated to pursue a career in art (Morris, 1919, p. 18).

Calls for a new way to educate the artist also came from some 20th-century artists including Johannes Itten, Lyonel Feininger, Wassily Kandinsky, Lazlo Maholy Nagy, and Joseph Albers—all of whom were at one time or another teachers in the German Bauhaus. While associated with the Bauhaus all these artists contributed concept statements expressing concerns for artistic form and for the artist's education in learning how to achieve it. Johannes Itten, for example, argued that to experience a work means to re-experience it noting that there is no great difference between a person who experiences a work and one who represents their experience in a work. Every human being, Itten believed, can be taught to draw a circle, but not everyone was capable of experiencing it. Experience, he argued, was a faculty of the mind and spirit being in one sense a material experienced physically and in another sense a spiritual phenomena produced by the spiritual faculties in the individual. To perceive, in his view, is to be moved which in turn means to form, making everything that is alive reveal itself through movement which either must move or fail to exist (Itten, 1921).

Paul Klee, like Itten, also urged a new mental-physical involvement with the art object. This he referred to as the new "I" and "you," the artist and the object in a new optical-physical relationship. The object, he observed, grows beyond its appearance through knowledge of its inner nature. The "I," he felt, draws conclusions about the inner nature of the object from the appearance of its exterior thus humanizing it and bringing it into a resonance with the object which transcends optical fundamentals. In the eye he claims, "all ways come together merged into form which is a synthesis of outward sight and inner vision." (Klee, 1923, p. 73)

Wassily Kandinsky shared much the same point of view as Itten and Klee but put more of his thoughts on educational matters in writing. Some of his better recognized essays include discussions of the elements of form, the value of teaching, a theory of painting and investigations of visual problems, and the value of analytical drawing. He was first invited to teach at the Bauhaus in 1922 and remained on its faculty until its dissolution in 1933. His Bauhaus experience inspired his most famous writings, *Concerning the Spiritual in Art* first published in the *Bauhaus Journal* of 1928 and discussed in the previous chapter and *Point and Line to Plane* which will be discussed in more detail here.

Lazlo Maholy Nagy also supported this view of artistic form both as an editor of Bauhaus publications and as a teacher and administrator. In 1923 he was appointed head of the metal shop, and was co-editor of the Bauhaus books, writing two volumes himself. In 1937 he became the director of the New Bauhaus (Chicago) which in 1938 became the Institute of Design. Maholy Nagy and Joseph Albers in 1923 jointly headed the preliminary course, Maholy Nagy teaching visual perception and Albers a course on the study of materials.

Joseph Albers is best known for his Gestalt of color ideas in *Interaction of Color* published by Yale University in 1963. His ideas that color is the most relative medium in art and that, in context, color provides innumerable readings and is independent of form and placement are well known in the field of art. What is less well known are his views on education which in 1928 he noted as being one's own experience. In an essay on creative education, Albers claimed that experimenting was better than formal study; education in art should be experimentally organized more on technological or economical concerns; and we should not encourage individualism as it stresses separateness. The task of the school he believed was to integrate the individual into the society and the economy (Albers, 1928).

As to the education of American artists and teachers in the new form concept, at least two schools seemed to exert a major influence: Yale University where Albers held the post of art department chairman and the New

Bauhaus-Institute of Design directed by Maholy Nagy. The influence of the Institute of Design (I.D.) is especially noted by John Chancellor who calculated that by 1955 the Institute had graduated some 1,500 teachers, designers, and architects as well as a good percentage of professional artists (Chancellor, 1955, p. 210). Chancellor also believed, perhaps erroneously, that before the Bauhaus there were no schools of design and that the Institute was lineal heir of the Bauhaus of the 1920's. Peter Seltz, an I.D. graduate, has recounted the institute's early history beginning with Maholy Nagy's founding of the New Bauhaus in 1937, its change into the Institute of Design in 1938, and its merger with Illinois Institute of Technology in 1944. Seltz believed much of what was taught in the founding years was misinterpreted by students adapting I.D.'s concepts in the newer U.S. schools of design which, in his view, sought to invent modernistic products. Seltz notes that in 1952 the Institute sought to correct this misconception by creating a new graduate program in art education to train the teacher as a creative thinker and more understanding teacher. Seltz and coauthor Koppe (1955) described art education at I.D. this way:

> The student explores a specific problem such as the meaning of line for example, within a given space, in drawing, sculpture, photography and again in analytical seminars. The early phase of the work emphasizes the pure act of doing, almost like dance the approach is both physical and emotional. Free arm and finger movements, squeezing of clay, experimenting with wire liberates the student from preconceived aesthetic notions and help him rely on his own ingenuity (p. 208).

Clearly these artists and others whom they influenced began to exert a strong influence for change in both U.S. college and high school curricula. Those affected at the college level included both the newer private schools of art and design and the art and design programs of the state university and college systems. While both the Institute of Design and Yale have had a major, direct impact on the education of the American artist, nearly all college and public schools have been influenced by the ideas of such artists as Kandinsky, Klee, Itten, Maholy Nagy and Albers, all of whom have contributed to changing the American school art curriculum. In all probability the most notable influence at the college level was the introduction of the two-dimensional and three-dimensional design courses as foundational study at both the college and high school level.

While the new foundational courses in the 1960's became the most noticeable change in the college curriculum, the form-Gestalt concept also had an impact on the fine arts curriculum through the introduction of several new Gestalt drawing and painting theories. Itten, Albers, Maholy Nagy, and Kandinsky all later published the ideas they developed while constructing the new curricula in the Bauhaus. Perhaps the greatest influence in American education was Kandinsky's *Point and Line to Plane* book, first published by the Solomon R. Guggenheim Foundation for the Museum of Non Objective Painting. Undoubtedly, the interest in Abstract Expressionism and non-objective painting in New York provided a particularly good opportunity for Kandinsky's 1926 work to be revisited and to be elevated into a sort of conceptual manifesto for educational programs and for the New York School of Painting.

Point and Line to Plane which describes the function of the elements of composition is not easy to describe succinctly because of both Kandinsky's use of metaphor and his efforts to move the discussion to a spiritual plane. Understanding Kandinsky is not, however, all that difficult if one takes into account his underlying goal of making the case for the objectification of feeling in form. One needs, nevertheless, to get past the music, dance, and language analogies used to support his theory of composition in painting and the rather absolute feeling states he ascribes to different compositional relationships. Taken as a Gestalt argument, Kandinsky's concepts deal with the pictorial elements of point and line and plane with regard to their inter-relationships and function in articulating the artist's feeling pictorially. In his discussion of the point, which he calls zero, and its relations to the picture plane he points out at least two considerations: (1) the relation of the size of the point to the size of the plane and (2) the relative sizes of the point on the plane.

Compositionally, Kandinsky is much along the same lines as Gibson and Arnheim. He discusses the feeling states most likely to be associated with different configurations of the elements of point, line and plane. Believing that inanimate forms express, he examines the point with respect to its affect on the picture plane and the line in relation to its direction on the picture plane (i.e., whether it is horizontal, vertical, or diagonal) and to its function in forming the primary forms of the triangle, square, and circle. He treats the basic plane or BP as expressive form itself through dividing a square plane into four equal parts assigning feeling states according to their position above or below or to the right or left half of the picture plane. Kandinsky, supporting the objectification of feeling, views the above positions as reflecting great looseness: The lower positions give the impression of condensation, heaviness, or constraint, the left half positions a feeling of freedom and right half ones a feeling of constraint. Thus each of the four sections of the picture plane exhibits different tensions because of its particular location on the basic plane.

Taken as a whole, *Point and Line to Plane* contributed at least a needed verbal analog to explain the painter's dialectic of thesis antithesis or push/pull with the iconographic features of the painting surface. Because most artists thought that it was something to be felt rather than be linguistically analyzed, Kandinsky's conceptions may have helped art theorists to formulate a description of the modernist position in painting and provide a rationale for revising the education of the 20th century artist.

Since 1960 a number of other drawing and design texts have been developed for postsecondary art foundation drawing and design courses. Some of the best known include *Design Principles and Problems* by Zelansky and Fisher, (1984) *Art Fundamentals* by Ocverk, Bone, Stinson and Wigg, *Design through Discovery* by Belin and *Design Basics* by Lauer (1984). The format most often used in these texts is to address the so-called elements of art and principles of design. The elements generally discussed include line, shape, value, texture, color and space, and the principles reviewed usually include the organizational problems of balance, continuity, and emphasis. Because artists generally are suspicious about these so-called elements and principles, the elements are approached mostly as expressive content and the principles mostly as practices for establishing visual order.

In addition to these elements and principle texts, there were a few other design and drawing texts which more specifically address the Gestalt problem from the fine arts viewpoint in drawing and painting. Representative texts of this type include

• *Basic Design: The Dynamics of Visual Form* by de Sausmarez (1971). Focuses on the study of elements and forces.

• *Drawing a Search for Form* by Mugnaini and Lovoos (1965). Addresses the concepts inherent in square and circular forms.

• *Graphic Games* by Baumgartner (1983). Stresses movement of equal elements on surfaces.

• *Vision and Invention* by Harlan (1986) and *Design in the Visual Arts* by Behrens (1984). The following paragraphs describe these books in greater detail.

Calvin Harlan's *Vision and Invention* differs from most elements and principles texts mainly through his Gestalt view of point and line as repetition, position, spatial intervals, pattern and motif. Citing Wertheimer's findings, Harlan points out that objects, shapes, figures, and qualities are related to one another perceptually through four means: (1) proximity, (2) similar form pattern, (3) similarity of direction, and (4) closure (Harlan, 1986). To confirm the problem as being a Gestalt issue, Harlan provides examples of compositions with single and multiple points on the picture plane. He also provides sample compositions using vertical, horizontal, diagonal, and curved lines in ways reminiscent of Kandinsky's exercises in *Point and Line to Plane* although no references to Kandinsky are made in this section of his text. To confirm that these Gestalt judgements are innate, Harlan provides samples of scribbles from Rhoda Kellogg's kindergarten children, visual phosphene forms electrically generated in human brains, and prehistoric conventionalized figures and symbols. These examples are apparently in support of Harlan's main claim that art is the objectification of feeling through intuitively determined expressive form.

Behrens in his *Design in the Visual Arts* shares Harlan's views in recognizing the importance of the Gestalt. In the chapter entitled "Composition and Gestalt," Behrens defines the term Gestalt as implying composition, arrangement or organization which can be described through distinguishing the differences between *composition* and *disposition*. Composition, he believes, is the construction of works in regard to their structural features; disposition, the construction of works according to their symbolic, representational or pictorial significance (Behrens, 1984). Behrens does treat Gestalt concepts historically through recounting Ehrenfel's tachistoscope research and the experiments of Wertheimer, Kurt Koffka and Wolfgang Kohler with the strobe light to simulate what was called apparent movement. These studies, according to Behrens, led to the discovery of the principles of perceptual organization or unit-forming factors which he defines as the tendencies in human perception to decide which parts or features of a field will be seen as belonging to one another and which will be seen as belonging apart.

Behrens also treats the Gestalt problem through discussing the principle of similarity, proximity and contiguity grouping, closure, and validation. Similarity he defines as the theory that things which look alike will tend to be seen as belonging together; proximity and contiguity grouping as grouping which occurs through proximity or time; closure as the action of the viewer who fills in the gaps and validity as the requirement that the viewer recreates the work through personal consciousness.

Again, more texts and more experiments could be cited which will further support that a form-Gestalt Paradigm conception of art exists. The philosophers, psychologists, artists, and educators already cited should, however, be sufficient enough to meet Kuhn's criteria that for a paradigm to exist it must have a concurrence among the professionals which inhabit the field, serve as a model for the conduct of historical research, and form a system of shared beliefs among scholars as to the nature of appropriate forms of study.

While the form-Gestalt paradigm has had only a relatively short history, beginning in the mid-19th century, it may well have been even more influential in the arts and education during that time than the schemata and motif paradigm previously discussed. This may be due in part to its influence in the visual arts in our own time and in part to our having access to such an extensive amount of literature in support of its claims. Its influence on our schools and college programs, especially in foundational design courses, puts it in on a par with the more traditional forms of schema and motif still practiced in the drawing class. It may, indeed, be seen by some as the dominant view practiced in our school and college art curricula, if only because of its emotional appeal to the human spirit and its rational appeal for more objective and structured forms of art study and practice.

Linguistic-Metaphorical Paradigm

Philosophical Definitions

The theoretical beginnings of the linguistic-metaphorical paradigm can be traced back to the time of Locke, Berkeley, and Hume through their claims that: (1) ideas exist in objects, (2) objects are only what we can observe factually about them, and (3) objects change over time. It was Hume, in particular, who pointed out that relationships between things at different times are contingent, that there was no necessary inference from past to future, and that physical objects can change over time.

The two 20th-century philosophers most influential in shaping the linguistic-metaphorical paradigm were Morris Weitz and Claude Levi-Strauss. Both were influenced by empiricist values but posed somewhat different conceptions of art. Weitz was influenced by the idea that objects are nothing more than what can be factually observed and, because perceptions change over time, no past theories are adequate enough to explain them. Weitz, therefore, questioned all past aesthetic theories including what he called Formalism, Voluntarism, Emotionalism, Intellectualism, Intuitionalism, and Organicism. He claimed that no classical theory was fully adequate to explain what a work of art is. Levi-Strauss, an anthropologist influenced by the ethnographical values of Rousseau, made a different claim—that art was a sign linked to social behavior or ritual which could not be understood independent of the social forces bringing it into being. Both philosophers, while arguing from somewhat different epistemological positions, were accepting of the notion, that a concept of art could be based on a metaphorical symbol interpreted through language.

Weitz's position as outlined in his essay, "Can Art be Defined," argues that no art theory has the necessary and sufficient properties to allow it to be logically justified, thus making a single theory of art logically impossible. Weitz does, however, believe that by keeping the concept open some (orderly) discussion could be developed in order to extend an existing concept or invent a new one to deal with each new case (Weitz, 1959).

Art is for Weitz a concept, thus requiring professional critics to revise their decisions when new conditions, new art forms, or new movements arise. The primary task of aesthetics, for Weitz, is not to seek a theory but to elucidate a concept. Concepts can be developed, according to Weitz, through the reconstruction of older theories as a basis for providing argument or for establishing criteria for judging excellence in art. He did not view existing theories as worthless because they can help decide what to look for or at in a work of art. Aesthetic theory, Weitz believes, are summaries of recommendations to attend in certain ways to certain features of art, or rather to know how we can talk about talk about art.

93

Levi-Strauss's views on art, on the other hand, are shaped by the post-Kantian view of Hegel that while art and science are of equal value they need to be judged on somewhat different terms. Levi-Strauss also accepted Rousseau's social contract to deny the self through adopting the idea that I am another who thinks through me and causes me to doubt whether it is I who is thinking: This merges the society of nature and the nature of society through seeing the individual as identical to others (Levi-Strauss, 1983).

Unlike Weitz, who questioned the relevance of the past, Levi-Strauss accepted the hidden primitive past life of humankind as offering insight into the present. In his view, to discuss art, one was obligated to understand the social conditions which brought it into being and consider social facts as things, thus making works of art social fact.

> One cannot study gods while ignoring their images; rites without analyzing the objects and substances manufactured and manipulated by the officiant; or social rules independently of the things which correspond to them. (Levi-Strauss, 1983, p. 11)

Through his commitment to the anthropological method, Levi-Strauss contributed to the development of a concept of art based on models offered by primitive cultures. The ritual practices of ancient cultures, in his view, permitted the construction of models which could be manipulated and therefore used as a means for understanding the present. This method, which he viewed as alternating between the deductive and empirical, permitted the use of subjectivity as a means for objective demonstration. It thus became possible, he believed, to make the case that because I was there such a thing happened, and therefore others could believe that they were there themselves.

The model Levi-Strauss offers is the world of myth and ritual. He defined ritual as the acting out of a myth or social taboo which he believed formed the basis for human society being a society. The ritual can also be seen as a riddle a presenter offers to an audience to serve as metaphorical analog for discussing the moral message being conveyed. Jack Burnham adapted Levi-Strauss's anthropological view into what he called "system aesthetics" which, according to Burnham, focuses on relationships between organic and nonorganic systems in neighborhoods, industrial complexes, farms, transportation systems, information centers, recreational centers, and other human activities. Burnham sees what he calls modern didactic art as something not residing in material entities but rather in relations between people and their environment. To him the artist operates as a quasi-political provocateur owing no responsibility to the output of objects which might somehow beautify or modify an environment (Burnham 1974). Burnham sees art as a means of breaking down boundaries between art and society through aesthetic and social problem solving on a multilevel interdisciplinary basis. Artists embracing this view include environmental artists Robert Smithson, Les Levine, and Allan Kaprow.

Embracing both Hume's ideas that relationships between things at different times are contingent and Weitz's open concept, Burnham is accepting of both the notions that art has no higher meaning than its assigned context and that it is only a fragment in an art system. Supporting his idea that art is essentially a non-object Burnham (1974) states,

> a sculpture that physically reacts to its environment is no longer to be regarded as an object. The range of outside factors affecting it, as well as its own radius of action reach beyond the space it materially occupies. (p. 22)

Burnham also endorses the anthropological view of Levi-Strauss in believing that art is ritual. By accepting the American Indian belief that all objects are art, Burnham rejects the notion of art as objects to be curated in museums. He proposes rather that art should become part of a universal code which is cyclical and nonlinear, or in his words an expendable container for the transmission of lived truths. This process is, in Burnham's view, the emerging new art paradigm which is neither an "ism" nor a collection of styles but rather a novel way for the artist to re-arrange surfaces and space and reject the role of tool maker to become the maker of aesthetic decisions.

Historical Definitions

The literature in art history probably first reflected the need for a new art paradigm in 1974 when calls for change appeared in articles published in the *New Yorker, Atlantic, Art History* and *Art Bulletin* magazines. Calls for a new art history also have been proposed in the writings of Harvard's Norman Bryson, Albert Boime and Svetlava Alpers, and Michael Baxandale.

Hobbs views this new art history as coming about through the new critical theories represented in semiotics. He credits the influence of semiotics for fostering the notion of art as a cultural product considered as a text, a formal system of signs in which art is not conceived as an object but rather as a space between the object. Art is, in his view, open to other texts thus giving it intertextuality (Hobbs, 1991).

What Hobbs calls the new art history is reflected in a number of different philosophical views and historical forms including deconstructionism, appropriative, post modern, pop and post pop. The art historical view is no longer focused on individual works of art but rather on codes of meaning in contexts rejecting notions of subjectivity, genius, artistic expression, or aesthetic response. The new art historians have seemingly rejected the traditional art history view of prioritizing artists and artistic intentions, assuming instead that all cultural productions are political and are no longer involved in direct expression of the artist's personality.

The new art historian generally considers the conceptions advanced by art historians as important as or even more important than the art itself. Art history in this revisionist view is more like social anthropology especially when it seeks to develop such things as

- A social history of art.

- A feminist or Marxist history of art.

- A women's history of women's art.

- A history of art of the colonized countries.

- A history of the confrontation of high arts and popular arts

- The histories of institutions responsible for teaching, publishing, exhibiting and preserving art.

Art history from such a view suggests further that there may well be as many art histories as there are art historians.

The Artists and Their Work

In spite of the revisionist philosophical and historical claims that a new paradigm exists only as text, artists in this new paradigm still do make art objects which still are looked at as being both objects for contemplation and as reflecting the social conditions influencing them. Some artists, like those mentioned by Burnham, continue to work in a deconstructionist mode. These include Sherry Levine, who copies modern photographs. Cindy Sherman, who creates feminist works, and conceptual artists, Daniel Buren and Hans Haake. All these artists claim to challenge the traditional views of privilege, male domination, and the cult of individual creativity.

Other contemporary art styles also reflect the linguistic-metaphorical paradigm through using personal images which range from being objects as both a thing in itself and for all practical purposes, non-things. These different styles include:

- Conceptualism where the object reveals only the plan for conceiving it;

- Pattern or decorative art such as appears in Miriam Schapiro's garments as feminist concerns;

- Graffiti Art by Keith Haring, Jean Michel, Basquait, and Kenney Scharf;

- Neo Naive and Bad Painting by Roy De Forest and Jonathan Borofsky and New Image;

- New Wave and Neo-Expressionist paintings by Susan Rothenberg and Helmut Middendorf.

These artists varyingly express abstract concepts or, feminist values, reject establishment values or culture, and promote antistyle or social concerns, yet all seem to draw on familiar forms of imagery including the human figure, animals, fragments taken from prehistoric forms, appropriated images, merged art forms, words and letter forms or manipulated images from computers, copiers and videos. All, it would seem, have one other factor in common and that is the use of metaphor and language.

The use of metaphor as illustrative power is, according to Turbayne, to say no to old associations, (things which have gone together or are already sorted) and yes to new associations by crossing old sorts to make new ones (Turbayne, 1971). Metaphorical thinking, according to Behrens, is something artists constantly employ in a visual work, a way of conveying some feeling or thought not essentially new. An art metaphor occurs in Behrens' view when an object, person, or event is represented as if it were some other object, feeling, or event from which it usually differs (Behrens, 1984).

Artists can, according to Behrens, create visual metaphors through (1) binocular disparity, (2) bisociation, (3) humor, (4) unit making, and (5) inventive modification. Behrens describes binocular disparity as facilitating the viewer's ability to see two different images as one; bisociation as grouping disparate images together on the basis of common linguistic terms (such as passages) and humor as the use of jokes, puns, or witty remarks to create confusion between two or more distinctive things. All such devices, according to Behrens, are used in a creative taxonomy where a new object appears to demonstrate a surprising similarity between two things previously thought to be different (i.e., making the strange familiar), or a surprising difference between two things normally considered similar (i.e., making the familiar seem strange) (Behrens, 1984).

The Education of the Artist

It is difficult to identify specific schools providing a specialized curricula for the education of artist teachers in the metaphorical paradigm because the rejection of art traditions can also lead to rejecting educationally what is to be taught and how it is to be taught. One example of such a school documented in the literature is the development of the California Institute of the Arts (CIA) as presented by Judith Adler (1979). She calls her book, *Artists in Offices* an ethnography of an academic art scene. It provides a critical view of the 1960's artist designing a new paradigm school within the staid traditions of the Disney family sponsorship. While her text is mainly about the excesses of counter-revolutionary artist-administrators creating chaos in the management of the school she also has something to say about the excesses of the program, the faculty and the students.

Adler's analysis of the educational milieu at the CIA provides a number of important, but also biased views of their paradigm. She found that when new movements in art are embraced and speedily discarded, historical records are bypassed in favor of pursuing more current values. Thus, Adler noted, a teacher in a field in which the main tradition is the breaking of tradition becomes in effect a teacher without a field. Without a stable craft tradition and a sense of what occupational skills to impart, arts teachers at CIA, she claims, found their authority as masters of a craft greatly weakened or absent. Artists were, in the minds of CIA faculty, people who exist in an art world regardless of what it is they do (Adler, 1979).

Further, Adler notes, CIA students, less willing to wait 30 years to become artists, were eager to learn clues about the latest development in a changing art scene before that scene and their potential for recognition were gone. This, she thinks, pushed the student to seek younger teachers more in "the know," and to take glee in the bashing of older faculty. According to Adler, faculty in such a rapidly changing art scene face feelings of obsolescence in their media and helplessness in training students to survive in an art market not controlled by their profession. Students adapt to this situation, she believes, mostly through believing that contact with their peers and access to tools and hardware are the principal reasons for attending school. Faculty, she believes, can become entertainers to substitute winning and seductive ways for their absent occupational authority.

Other schools and universities in addition to Cal Arts have, of course, adopted the new paradigm in their curriculum but in a much less dramatic form and certainly with less administrative zeal. While it is hard to name more than one or two who have adopted a whole new paradigm look, many have introduced the metaphorical linguistic paradigm into the foundational drawing and design courses and into the painting, sculpture, craft and printmaking studios. Most certainly this approach is more popular with younger faculty who recognize that time is on their side and this approach will exert more influence in shaping the education of tomorrow's artists and teachers.

Several new foundational texts also have been introduced and are being used in an increasingly larger number of universities and schools. Included are Behrens's *Design in the Visual Arts* (1984), *Art Synectics* by Roukes (1982), *Visual Workouts* by Johnson (1983) and *Drawing* by Betti and Sale (1986). In *Design in the Visual Arts* Behrens effectively treats the notion of art as metaphor and illustrates various art styles in the metaphorical-linguistic paradigm. In *Visual Workouts* Johnson provides over 70 art problems as metaphors including such assignments as three-image narrative, object-word narration, time capsule, video sequence, wordlist painting, visual installation piece and a personal shelter.

Claudia Betti and Teel Sale in their text, *Drawing*, provide a much more conceptual discussion of the paradigm. While admitting of an eclectic view, their text argues strongly for the new paradigm. The authors advance, for example, two approaches to understanding studio concepts including the use of (1) ideas which transform traditional approaches to the picture plane and (2) contemporary theme approaches. To transform the picture plane, the authors pose several studio problems in what they call the assertion and denial of the picture plane. They see this as being accomplished through (1) dominance of the edge, (2) negotiations of the edge, (3) arrangement of images and (4) division of the picture plane.

Dominance of the edge is accomplished through changing the traditional rectangular plane into shaped forms similar to those invented by Frank Stella, Ellsworth Kelly and Jonathan Borofsky and through internal framing practices such as those used by Yvonne Vacquett and Jim Nutt. Negations of the picture plane are efforts to make the viewer imagine that if the plane were extended in any direction the image would also extend unchanged such as occurs in works by Jackson Pollock, and Jean Dubuffet. The arrangement of images is viewed as a matter of deciding relationships between positive and negative spaces to bring attention to the shape and size of the plane on which the images are placed such as occurs in the works of Claes Oldenburg and Morris Louis. Division involves using a grid that divides the picture plane into units or segments as appears in works of David Salle, Rob Erdle and Pat Steir (Betti, & Sale, 1980).

Thematic development is described by the authors as a sustained series of drawings with an idea or image in common. The themes discussed are those developed by individuals, by groups, or as shared concepts. Individual themes include such things as the working drawings of Claes Oldenburg, the bathrobe series by Jim Dine, and the non-objective images of Vincent Falsetta. Group themes occur when members of the same school share common stylistic or subject interests like the commonplace objects used in the pop art of Tom Wesselmann and Andy Warhol. Emanating from art history shared themes, according to the authors, are raids on predecessors' subject sources such as occurred in the works of Larry Rivers, Roy Lichtenstein and Mel Ramos.

Perhaps the most comprehensive text for advancing the metaphoric-linguistic paradigm is *Art Synectics* by Nicholas Roukes (1982). Roukes's chapters all center on either metaphor or linguistics, and include such topics as analogs, signs and symbols, myth, ritual, and paradox. Analogy he defines as the equality of agreement in likeness or proportions between things; symbols, as signals or signs useful for codifying knowledge and experiences; myth and myth making, as providing the amalgam of its relations and mediations; ritual, as action by a savage society to act out events; and paradox, as characteristic of a work which enables it to both contain and express different meanings.

Each chapter includes activities designed to provide experience in solving these concerns in a studio context. In analogy, the student pursues a number of analogical design problems such as finding design likenesses, using nature for design analysis, projecting personal feelings into objects, discovering relationships between dissimilarities, and creating visual puns. In the chapter, signals, signs and symbols, students create graphic equivalents for mechanical processes, design symbols that portray a life style, alter a common object with graffiti, and use graphic signs as a basis for creating abstractions. In the chapter myth and myth making, Roukes assigns students the tasks of reinterpreting ancient myths, portraying the alter ego in three-dimensional form, and making mythological machines and modes of transport. In ritual, game and performance, he recommends students make wearable art; create an interdisciplinary mixed-media art event, a ritual object, an inflatable media bubble, and an architectural environment; and play an art game. In paradox, students attempt to create a graphic labyrinth and make a surreal totem, a landscape in a box, and a perspective drawing using part of the human anatomy.

Again, more examples from the literature in art theory, art history, aesthetics and the studio could be offered though, I believe, the examples already provided are sufficient enough to demonstrate that a paradigmatic concept of art as metaphor and language can be said to exist. The concept exists as a paradigm because the citations from the literature of art suggest that a concurrence exists among professionals on the structure of the concept and its utility as a model for the conduct of research and as a system of shared beliefs capable of supporting appropriate forms of study. Furthermore, while the paradigm has been in existence for no more than two decades and may still be noted as emerging, the attention given in the literature of art suggests that it will both sustain and grow in force in the school and college curriculum for many years to come.

Summary

The three paradigm conceptions of art as schema-motif, art as form-Gestalt and art as linguistic-metaphorical as adumbrated in this chapter suggest that some currently held beliefs regarding a disciplinary conception of art production and art history may need examination. These paradigms challenge whether a so-called discipline based art production or art history approach can be truthfully said to exist. Without a concurrence among practitioners that a coherent concept of the discipline is possible we may properly conclude that no necessary or sufficient conditions exist to consider those who either work in the studio or engage in the study of art history as functioning in a paradigm community. Without concurrence on the concept, there is, in all probability, as many differing views of studio production and what constitutes art history scholarship as there are theories about such matters. More importantly it would seem unlikely, therefore, that any curriculum using art production or art history can be said, to reflect an "artist's" or an "art historian's" point of view to justify its use in constructing a curriculum in art.

On the positive side, the existence of these paradigms also raises serious questions as to whether conceptual barriers need to exist between members whose concerns are about thinking or making art. Furthermore, if such barriers do exist they may be more a consequence of what members do in the various art institutions they serve rather than reflecting any conceptual difference in their beliefs about art. The elimination of such barriers also suggests, moreover, that both older and newer conceptions of art remain viable as means for constructing coherent curricula and programs reflecting agreement among members from different professional modes of inquiry.

The question thus to be posed in Chapter IV is whether these conceptual paradigms cohere with various art curriculum conceptions currently being advanced in the instructional literature of art education. To demonstrate the possibility of such a coherence an analysis of a variety of texts used in art instruction in American elementary and secondary schools will be attempted.

References

Abrams , M. (1953). *The mirror and the lamp*. Oxford: Oxford University Press.

Albers, J. (1928). Creative education In E. Stein, (Ed.), *The Bauhaus* (p. 142). Cambridge: M.I.T. Press.

Albers, J. (1963). Interaction of color. New Haven: Yale University Press.

Adler, J. (1979). *Artists in offices*. New Brunswick: Transaction, Inc.

Arnason, H. (1986). *History of modern art*. New York: Harry N. Abrams, Inc.

Arnheim, R. (1966). *Toward a psychology of art*. Berkeley: University of California Press.

Arnheim, R. (1969). *Visual thinking*. Berkeley: University of California Press.

Baumgartner, V. (1983). *Graphic games from pattern to composition*. Englewood Cliffs: Prentice Hall, Inc.

Behrens, R. (1984). *Design in the visual arts*. Englewood Cliffs: Prentice Hall, Inc.

Betti, C. and Sale, T. (1986). *Drawing, a contemporary approach*. New York:CBS College Publishing.

Burrell, G. and Morgan, G. (1985). *Sociological paradigms and organizational analysis*. Portsmouth, NH: Heinemam.

Burnham, J. (1974). *Great western salt works*. New York: George Braziller, Inc.

Chancellor, J. Institute of Design. The Rocky Road to the Bauhaus. Chapter 9, p. 210. In E. Stein (Ed.) *The Bauhaus*. p. 210. Cambridge: M.I.T. Press.

Collingwood, R. (1953). *The principles of art*. New York: Oxford University Press.

Collins, B. (1987). A methodological critique of the teaching of art history: Or what's wrong with Janson and Gardner. *Forum, 1 (1)*, 18-25.

Dewey, J. (1934). *Art as experience*. New York: G.P. Putnam's Sons.

Edwards, B. (1978). *Drawing from the right side of the brain*. Los Angeles: J.P. Tarcher Press.

Gardner, H. (1959). *Art through the ages*. New York: Harcourt, Brace and Company, Inc.

Gibson, J. (1966). A theory of pictorial perception. In G. Kepes (Ed.), *Sign image symbol* (pp. 92-107). New York: George Braziller, Inc.

Gombrich, E. (1972). *Art and illusion*. Princeton: Princeton University Press.

Habermas, J. (1971). *Knowledge and human interests*. Boston: Beacon Press.

Harlan, C. (1986). *Vision and inventions*. Englewood Cliffs: Prentice-Hall, Inc.

Harrison, A. (1978). *Making and thinking: A study of intelligent activities*. London: The Harveston Press Limited.

Henri, R. (1958). *The art spirit*. New York: J.B. Lippencott Company.

Hobbs, R. (1991, May). Museum ethics and the new art history. Paper presented at the Ethics of Change Seminar, p.6. Florida State University.

Hochberg, J. (1988). Problems of pictorial perception. In G. W. Hardiman & T. Zernich (Eds.), *Discerning art*, pp. 366-389. Champaign: Snipes Publishing Co.

Hoffman, H. (1948). *Search for the real*. Cambridge: The M.I.T. Press.

Itten, J. (1921). Analysis of old masters. In E. Stein (Ed.), *The Bauhaus*. Cambridge: M.I.T. Press.

Johnson, M. (1983). *Visual workouts*, Englewood Cliffs: Prentice-Hall, Inc.

Kuhn, T. (1970). *The structure of scientific revolutions*. Chicago: University of Chicago Press.

Kandinsky, W. (1947). *Point and line to plane*. New York: Dover Publications, Inc.

Klee, P. (1923). Ways of nature study. In E. Stein (Ed). *The Bauhaus*. Cambridge: M.I.T. Press.

Langer, S. (1953). *Feeling and form*. New York: Charles Scribner's Sons.

Lanier, V. (1972). Objectives of teaching art. *Art Education, 25*(3), 15-18.

Lauer, D. (1979). *Design Basics*. New York: Holt, Rinehart, and Winston.

Levi-Strauss, C. (1983). *Structural Anthropology (Vol. 2)*. Chicago: University of Chicago Press.

Logan, F. (1955). *Growth of art in American schools*. New York: Harper and Brothers.

McWhinnie, H. (1989). *Hoyt Sherman and history of art education*. Unpublished manuscript, University of Maryland, College Park.

Mendelowitz, D. (1967). *Drawing*. New York: Holt, Rinehart and Winston, Inc.

Mittler, G. Learning to look/looking to learn: A personal approach to art appreciation at the secondary level. *Art Education,* March, 1980 (pp. 17-21).

Morris, W. (1919). Arts and crafts circular letter. In J. Stein (Ed.), *The Bauhaus*. Cambridge: M.I.T. Press.

Mugnaini J. & Lovoos J. (1965). *Drawing a search for form*. New York: Reinhold Publishing Co.

Nicolaides, K. (1941). *The natural way to draw*. Boston: Houghton Mifflin Company.

Ocvirk, O., Bone, R., Stinston, R., Wigg, P. (1985). *Art foundation talks theory and practice*. Dubuque: William C. Brown Publishers.

Panofsky, E. (1955). *Meaning in the visual arts*. Garden City: Doubleday Anchor Books.

Pearse, H. (1983). Brother can you spare a paradigm? The theory beneath practice. *Studies in Art Education, 24*(3), pp. 158-163.

Pearse, H. (1992). Beyond paradigms. *Studies in Art Education, 33*(4), 244-251.

Podro, M. (1983). *The critical historian of art*. New Haven: Yale University Press.

Purser, S. (1973). *The drawing handbook: Approaches to drawing*. Gainesville: Parser Publications.

Roukes, N. (1982). *Art synetics*. Worcester: Davis Publications, Inc.

Seltz, P. & Koppe, R. (1955). The education of the art teacher. *School Arts*, April 1955.

Semper, G. (1852). Science, industry, art. In J. Stein (Ed.), *The Bauhaus*. Cambridge: M.I.T. Press.

de Sausmarez, M. (1971). *Basic design: The dynamics of visual form*. New York: Van Nostrand Reinhold Company.

Turbayne, C. (1971). *The myth of metaphor*. Columbia: University of South Carolina Press.

Weitz, M. (1959). *Problems in aesthetics*. New York: The Macmillan Company.

Weitz, M. (1959). The role of theory in aesthetics in *Problems in Aesthetics*. New York: The Macmillan Company.

Wolffin, H. (1950). *Principles of art history*. New York: Dover Publications, Inc.

Wygant, F. (1983). *Art in American schools in the nineteenth century*. Cincinnati: Interwood Press.

Dubuffet, Jean. *Site à l'homme assis*, (Gift of Robert M. and Anne T. Bass and Arnold and Mildred Glimcher, in Honor of the 50th Anniversary of the National Gallery of Art, © 1993 National Gallery of Art, Washington, 1969-1984, polyester resin/cast and painted, height: 3.048 (120).

Chapter 4

Paradigms for Art Teaching

To claim that differing paradigms for thinking about and making art exist does not guarantee that they directly influence the art teaching programs of schools. This chapter, therefore, explores the possibility that the paradigms outlined in Chapter III actually function in schools while at the same time recognizing that the goals of American education are much broader than art. Public education in America, and other countries, is principally concerned with the acculturation of the young into the values, traditions and customs of the society. Because the U.S. is a democracy with the responsibility for education vested in individual states, American schools are, fortunately, free to adopt differing conceptions of education and art to influence how art is taught in them.

To achieve American educational goals, those responsible must go beyond thinking of schools as storehouses of knowledge and see them as institutions effecting positive changes in the social and intellectual growth of children and youth. This requires that we in art, like our colleagues in other subjects, contribute to shaping a broad range of student behaviors. This broader contribution has over time been reflected in the various goals pursued by our field. In reviewing the art education literature it is, therefore, important to differentiate between educational goals that are social, developmental, or intellectual and those that are essentially aesthetic. This is not always an easy task, however. For when the goals of an art paradigm are socially focused, the distinctions between them and the goals of general education are for the most part blurred; where artistic conceptions are more rational, individualistic and idiosyncratic, values may be only implicitly evident. Also, because schooling in art involves children and teachers experientially, there is a need to think of art activity as being important in its own right as well as being the means for transmitting aesthetic knowledge and experience.

Because American goals of art education are related to the overall purposes of schooling, art education literature is rarely, if ever, focused solely on aesthetic conceptions of art education. Texts with such titles as *Mind Your*

Child's Art, Creative Teaching in Art, Art in Everyday Life, Meaningful Art Education, The New Art Education, and *Education Through Art* suggest that they include more about current educational trends and artistic tastes than about which aesthetic goals are pursued. School budgets also weigh heavily in determining which kinds of materials are published and at what level. When school populations and enrollments in art teacher education programs are on the increase, the number of college-level texts also increase; when enrollments decline so do the number of college texts. Similarly when enrollments in college Art for Elementary School courses exceeds the enrollment in secondary, so too does the number of general education texts for the elementary school far surpass the number published at the secondary level.

A review of the current art education literature leads to the general conclusion that most art education publications are directed toward general education in art at the elementary level. This affects both the content of the college level art education texts available and the kinds of curricula published in such commercial magazines as *School Arts* and *Arts and Activities* and in the series publications offered by various school art commercial publishers and art materials manufacturers. With the exception of the more scholarly articles published in the National Art Education Association periodicals, *Art Education* and *Studies in Art Education* and the occasional papers published by CEMREL, the Getty Center, and Arts Propel, few texts can be said to be primarily directed toward explicating the conceptual paradigms previously identified.

These restrictions in scope and the other limitations mentioned on the art education literature section require an especially prudent selection of the works to be discussed and analyzed to accurately reflect the aesthetic paradigms. This chapter will, therefore, include only one college level text as a paradigm exemplar and review only a limited number of the supporting texts and school level curriculum series. The three texts forming the principal basis for this discussion are Lowenfeld and Brittain's *Creative and Mental Growth* (1975), McFee and Degge's *Art, Culture and Environment: A Catalyst for Teaching* (1977), and Feldman's *Becoming Human Through Art* (1970)—all of which provide conceptual arguments for the paradigms practiced in schools. This chapter's purpose is to demonstrate both that conceptual linkages exist between them and that the paradigms identified in Chapter III along with this text's philosophical analysis can be used to critically examine the curriculum statements addressed in the next chapter.

Some Earlier Efforts Toward Conceptions in Art Education

It was Manuel Barkan who first advanced the notion that different conceptions of art inform the curriculum in American schools. In his *Foundation For Art Education* text (1955), he outlined the creative process as having three distinct forms:

1. Imitation—impressions creating images that later become ideas.

2. Imagination and Intuition—meanings formed by individuals as imagined.

3. Intuitive Intellectual Interaction—sensation becoming meaningful in intellectual awareness.

In the 1960's, Dale Harris also outlined differing conceptions of art and differing perceptions of human response in his review of theories on the psychology of drawing. Harris (1963), in his *Children's Drawings as Measures of Intellectual Maturity*, provides a broad range of views and reports of scholarly studies dealing with perception and artistic form. Harris organized his psychological theories in two categories: (1) theories that imply an inherent organization such as those used in Gestalt concepts and (2) theories that assume organization in drawing as given in experience which limits concepts to language. Under theories suggesting inherent organization, Harris describes two different types: 1. Nativistic theories propose that organization in drawing results from properties either in the work or in the nervous system of the individual. 2. Organismic theories he believes, are clearly more holistic than behavioristic in their thinking.

Under nativistic theories he includes art education theorists Gustaf Britsch, Henry Schaefer-Simmern, Rudolf Arnheim and Herbert Read. Schaefer-Simmern, in particular, is cited as supporting a nativistic approach through his claim that in drawing, as well as in all artistic activity, there is an intrinsic or inherent character whereby it evolves from simple to more complex forms. Lowenfeld, on the other hand, was viewed by Harris as somewhat of a maverick. He saw Lowenfield's theories of children's drawings as more "Gestaltish" than "organismic" and Lowenfeld himself as concerned primarily with concept formation. Harris (1963) noted that to Lowenfeld

> the function of art education is not so much to bring awareness of the content of the unconscious as to activate passive knowledge. The mechanism is the development and enhancement of the self, or ego, through creating pleasing results with color, line and form and through highly individual ways of viewing the world. (p. 183)

Harris's list of scholars supporting his second theory (that organization in drawing is given by experience) includes Florence Goodenough, author of the Draw-a-man test; psychologist Jean Piaget; art historian E.H. Gombrich; and art educator June McFee. Harris, claims that Florence Goodenough's theories given in experience sought to be the most rigorously empirical and that she was the first to give a comprehensive account of children's drawings wholly in empiricist terms. In support, Harris quotes Goodenough as saying "no theory of drawing can be formulated apart from consideration of perceptual processes" (Harris, 1963, p. 185).

Harris also cites several other organization-from-experience theories which support (1) cognition contents as hypothesized and understood as being built up empirically; (2) perception as involving both synthesizing and analytic processing; (3) discrimination as involving analysis, comparison, and abstraction; and (4) drawing as the development of a system of verbalized concepts. Harris (1963) in support of Goodenough's view claims:

> Drawings of the objects are based on concepts; concepts are based on experience with objects. Experience increases the aspects of objects that are reacted to, understood and incorporated in drawing. Not only are the number of these aspects increased by experience; the *relationships* [sic] among them are grasped more completely, Thus with experience a larger number of concrete aspects and what is more important, more abstract aspects are understood and used in drawings. (p. 195)

Harris (1963) placed June McFee in the drawing-from-experience category because she envisioned the need for (1) abstract handling of information, (2) cognitive understanding, (3) awareness of visual details and (4) use of both postural and visual receptors for getting information from the environment. Harris placed Gombrich in this group because Gombrich supported schema as designating the particular concepts and techniques that control the artist's choice of subject matter and his ways of handling it (p. 202).

While Harris, like Barkan, describes a number of drawing theories that cohere with the Chapter III paradigms (schema-motif, form-Gestalt and linguistic-metaphorical), he also saw them in only two forms: (1) those theories depending on responses to organizational features of the drawing and the emotional circumstance involved in its making or viewing and (2) those organizational processes that encourage continuous individual cognitive growth through increased perceptual differentiation. Harris thus classifies these drawing theories into two philosophical orientations, rational and empirical, and does not include a neo-idealist position which unites the rational and empirical traditions.

The Schema-Motif Paradigm in Art Education Today

As Harris notes, Lowenfeld was committed to the enhancement of the self, to the activation of passive knowledge, and to pleasing visual results. He, therefore, offers the best example of an art educator supporting the art as schema-motif paradigm. Lowenfeld's views are mostly contained in his art education classic, *Creative and Mental Growth* (1947), which has undergone numerous revisions. This text's staying power is amply demonstrated by the publication of its eighth edition (1987) co-authored by the late Lambert Brittain.

Lowenfeld made two fundamental assumptions in defining the creative act: (1) that the ends of art are understood through a dialectic occurring between the maker and the thing formed and (2) that the thing formed (art) was a deliberate and intelligently articulated expressive form. Lowenfeld's commitment to the dialectic is evidenced in his additional claims: (1) that the act of creating itself provides new insights and new knowledge for further action and (2) painting and drawing is a constant process of assimilation and projecting—taking in through the senses a vast amount of information, mixing it up with the psychological self, and putting it into a new form suitable to the expressive needs of the artist at the time it is created. Lowenfeld also accepted the notion of art as beginning with an idea or thought about something that was, in effect, a confrontation with self or with experience (Lowenfeld, 1975).

Lowenfeld, furthermore, argued that expression was connected to the ability to recall events occurring through the highlighted intensity of our emotions thus enabling us to remember certain events and see them in detail. In spite of his admonitions against student copying, Lowenfeld also believed that imitation was an important factor in learning.

> One of the most important means of communication-language is initially conceived by imitation. The importance of imitation as a means of learning therefore, cannot be overlooked. Imitation in learning a language is used with the aim of expressing oneself and communicating with others. (Lowenfeld, 1964, p. 21).

Thoughts and ideas could also, according to Lowenfeld, be expressed creatively, especially when the self was fully identified in expressing. What mattered, in his view, was how the thing is expressed rather than what content was expressed.

Both Lowenfeld's concept of child art and his teaching methodology were connected to the development of schema and deviations from it. In *Creative and Mental Growth*, Lowenfeld traces the child's development of schema through five stages:

1. The scribbling stages from 2 to 4 years.

2. The pre-schematic stage, from 4 to 7 years.

3. The schematic stage, from 7 to 9 years.

4. The gang age from 9 to 11 years.

5. The stage of reasoning from 11 to 13 years.

Through the attention given the developmental stages, Lowenfeld outlines a morphology of expressive growth stiltified at the schematic stage through the repetition of schema and resolved in later stages through deviations from schema in a path toward more realistic modes of representation.

Unlike Gombrich who believed artistic schema are learned from other pictures, but like Kellogg, Reed, and Arnheim, Lowenfeld believed that schema develops phylogenetically. Also, where Gombrich speaks of altering existing stereotypes through correction of perceptual fit, Lowenfeld views this change as a deviation from schema accomplished through the activation of passive knowledge. Schema is, for both Gombrich and Lowenfeld, a representation of an object but for Lowenfeld one that also originates in both visual and nonvisual experiences determined by the emotional and kinesthetic experiences of the child, the touching impressions received by the child, or the functions or behaviors of an object. The mature artist like the child, he thought, may also show a lack of involvement by repeating a technically proficient piece of art or a certain mannerism without change, becoming caught in a stereotyped repetition of his own techniques (Lowenfeld & Brittain, 1975, p. 33).

Finally, Lowenfeld also believed that (a) the art content employed by the young child was the same as that used by the professional artist, and (b) the child knows in a passive way more than he or she ever uses. It is, according to Lowenfeld, part of the teacher's role to activate passive knowledge. The aim of child art instruction is therefore to encourage deviations in the schema or stereotypes in drawing through the exaggeration of important parts, neglect or omission of unimportant or suppressed parts, or a change of symbols for unimportant parts. When teacher interaction is needed, Lowenfeld's method is not at all unlike that of Nicolaides who emphasized identifying with the thing or the event as the means to face one's own feelings and emotions. Subject matter, or the thing represented, was also secondary for Lowenfeld; it needed only to be important to the child and not to pressure him or her to perform in a certain way. To overcome schema or stereotypes Lowenfeld suggested that the teacher provide the means to (1) encourage the child to identify experientially with the work, (2) motivate the child to define the expressive idea, (3) clarify the meaning of the work in progress, or (4) divert attention to content through the challenge of using newer media.

Lowenfeld's students, Lambert Brittain (1979) and Kenneth Lansing (1976), supported his developmental stages. However, they somewhat deemphasized his interest in the activation of passive knowledge and his deviation from schema message, and avoided altogether his valuing of imitation. Still other art educators support Gombrich's position of valuing historical schema. They include Robert Kaupelis (1983), Brent and Marjorie Wilson (1983), Kenneth Lansing and Arlene Richards (1981), and Al Hurwitz and Stanley Madeja (1977). Kaupelis (1983), for example, believes most artists begin by copying the comics and that most art is born from art. The Wilsons (1983) go much further, claiming that drawing development is dependent upon borrowing and employing the images of the art of a culture; they note that all graphic language relies on a culturally specific vocabulary and style.

The Wilson's study of the children of Nahia, an Egyptian village in Giza, convinced them that despite of a lack of comic books, magazines, advertisements and book illustrations the Nahia children influenced one another. The findings of their study (Wilson & Wilson, 1983) include the following:

- A given "graphic language" is largely composed of a culturally specific standard "vocabulary" of shapes and configurations.

- Perceptions of objects in the every day world have less effect on how objects are drawn than the standard cultural symbols used for depicting objects.

- If young people have few graphic configurations available to borrow from adults, then they borrow them from other children.

- The fewer the graphic influences the more impoverished and predictable a style will be. (p.14)

Teaching Drawing Through Drawings

At least three texts advocate schematic approaches to the teaching drawing: 1. *Teaching Drawing from Art* by Brent Wilson, Marjorie Wilson, and Al Hurwitz. 2. *Children and Their Art* by Charles Gaitskell, Al Hurwitz, and Michael Day. 3. *The Elementary Teachers Art Handbook* by Kenneth Lansing and Arlene Richards. The first text listed is almost exclusively directed toward this point of view, while the other two advocate using schematic approaches along with others.

Brent and Marjorie Wilson in collaboration with Al Hurwitz (1987) presented a schematic curricular approach in their text, *Teaching Drawing from Art*. They begin by citing Gombrich's claim that to build an image you have to start somewhere and the easiest starting point is a minimal model of what you want to represent. They also claim that drawing development is dependent on employing the images of a culture and that every image we draw owes something to the graphic images of others. Further, the authors point out that children have little choice but to borrow the images of others and that without such images the language of drawing would be much poorer.

Wilson, Hurwitz, and Wilson recommend the following steps in the teaching of drawing: (1) remove intrinsic biases; (2) set conditions for organic unfolding; (3) provide information about the ideas, styles, techniques, and skills employed by professional artists; and (4) develop ways to teach drawing through drawings. The studio models provided in the text include observational drawing approaches to composition, memory drawing, action drawing, illustrative drawings, and talking and writing about drawing. Although they advocate the use of other more traditional methods of teaching drawing, these follow chapters on "Teaching Drawing Through Works of Art" and

"Going for Style" in which students work in "the style of" Edward Munch, Saul Steinberg, Paul Klee and Goya.

Although authors Lansing and Richard claim their text supports different art learnings, *The Elementary Teacher's Art Handbook* is essentially a studio text which begins each studio medium or mode with a reproduction and a biography of an artist which they refer to as an exemplar. The authors claim at least four purposes for the book, but helping teachers integrate art history and art appreciation into productive art activities seems paramount. They approach the making of art through (1) instruction in the techniques used in drawing, painting, printmaking, sculptures and crafts; (2) the study of composition and understanding of art works; and (3) knowledge of the qualities that characterize certain works of art. Although instruction in art history is also one of the aims, their approach is directed more toward the enhancement of studio instruction than toward teaching art history. The text's approach to style, for example, is to show different styles, but also to understand unique solutions to problems, use different approaches to technology, use principles of composition, and discover the differences between great and mediocre art. As the authors note, to bring art history and appreciation into a school's art program, the teacher should correlate them with instruction in the productive aspect of art. Most children, they claim, are interested in making art not talking about it (Lansing & Richards, 1981).

Like the Lansing and Richards text, *Children and Their Art* also advocates the use of schema in teaching drawing. Authors Gaitskell, Hurwitz, and Day (1982) suggest that to teach composition some professional work emphasizing certain elements of design can be brought to the attention of even those pupils who are still in the early symbol stage. The work of Matisse, Picasso, Rembrandt, Tiepolo and Daumier are offered by the authors as positive models for teaching drawing.

Art As Coming From Art

Two texts, *The Joyous Vision* by Hurwitz and Madeja (1977) and *Discovering Art History* by Gerald Brommer (1988) support the notion of art coming from art. In *Joyous Vision* the authors claim that it is entirely conceivable that a complete art program based on the study of professional art works could be designed (Hurwitz & Madeja, 1977). To support this, the authors offer examples of studio approaches that they feel will build on some formal or theoretical concern of an artist, a particular work or a movement. It is, however, in the Brommer text that we find the most traditional view of teaching art history through the evolution of style.

Discovering Art History by Gerald Brommer (1988) is one of the most widely used pre-college texts on art history. It could be described as a secondary-level Jansen or Gardner history of Western art text with a decidedly multicultural/DBAE influence. The author does make an effort to identify other-than-Western cultural influences through the introduction of multicultural timelines and independent DBAE-type projects in analysis, aesthetics and studio. However, the principal approach of the text is through a chronologically sequenced study of Western art.

Brommer claims that if the reader follows the progression of styles, contemporary movements such as new expressionism or abstraction can be understood more easily. He also believes the materials artists use and the kinds of subject matter they express should be discussed prior to viewing the evolution of historic style and so devotes the first four chapters to materials and subject matter.

Brommer handles content primarily by recounting world history and by tracing the evolution of artistic style. He shows the evolution of style both within and between epochs up to the middle of the 18th century. At this point, however, an approach that appeals to adolescents, he departs from his chronological mission and becomes more concerned with a comparison of styles or expressive intents which he views as being on a continuum between what he calls Classic/Intellectual and Romantic/Emotional. Here, Brommer takes a more contextual rather than stylistic view, a view he maintains throughout the remaining chapters. Brommer looks at the New Classicism, Romanticism and Realism as essentially opposing views in late 18th and 19th-century art; at 20th-century art as the effect of intellect, emotion and imagination on the "isms"; and on American art from 1900-1950 as a particularly American response to changes from both within and without. In spite of this shift, references to style and surface features are still the principal means used to organize and discuss the artists and their art forms.

The Form-Gestalt Paradigm in Art Education Today

June King McFee first came to the attention of the field of art education through the publication of her text, *Preparation for Art* (1961 revised in 1970) in which she argued that art education was not a distinct discipline because it was linked to many different fields. She based her content on two premises: (1) art is a form of human communication and (2) the production and appreciation of art are kinds of human behavior. Although she believed that several fields including anthropology could contribute to the understanding of art, McFee's aesthetic viewpoint contained strong formalist tendencies. As McFee (1970) notes

> Aesthetic judgement is dependent neither wholly on the characteristics of the object nor on the individual. It is the result of the transaction of the individual's capacity to respond to the qualities inherent in the object. (p. 7)

McFee is probably best known for her perception-delineation theory (P-D). She actually viewed it as an eclectic model, believing it to be more of an hypothesis than a true theory. It is presented as having five stages: (1) the overall readiness of the child to respond cognitively, both perceptually and conceptually; (2) the psycho-cultural transaction within the classroom environment; (3) the child's habits of informational handling; (4) creative delineation of his or her response; and (5) evolution, feedback, and transfer (McFee, 1970). Harris claims McFee placed different evaluations on Witkin's research (Witkin, 1954) and corrected Lowenfeld's visual and haptic modes to include Witkin's field-independent and field-dependent modes of space perception. McFee also, he thought, drew a distinction between visual concepts and cognitive concepts or between visual and cognitive learning. In her own work, McFee asserted that, "children who are aware of the existence of the constancies—color, size and shape—can reduce their limiting effects by learning to observe visually as well as cognitively" (McFee, 1961, p. 60).

McFee first discussed her ideas on training in art in her 1961 edition, noting that when art is thought of primarily as a means of self-expression, it is not fully used. Children, she felt, should be encouraged to look for ideas outside themselves as well as inside. The outside, for McFee, was to be found in the aesthetic qualities of the physical world where children could learn to find satisfaction in improvement of their skills (McFee, 1961, p. 203). McFee approached perceptual training mainly from a Gestalt or field psychology bias. Her recommendations were to help children handle visual complexity through (1) searching for pattern; (2) using verbal descriptions of space, (e.g., behind, above, below) (3) exploring constancies in shape, form, color, and size; (4) manipulating similar things as a unit; (5) taking an average of different things; (6) completing visual wholes through continuation; and (7) recognizing visual patterns in figure and ground.

In her 1970 revision, McFee expanded on these visual ideas by presenting foundational art activities, namely: (1) learning to see in space and light, and (2) design and art in society. In training students to see, McFee suggested teaching children to recognize size and distance changes, shape changes in space, circle changes in space, changing space through alternative points of view, changing value through light, and understanding space through variation in design. It was not until *Art, Culture and Environment* (1977) co-authored with Rogena Degge however, that McFee first outlined how these ideas could be applied to the teaching of drawing.

In *Art, Culture and Environment* the authors devote an entire section to activities in seeing and drawing. These activities designed for individual students or groups of students, are organized into seven areas at four sequentially different levels of complexity. The areas are listed in what McFee and Degge call a logical sequence to build on one another and the levels are selected according to the readiness of the student. The areas and their high-lights are:

1. Area A—Learning to see and draw the details and relationships in space. In this section, children complete exercises on exploring detail, go beyond stereotyped images, explore surfaces, and apply other areas and levels of drawing.

2. Area B—Learning to see and draw the details and relationships in space. The student performs exercises comparing sizes, learning how things look and how they are, creating illusions in space, and analyzing changes in film and videotape.

3. Area C—Learning to see and draw shapes changed by viewpoint. The students participate in exercises to discover multiple images and differing viewpoints, and analyze shapes and foreshortens.

4. Area D—Learning to see and draw the structure of things. Through the exercises, students analyze structure, remember structure, analyze how structure affects form, and study form as movement.

5. Area E—Learning to see and draw in different lights. Children look for lights and shadows, create forms with light, change light sources, and use light as a means of expression.

6. Area F—Learning perspective systems. Students work on exercises that look for perspective, make things look further away, see up and down and left and right, and use perspective systems.

7. Area G—Learning to see and draw the emotional qualities in things. Students analyze drawings, use line to express feeling, project emotions, and draw subtle qualities and nuances. (McFee & Degge, 1977)

The authors' rationale for learning how to draw reflects McFee's original eclectic interests in educating through art, including perception, aesthetics, structures, cognition, communication and visual organization. Although all of these goals are to be pursued, the authors' Gestalt-form interest seems to be the central focus of the instructional plan. They aver that children need to "see better" to effect changes in their environment, yet the overall goal of instruction is, they note, "to understand how all the parts work together" (McFee & Degge, p. 27).

According to McFee and Degge, things working together is best understood through seeing and designing, especially through the Gestalt process of: (1) organizing visual elements; (2) achieving variety in order; and (3) looking for similarity and dissimilarity, relatedness, grouping, and kinesthetic feeling. In this effort, the authors take Arnheim's view that objects carry self-evident expression through directed tension, which is accomplished through the organizational processes of the brain expressed as visual patterns in an organized whole or physiological equivalent of what is experienced. The method advocated is to see objects, shapes, figures and qualities as related to one another perceptually through proximity, similar form patterns, and similarity of direction and closure. Thus, the relatedness is achieved through what Gestaltists call the principles of similarity, proximity and contiguity grouping, closure and validation.

Other art education texts that have also supported both McFee's perception-delineation theory and other form-Gestalt conceptions, with a brief look at their support, they are

1. Hastie and Schmidt's *Encounter with Art* (1964). Supports McFee's Perception-delineation theory including her stages of readiness, psychological environment, information handling, and delineation.

2. Dimondstein's *Exploring the Arts with Children* (1981). Claims students search for objective form is a means for obtaining wholeness.

3. Lansing's *Art, Artists, and Art Education* (1976). Supports the importance of a "good Gestalten" composition.

4. Mattil and Marzan's *Meaning in Children's Art* (1981). Proposes building mental images through recall, observing detail and shapes tied together through pattern and distribution.

5. Linderman's *Art in the Elementary School* (1990). Proposes children use viewing devices for arriving at a dynamic, integral, unified whole.

Among the precollege art teaching texts designed for school use that embrace a form-Gestalt conception. Some focus on making art and some emphasize the history and criticism of art to the full or partial exclusion of studio activity. Texts focusing primarily on art production include Townley's *Another Look* series (1981), Hubbard and Rouse's *Art, Meaning, Method and Media* (1981) series and Hubbard's *Art in Media* series and *Art in Action* (1987) series. With respect to texts which focus on art history and art criticism I include Mittler's *Art in Focus* (1989) series, Kay Alexander's *The Spectra Program* (1988) and the Hollingsworths's *Smart Art* (1989).

Art From the Picture Plane

Mary Townley's *Another Look* series comes the closest to reflecting McFee and Degge's perceptual approach to drawing. This series designed for classroom use is presented in three 12" x 18" books with a total of 16 chapters or units presenting specific features to be noticed about the shapes or forms pictured. Some units show objects more clearly than they might be seen in the environment, some show how artists deal with these objects in personal ways, while others show how visual skills can be used for understanding other subject areas. The stated aim of Townley's series is to achieve student visual literacy, thus enabling them to look at their surroundings with a new understanding. The large-format art reproductions and photographs are organized according to form type and are designed to permit the student to both cut them out and move them around so that different works can be seen in different contexts (Townley, 1981).

The Townley books, sequenced according to three elementary grade levels, are organized around the elements and formal qualities of art under these headings: shapes of objects, location of objects, position of objects, structure, space dominance and scale. Seeking essentially Gestalt solutions, the lessons on shape require the student to recognize different kinds, such as open and closed, geometric and free, straight and curved, symmetrical and asymmetrical. The exercises on the location of objects require seeing objects as separated and touching, joining and so forth; on the positions of objects, to recognize vertical, horizontal and diagonal compositions; and on structure, to identify design motifs which are skeletal, spiral, and so on. Lastly on space, to characterize space as negative and positive and on scale, to see it as standard or nonstandard. Students study these art forms involving various elements and formal properties, then write about what ideas they inspire and finally create some work of their own employing the concept (Townley, 1981).

Art As Phenomenological Inquiry

The Hubbard and Rouse series, *Art, Meaning, Method and Media*, was the first of several grade-level art texts appearing in the 1970s that were designed for schools. Though reflecting both that period's concern for stating objectives behaviorally and for introducing cognitive content into the school art program, its major aim was to help students make art using a variety of media and applying the elements and principles of design (Hubbard & Rouse, 1981). The series, according to its authors, provides a tested, year-long, art program spanning six consecutive years. Organized on three levels, it builds cumulatively on the content of the preceding year's work. While the series was originally designed for classroom teachers with no special preparation for art teaching, the authors suggest it could also be used by certified art teachers as well.

The content is organized according to six tasks/categories: (1) learning to perceive, (2) learning the language of art, (3) learning about artists (4) criticizing and judging art, (5) using art materials and (6) building productive abilities. The authors believe the assigned tasks help build the kinds of knowledge, attitudes and abilities needed in the study of art, but recommend that every child be given the greatest opportunity for success in art that can be devised (Hubbard & Rouse, 1981, p. iv).

In these tasks, learning to perceive art is achieved through the careful development of the five senses: learning the language of art, using the elements and principles of art, knowing about different kinds of artists and art, criticizing art, using texts and materials, and building artistic abilities to produce finished art work. Moving through the levels, the tasks become more sophisticated and complex and move sequentially from simple forming in line, shape, color, and texture to using the elements in picture making and finally to discussing pictures based on to the concepts or theme expressed in the work. As children work through the series, the elements are combined, compositional features become more complex, and the vocabulary level increases with progressively more emphasis given to more sophisticated forms of picture making and use of the artistic elements and principles.

Hubbard's *Art in Action* series expands on the earlier Hubbard and Rouse texts both by broadening its scope to include lessons for students in the middle, junior, and senior high and by introducing the self-instructional strands model he developed at Indiana University (Hubbard & Zimmermann, 1982). The series is organized sequentially according to levels of reading difficulty. At the beginning level, the reading level is less difficult, the reproductions of art are much larger and more colorful, and the content is sequenced beginning with the identification and awareness of elements and principles and moving on to experiments with materials, techniques, and composition; perceiving visual relationships; and finally developing original and uniquely creative art solutions. Although more attention is given to the elements at the higher levels, the content itself centers on design, drawing, paintings, and sculpture. Lessons begin with an art reproduction followed by inductive questioning, and ending with the making of a studio product. According to the author, the series combines critical thinking skills with creative observation to introduce students to the subject matter of art, and to help them understand art and value it.

Hubbard's multidisciplinary approach to art learning emphasizes both his critical methods for analyzing art and his cognitive perceptual approach to creating art, thus encouraging the student to develop both an appreciation of art and a more cognitive approach to creative expressing. Although each lesson begins with the analysis of an art work, it does not seem to be directed toward students either making art in the styles of mature artists nor developing meta-critical skills. In spite of the attention paid to critical and historical knowledge, his approach seems more directed toward the achieving of Gestalt-form in aesthetic objects. His sequence begins with visual elements and relationships; then analyzes expressive features, form, and content; and lastly evaluates art concepts. Such a sequence suggests that the student is more likely to find solutions in the studio rather than through critical or meta-critical discourse.

Art As Intuitive Expression

Gene Mittler's work, *Art in Focus* (1989), is one of the better known art history/art criticism texts used in schools. The author's stated purpose is to help students acquire the knowledge and understanding needed to make and support decisions about works of art. While the introductory chapters are directed toward the students developing cognitive approaches to art history and criticism, the art history section of the text is more traditionally organized with its content approached chronologically through the epochs of Western art arranged from prehistoric to modern.

Mittler begins his book with a review of his art criticism and art history operations borrowed from Edmund Feldman's functional styles (Feldman, 1974), which he outlined in *Art Education* (Mittler, 1980). His functional tendencies are however moderated through both his Gestalt approach to style and motif and his art-from-art approach to the history of Western art. Like Brommer, Mittler also offers a multicultural approach but only in the latter part of the text.

The sequence of Mittler's art history and art criticism operations involve (1) description, (2) analysis, (3) interpretation and (4) judgment. He suggests that to understand art one needs to (1) phenomologically inventory surface features, (2) research historical context, (3) examine relations between forms, and (4) interpret and judge the value of the work as an aesthetic object. It is however in the feelings and impressions of the perceiver that Mittler finds the means for making artistic judgment and determining artistic style (Mittler, 1989). Mittler, while showing concern for the social and political conditions of the various art epochs (including women's issues and multiculturalism), still approaches art history through the evolution of style where the new owes its beginnings to the old. Mittler is also committed to an intuitive study of imagery through: (1) critical questioning of works with regard to value, perspective, color, composition, shape, positioning, space; (2) expressiveness, in the chapters on "Sight and Feeling," and the "World of Light and Shadow"; and (3) studio activity, requiring students to use shape, space, value, color and scale. Intuition is particularly evident in his comparison of artists VanEyck and Masaccio where student questioning requires attention to shapes, perceptual differentiation, space, color, line, materials, and techniques (Mittler, 1989, p. 213).

Patricia and Stephen Hollingworth's how-to book, *Smart Art* (1989), is one of several whose approach to classifying and critiqing art uses a form-Gestalt, phenomenological approach. The authors also use Feldman's theories of art—imitationalism, emotionalism and formalism—and claim, like Mittler, that their aim is to help students learn how to talk about art. Their method is to first classify the work according to Feldman's theories and then critique it in four sequential steps: (1) description of the art elements, (2) analysis of design (3) interpretation of the meaning and (4) judgment of the work. The teacher is instructed to photocopy the exercises in the book, hold group discussions on each activity, and provide art materials for student use. The class begins with a discussion of lines, shapes, colors and textures which are later applied to the art work exercises. Students are then given a series of questions on how to think about what art is and asked to answer the questions raised about the art works of William Merritt Chase, Leonard Baskin, Frank Stella, Edward Munch and others. Following these steps in classifying and critiquing art, the next series of exercises requires the student to describe the art elements of line and shape, color and texture; and to analyze the principles of design, through learning about repetition, variation, proximity, focal point, balance, space, and value. The student is also asked to interpret the meaning of the work through making guesses based on its use of lines, colors, and subject matter. Judging the work, which is the last exercise, requires the student to rank order works according to form and content and personal preferences. While the authors' aim appears to be the discussion of art works, the method employed seems directed more toward describing and evaluating the work phenomonologically as a way to encourage art valuing. Moreover, although they emphasize language growth for use in dialogues, the authors still place their greatest emphasis on the individuality of art works and on students' individual emotional, evaluative responses.

Kay Alexander's *Learning to Look and Create: The Spectra Program* (1988), is another example of a form/Gestalt approach to curriculum development but organized in a useful loose-leaf and slide format. The Spectra Program consists of seven sets of art lessons with accompanying slides for art instruction in grades Kindergarten through six. The lessons in grades K, one, two and three introduce basic concepts and vocabulary in the field of art and are sequenced according to developmental levels. The lessons in grade four are organized around the elements of line, shape, color, space, form, and texture and are presented as lessons in composition. The grade five lessons treat American art chronologically and the grade six lessons constitute a brief survey of Western Art. Most, although not all, lessons end in a studio experience. The elements addressed include line, shape, color, space, and texture, and the principles of design covered are repetition, movement, contrast, balance, emphasis, unity, and variety. Among the studio modes offered are painting, drawing, design, clay, textiles, murals, mixed media, sculpture, masks, puppets, and print making. Lessons culminating in art production typically focus on the use of a medium and on studio skill development. The slides furnished with each graded set are used both to motivate and to illustrate applications of the concept to be learned in the lesson. The "just look" lessons focus on analyzing or describing a principle or element through a guided question and answer discussion after viewing a slide of an artist's work and receiving art historical information about the artist's life.

Alexander describes the program as one that teaches perceptual skills, skills which she feels will teach the child to not only see a work but experience and understand it aesthetically. She believes that art judgment, although involving the use of critical and historical information, becomes more valid when the student's knowledge is based on personal experiences with works of art. In order to help the students exercise judgment, she recommends the use of an art questioning process to draw out students' ideas which she then follows up on with a discussion of the elements and principles as applied to the composition (Alexander, 1988).

While the lesson goals are to help the student develop aesthetic judgment, this can occur, according to Alexander, either through writing or talking about the elements or principles in the work or through creating a work. The studio experience, in her view, provides a balance between perceptual and hands-on skills and continuing to learn aesthetically while creating. Though the goals of the series are broadly based on the domains of art history, art criticism and art production, she also believes that the art experience goes beyond the school's "basic" subjects. It is, therefore, a way of knowing different from ordinary language because it deals with symbols that cannot be expressed in any other way.

The Linguistic/Metaphorical Paradigm in Today's Art Education

One of the best arguments for a linguistic/metaphorically based curriculum is found in Feldman's text, *Becoming Human Through Art* (1970). This text logically develops what an empiricist paradigm entails and how it might function in a school art curriculum. Feldman is probably best known for his art history text, *Varieties of Visual Experience* (1967), which takes a generally Marxist or Socialist view of art history. In *Varieties*, Feldman organized art history functionally rather than chronologically; dealt with the elements and principles of art structurally rather than expressively; and approached the various artistic forms more as humanistic transactions than as objects to be curated and exhibited (Feldman, 1967).

In *Becoming Human Through Art* (1970), Feldman translates his social art history into an art teaching methodology which he believes is useful in constructing a school art curriculum. In both texts his anthropological view of art influences both his defining of the art object and the optimum conditions necessary for the viewers' response and interaction. In *Becoming Human*, Feldman's view of art is presented as an ethnographic triangulation of viewpoints taken from anthropology, art history and popular culture. Anthropologically, he defines art as both a technology and as a type of behavior; historically, as a behavioral encounter with historical works; and culturally as a means for communication. In defining the word "art," Feldman rejects the term (1) has evaluative meaning, (2) refers to objects curated for display, (3) signifies personality or genius and (4) indicates objects for personal adulation or adornment. To arrive at a truly new concept of art, Feldman believes, we cannot make distinctions between fine or applied art or treat art history as a logical progression toward a higher truth. Rather, Feldman finds art everywhere around us and integrally related to the kinds of persons we are (Feldman, 1970).

Art As Problem-Solving Activity

Educationally, he views art as ritual problem solving in which art becomes an instrument for solving significant human problems. In schools, Feldman views art activity as a means for the child "to appreciate his worthiness as a being who can evoke the considered reactions of other beings" (Feldman, 1970, p. 36). As a consequence, he views self-expression as being a competition in communicating the process of becoming more fully human. Feldman (1970) notes how we should respond to students:

> (1) We respond humanly to his work; (2) we help establish the ideas of art as communication; (3) we give the child as artist a sense of motion toward an aesthetic goal; (4) we prepare him for passage into adolescence; (5) we acquaint the child with the larger world he must eventually live in; (6) we provide him with a rudimentary model of critical discourse. (p. 46)

Feldman, moreover, views human behavior and responsibility in terms reminiscent of Rousseau and Levi-Strauss. For example, he believes that: (1) human beings should not be used as objects, (2) love determines what a person can incorporate into himself, (3) authentic learning begins with the longing of self to overcome the isolation that the human condition imposes, and (4) art is a tool for dealing with human situations which require expression. Morally he notes,

> The child's visual expression is more than artistic representation, it is a type of moral activity, one of the earlier opportunities a person has for acting like a moral agent. This is precisely what the tribesman does with his concern about illness, fecundity or about identifying a member of his group. He names and actualizes—that is, gives form to his hopes and fears and thus comes to terms with them. (Feldman, 1970, p. 180)

Feldman also views the art curriculum as being humanistically based in four areas.

1. Cognitive Study—Understanding the world. Achieved through studying persons, groups, and physical communities through art.

2. Linguistic Study—Learning the language of art. Achieved through the study of line, shape, and color as experience.

3. Media Study—Exploring the varieties of the language. Achieved through the interaction of the medium and the meaning.

4. Critical Study—Mastering the techniques of art criticism achieved through systematizing talk about art.

It is, however, in the domain of cognitive study that he most clearly reveals his sociological and anthropological ideas.

Feldman's description of how cognitive study would function in the school provides a clear view of how his concepts might influence the school art program. As previously noted, Feldman views cognitive study as the study of persons, groups and physical communities through art, which for him should exist in a curriculum geared to understanding the world through: (1) meeting people, (2) discovering groups, and (3) exploring places. The studio content described in "meeting people" includes developing visual approaches to personal imagery, preserving someone's memory, and reading the images of people. The subject matter content for "discovering groups" includes making images of groups we belong to and of group life in the movies and on TV. "Exploring places" includes the study of man-made communities, practical objects, and city planning. The practice lessons assigned to each form of study suggests, first, to engage the student in a discussion of the work, then develop a hypothesis or concept to explore and, lastly, test the concept through constructing an art work, dance or play, writing an essay, or propose some political or social action. Studio activities offered in the other sections of the text such as "Learning the Language of Art" and "Studying the Varieties of Language," also follow the look, discuss, hypothesize and test approach.

Art As Contextual Study and Criticism

Several texts in art education support the metaphorical/linguistic approach to art teaching including

1. Kaufman's, *Art and Education in Contemporary Culture* (1966) supports an inductive or structured approach to learning which he feels can coalesce a variety of behaviors into a structured pattern to achieve validation and permanency (p. 248).

2. Chapman's *Approaches to Art Education* (1978) advocates the curriculum functions of personal fulfillment, transmission of the cultural heritage, and development of social consciousness (p. 122).

3. Eisner's *Educating Artistic Vision* (1972) advocates teachers as models for what people "do" in the field of art through making and criticizing art in a changing educational environment (p. 162).

At the public school level, a number of other curriculum publications also support the linguistic/metaphorical paradigm. These include the *Understanding and Creating Art* series (1986) by Goldstein, Saunders, Kowalchuk, and Katz; Chapman's *Discover Art* (1987) and *Teaching Art* (1989) series; and Ragans's *Art Talk* (1988).

Understanding and Creating Art is a two-volume series for grades seven and eight which, according to Goldstein *et al.*, provides a balanced art curriculum in five basic areas: (1) responding to works of art, (2) understanding the content of art, (3) producing art, (4) understanding the importance of art and of the expanding role of the artist, and (5) making art judgments. The series analyzes two "core" paintings in the grade seven text and three "core" paintings in the grade eight text; both texts contain reproductions of other artists' paintings, sculptures, photographs, architecture, crafts and drawings organized according to five themes: (1) the artist and nature, (2) the artist looks at people, (3) symbols and allegory through architecture, (4) heroes in history and (5) looking at the industrial world. The course objectives are sequenced according to the following: (1) awareness of natural and man-made environments, (2) expression through materials, (3) understanding self and others, and (4) visual discrimination and judgment. Course activities are sequenced as: (1) examining objects, (2) exploring elements, (3) applying principles, (4) designing in materials, (5) appreciating art and artists, (6) evaluating art work, and (7) applying aesthetic judgments (Goldstein, *et al.*, 1986).

The authors analyze the five major (core) works through an inductive questioning process designed to reveal the subject matter content and the expressive meaning or storyline of the work while also providing historiographic data about the artist and the object. The reproductions used to illustrate content in the various art forms are approached through an inductive questioning process which examines the art work through: (1) materials and techniques, (2) the elements and principles of organization, and (3) the expressive character of the work. This is then followed with a studio activity that begins with a discussion of an art work and ends with the student making and critiquing a work. Because the text aims to build the student's aesthetic growth through increased visual discrimination and judgment, one must assume the authors' primary objective is to educate students in art criticism. The process examines surface features, analyzes works according to subject matter and formal elements, and views artists as recorders of nature and visual communicators. This process clearly supports the idea that artists and art both serve a social function and that students are essentially "consumers of art."

Chapman's *Discover Art* series reflects many of the same social and educational values as her text, *Approaches to Art Education*. This series presents a sequential art curriculum for grades 1-6 which the author claims is an art program that develops perceptual awareness, provides for creative art activity, and teaches art appreciation and awareness of art in everyday life. Instruction at each level is organized around three instructional emphases—creating art, looking at art, and living with art. Each year's program begins with eight to ten lessons on the basic art concepts and the skills students are to use in the remaining lessons. In the lessons for grade levels 4-6, students (1) discuss the presented themes, (2) present their own ideas, (3) look at works of art which reflect artists' interpretations of natural forms, and (4) study a form and make a drawing of it (Chapman, 1987).

While the series goal is to help students create art and learn how and why people create it, Chapman's (functional) view requires that students do this through the study of: (1) the art occupations people choose, (2) the ways art emphasizes the physical environment and (3) the insights it brings for understanding other people in other times and places. Although art making is important to Chapman, she also believes art learning to be a search for solutions to cognitive art problems through investigation and study of what causes art to exist, how it is constructed and organized, and what social meaning it has for the person who creates it.

Chapman's more recent series, *Teaching Art*, offers the same basic content as the *Discover Art Series* though expanded in scope, improved in its visual appearance and reorganized into a loose-leaf format. The goals of creating art, looking at art, and living with art are essentially unchanged, but the social goals of art are more forcefully articulated, the visual aesthetic more effectively realized, and curriculum materials more flexibly presented. *Teaching Art* is packaged in two sets, one for grades 1-3 and another for grades 4-6. The lesson books in each set include 45 lessons for each grade level including objectives, suggestions for interdisciplinary activity and recommended hands-on activities. *Teaching Art* also includes a basic guide outlining strategies for teaching, the sequence and scope of the curriculum, and a guide to various art techniques and media. Also included are twelve 17" x 10" color prints, thirty-two 4" x 5 1/2" art card reproductions, and seven art games. Twenty-two additional color reproductions and two posters are available to supplement the series.

In the basic guide, Chapman articulates her belief that art serves human needs through producing shelter, clothing, and objects of spiritual meaning. She believes that art is created to express social customs and beliefs through efforts to honor leaders, teach religious beliefs, forward political aims, celebrate bountiful harvests, and commemorate victories and defeats. Educationally, she views the function of art education as transmitting knowledge about art and helping children develop a concept of art (Chapman, 1989).

Summary

The foregoing discussion illustrates that a number of important art-teacher education texts and school-level curriculum series do cohere with the conceptual paradigms of schema-motif, form-Gestalt, and linguistic-metaphorical. These paradigms then inform the concepts used both for educating the professionals who teach art and for determining the curriculum they recommend in schools. All writers do not agree on all matters within the paradigms, but this is due both to how scholars normally function in a paradigm and to the particular circumstances that shape the choices or emphasis they support.

The quantity and quality of the work of these professionals, though reflecting only a small portion of the literature available, should suggest that much thought and effort has already been expended in the construction of professionally important and viable curricular materials for educating students in all three conceptual paradigms. If a particular text may no longer be in print or may not be considered as "current", this has little to do with the importance of the concepts explicated or the curriculum materials developed which, for the most part, still have relevance to today's schools. Because we live in a world of change and because we also expect, as artists and educators, that the new will always be better than the old, we sometimes fail to recognize that we have not, as yet, even come close to beginning to apply what we already know is possible in the development of the school art curriculum.

So much of what has been done has yet to be fully tested in practice; our next steps, therefore, should be to explore in greater depth the work already completed, including Lowenfeld's work in "creative and mental growth," McFee's and Degge's work in Gestalt drawing, and Feldman's and Chapman's functional approaches to schooling. All should be considered as conceptions worthy of further study and development, and all three paradigm approaches should be viewed as foundational in the development of newer and more effective curricula. These contending paradigms individually or in concert do have much to offer to today's schools which are only just beginning to consider the catholicity of viewpoints now evident in the world art market, where styles ranging from realism to deconstructionism challenge both our intellect and our aesthetic sensibilities. Newer and more viable art education curricula for today's schools can emerge from these differing conceptions of art, some which use existing motifs, others which use highly intuitive forms of understanding, or relate art more closely to social and political life.

Because the effectiveness of the curriculum in each individual school can only be evaluated within the context of a particular classroom, taught by a particular teacher, and involving a particular group of students in a particular school and community, much more work needs to be done in order for these paradigms to accommodate what most art teachers face in their particular teaching situation. The goal of Chapter V is, therefore, to consider how these conceptions can be evaluated and further developed to meet the specific needs of the teachers, the students, the school, and the community.

References

Alexander, K. (1988). *Learning to look and create: The Spectra program*. Palo Alto: Dale Seymour Publications.

Barkan, M. (1955). *A foundation for art education*. New York: Ronald Press Co.

Brittain, L. (1979). *Creativity, art and the young child*. New York: Macmillan Publishing Co., Inc.

Brommer, G. (1988). *Discovering art history*. Worcester: Davis Publications, Inc.

Chapman, L. (1978). *Approaches to art education*. New York: Harcourt Brace Jovanovich, Inc.

——(1987). *Discover art*. Worcester: Davis Publications, Inc.

——(1989). *Teaching art 1-3*. Worcester: Davis Publications, Inc.

——(1989). *Teaching art 4-6*. Worcester: Davis Publication, Inc.

Dimondstein, G. (1974). *Exploring the arts with children*. New York: Macmillan Publishing Co., Inc.

Gaitskell, C., Hurwitz, A., & Day, M. (1982). *Children and their art*. New York: Harcourt Brace Jovanovich, Inc.

Goldstein, E., Saunders, R., Kowalchuk J., & Katz, T. (1986). *Understanding and creating art*. Dallas: Garrard Publishing Co.

Eisner, E. (1972). *Educating artistic vision*. New York: The Macmillan Co.

Feldman, E. (1967). *Varieties of visual experience*. New York: Harry N. Abrams, Inc.

Feldman, E. (1970). *Becoming human through art*. Englewood Cliffs: Prentice Hall, Inc.

Harris, D. (1963). *Children's drawings as measures of intellectual maturity*. New York: Harcourt, Brace and World, Inc.

Hastie, R., & Schmidt, C. (1964). *Encounter with art*. New York: McGraw-Hill Book Co.

Hollingsworth, P., & Hollingsworth, S. (1989) *Smart art*. Tucson: Zephyr Press.

Hubbard, G. (1987). *Art in action*. San Diego: Coronado Publishers.

Hubbard G., & Rouse M. (1981). *Art meaning method and media*. San Diego: Benefic Press.

Hubbard, G., & Zimmerman, E. (1982). *Artstrands*. Prospect Heights: Waveland Press, Inc.

Hurwitz, A. (Ed.). (1983). *Drawing for the schools*. Baltimore: Maryland Institute, College of Art.

Hurwitz, A., & Madeja, S. (1977). *The joyous vision: Source book*. Englewood Cliffs: Prentice Hall, Inc.

Kaufman, I. (1966). *Art and education in contemporary culture*. New York: The Macmillan Co.

Kaupelis, R. (1966). *Learning to draw*. New York: Watson Guptill.

Lansing, K. (1976). *Art, artists and art education*. Dubuque: Kendall/Hunt Publishing Co.

Lansing, K., & Richards, A. (1981). *The elementary teacher's art handbook*. New York: Holt, Rinehart and Winston.

Linderman, M. (1990). *Art in the elementary school*. Dubuque: Wm. C. Brown Publishers.

Lowenfeld, V. (1964). & Brittain, W. (1975). *Creative and mental growth (6th ed.)*. New York: Macmillan Publishing Co., Inc.

Mattil, E., & Marzan, B. (1981). *Meaning in children's art*. Englewood Cliffs: Prentice-Hall, Inc.

McFee, K. (1961). *Preparation for art*. San Francisco: Wadsworth Publishing Co., Inc.

McFee, K. (1970). *Preparation for art*. Belmont: Wadsworth Publishing Co., Inc.

McFee, J., & Degge E. (1977). *Art culture and environment: A catalyst for teaching*. Belmont: Wadsworth Publishing Co.

Mittler, G. (1980). Learning to look/looking to learn: A proposed approach to art appreciation at the secondary school level. *Art Education, 32 (3)*, 17-21.

Mittler, G. (1989). *Art in focus*. Mission Hills: Glencoe Publishing Co.

Ragans, R. (1988) *Art talk*. Mission Hills: Glencoe Publishing Co.

Townley, M. (1981). *Another look*. Menlo Park: Addison-Wesley Publishing Co.

Wilson, B., Hurwitz, A., & Wilson, M. (1987). *Teaching drawing from art*. Worcester: Davis Publications, Inc.

Witken, H. Personality through perception. New York: Harper.

Chapter 5

From Educational Theory To
Curricular Practice

This chapter relates the previously described conceptual paradigms for thinking about and making art with what occurs in art classrooms. If the things teachers and students do in classrooms could be categorized in the same analytical way that curriculum theory is organized, the task in this chapter would be a relatively simple one. Unfortunately, what individual teachers and children do in art classrooms varies enough to suggest that there may be as many instructional paradigms as there are art teachers, students, schools and communities. While it could be clearly demonstrated in Chapter IV that the conceptual paradigms of schema/motif, form/Gestalt, and linguistic/metaphorical cohere with what the art education literature describes as curricular conceptions guiding art programs, these conceptions, unfortunately, may not cohere with actual classroom practice.

When the school curriculum is viewed in the context of what students and teachers actually do in schoolrooms, it is more likely to reflect many different curricular conceptions. For any curricular concept to be said to truly exist there needs to be a symbiotic relationship between the curriculum theory and the actions of students and teachers in real schools. Thus, for an art curriculum to be something more than just a theoretical construct, it needs to actually function in a school setting and reflect what children, teachers, schools and communities value about art and education—a task requiring much thought and effort, that is, if we hope to see our theories and classroom practices are to cohere. It is the main goal of this chapter, therefore, to suggest some ways to reach answers to the curricular questions identified in the introductory chapter of who, what, when and where.

Two prior assumptions will guide the discussion in this chapter:

1. There are both useful and potentially fecund art curriculum theories and materials that can be used to guide what is taught in schools.

2. These theories and materials can make a contribution to the art curriculum construction process when they are understood, practiced, and evaluated in an art classroom setting.

To develop curricula in this manner, however, requires an understanding of (1) how various general curriculum concepts have developed historically, (2) how to proceed with the process of analyzing and evaluating existing art curricula and (3) how to develop and implement an effective curriculum in the art classroom. This approach to curriculum design rejects the notion that a teacher-proof curriculum is needed or one that supports getting teachers to teach art in one specific way. It, furthermore, recognizes the virtual impossibility of utilizing curricular materials without the teacher imprinting his or her personal stamp on that material. This chapter is, therefore, also about helping teachers judge for themselves whether the curricular activities in which they engage are educational or whether they are merely alternatives to teacher proofing.

PART I—UNDERSTANDING THE CURRICULUM CONCEPTUALLY

Knowing What a Curriculum Is

The total school curriculum can be described as,

- All the experiences a learner has under the guidance of the school (Foshay, 1969).

- A plan for learning (Taba, 1962).

- Questions about teacher thinking and doing (Connelly & Clandinin, 1988).

- All of the above.

Developing the total school curriculum involves considering much broader issues than are involved in merely thinking about learning in science, social studies, or art. In the broadest sense, the general curriculum reflects all of what we value about the American society, its people, its social institutions, and the desirable goals of education in a democracy. Since colonial times, the concerns of schooling have evolved from the first laws requiring the teaching of reading so that children could learn to read the bible to publications reflecting today's concerns for egalitarianism and multiculturalism. A brief review of the concerns addressed and the goals pursued in the evolution of the American school curriculum may increase the understanding of the curriculum as it is both influenced by and contributes to the overall goals of schooling in American society.

Education as Inquiry

During the 19th century the emphasis in American schools was placed on the notion of *learning as inquiry*, which was inspired by *the inductive method of science*. This theory held that one can learn best from direct observation and experience. Object teaching was a 19th-century educational reform based on this idea. Although supporters of object teaching tended to view the method as a kind of reading readiness to improve observation and expression, its methods were mostly influenced by the inductive method of science, that is, careful observation, the collection of data based on observation, and generalization based on observed relationships among cases.

Education as Reasonable Learning

Dewey's ideas on reflective thinking became systematized into a method in 1910 (Dewey, 1910). Grounded on a social framework, Dewey's conception and educational method was based on the idea that thinking is problem solving. Dewey argued that object teaching was a false method, because it assumed that an object had to be known before it could be used intelligently. Dewey, therefore, challenged the notion that learning must proceed from the simple to complex and claimed the most important concern should be the individual's purpose or the use someone intended to make of the object. In this way, Dewey questioned the inductive method and proposed a method beginning with the whole and proceeding to its component parts, a concept generally supported by Gestalt theory.

Education as Problem Solving

In the elementary school of the 1930's, the Progressivist supporters of Dewey attempted to implement his idea of active inquiry into units, activities, and projects. Field trips, excursions, observation and discussion all became important parts of schooling. Because the Progressives viewed education as inquiry, the scope of schooling was broadened at the secondary level to include helping students to think intelligently about social problems. Although this was not a new idea, the Great Depression helped make this objective become paramount.

The Progressive Education Association's famous Eight-Year Study of this period also viewed problem solving as a total process beginning with the definition of the problem and ending with an action. The thinking processes advocated included a number of goals including problem solving, critical thinking, reflective thinking, intelligent thinking and scientific thinking. The study also supported the notion that the best curricular results could be obtained when all the teachers in the schools agreed on the approaches involved and the language to be used in defining the process.

Education as Discovery Learning

During the late 1950's and early 1960's, "how scientists work" again became the model adopted by curriculum developers. The model developed, however, was discipline focused rather than socially focused. Discovery teaching in this era was a disciplinary effort to teach children to think like scientists rather than like children. It was believed that children discovering scientific concepts on their own would result in more effective learning and instill the desire for further and more significant discovery like earlier notions of education as inquiry. The discovery learning approach supported an inductive approach to learning where the student induces abstractions or generalizations from specific cases.

Education as Discipline

Curriculum builders who were proponents of learning as inquiry in the 1960's also later introduced the idea that the inquiry process differs from subject to subject. They believed that discovery behavior is specific to the subject matter domain in which the discovery takes place. Discovery, according to disciplinary proponents, requires different concepts and systems of logic when working in biology or in breaking hieroglyphic codes. This disciplinary conception was strongly influenced by Jerome Bruner (1960) who maintained that learning the fundamental structure of a subject through discovery would enable the student to solve all sorts of problems.

Education as Cognition

In the late 1960's and early 1970's, curriculum builders also turned to the ideas of Piaget who believed that the child plays an active role in his or her own intellectual development. Reinforced by research on the education of disadvantaged children and the work of Benjamin Bloom, curriculum theorists sought to develop higher level cognitive objectives that would encourage the development of thinking processes and self-impelled inquiry. Hilda Taba (1962) focused attention on teaching strategies that fostered autonomous thinking and teacher education programs based on the idea that individual thinking depends heavily on the nature of the thinking processes individuals have experienced.

Education as Relevancy

At the same time as the so-called disciplinary curriculum movement occurred, many young people began a renewed interest in the social sciences and the humanities in a search for educational experiences that could put them in touch with the "real world." Because of the Viet Nam conflict American society was rife with protests, demonstrations and demands for reform. America was, according to these reformers, a "sick society" in which the people of Appalachia, the migrant worker and the urban poor were made "invisible" and the issues of poverty, racial discrimination and the environment were being ignored. Many demanded a newer and more relevant curriculum which the young could use to combat social ills and make a better world.

The curricular response to relevancy in American public education was to create projects, mini-courses, alternative schools, external programs, contracts, individualized curricula, revision of existing courses and creation of new ones. The new concerns in the curriculum focused on the problems of environmental protection, drug addiction and the meaning of law; responses to these concerns led to educational alternatives emphasizing freedom of choice by selecting from a smorgasbord of school electives.

Education as Affect

In the early 1970's there was a resurgence of the idea that *cognitive goals do not* really matter. What did matter according to advocates was the learner's feelings and emotions. Supporters of this approach believed that learners should not be forced to learn what others select for them—

an imposition of the values and purposes of others onto the individual. The most profound influence on affective education movements was the philosophy of existentialism which critics viewed as a preoccupation with self through getting children to express their feelings and talk about their problems.

Over time the American school curriculum evolved through emphases reflecting object learning; learning as inquiry, as problem solving, and as discovery; and problem solving as reflective thinking. Today's emphases seems to reflect what some call an "activist" agenda proposing that the school's curriculum provide the means to alleviate the problems of people in the larger society. Some critics view this as replacing acting on thinking with acting on feeling. In the late 1970's and early 1980's the activist agenda, inspired by the political scandals of Watergate, tended to encourage a new cynicism. People were motivated to do their own thing and schools reacted by creating a system of values clarification to inspire more moral education.

One thing is certain in future curricular development: Swings in the educational pendulum will continue, especially, if those influencing curriculum reform continue to view curriculum design mostly as a political confrontation between forces supporting social control and social power. To say curriculum reform is merely a choice between training students for industry (social control) or freeing students to make their own decisions (social power) is to politicize it, that is, to view curricular reform as a political rather than an ethical or moral issue.

The general curricular theories and the art curriculum emphases discussed in Chapters I and IV suggest that it may be more appropriate to characterize curricular change as reflecting essentialist or contextualist positions rather than political ones. Essentialist curricula emphasize the activities which provide the greatest opportunities for individual problem solving. Contextualist curricula can be viewed as emphasizing either social control or social power depending on what one believes, that is, whether true freedom is achieved through helping students become more individualistic, self-reliant and self-motivated or whether individuals to be truly free must lose some of their freedom in order for others to be free. Individualism is, then, considered by some to be the ultimate freedom, and by others as something benefitting the economically advantaged at the expense of the socially disadvantaged and the poor.

Looking back at the changes in the American school curriculum, most theorists generally agree that we have to view the curriculum problem in different terms than we did 20 or 30 years ago. While the debates between the progressives and revisionists, the Gestaltists and behaviorists, and the various psychologies of education will continue, one fact seems clear: The teacher should be an active participant in developing the conceptual basis to be used in operationalizing the school's curricula. Some knowledge gained about the curriculum supporting this notion include: (1) the need for a more practical approach; (2) the need for theory in guiding curriculum practices; (3) the acceptance of different curricular viewpoints; and (4) the need to know if the curriculum is working.

The Need to Look at Practice

Past efforts to look at schools solely from the viewpoint of former practitioners while well intentioned did not produce the needed changes in schools. As long as practical wisdom was considered to be the domain of the classroom teacher and theoretical competence the domain of the teacher educator, there was no viable way to connect the theories of curriculum with what actually occurred in schools. In that milieu, curriculum development became mostly a matter of theoretical writings supported by forms of curricular criticism which more often than not reflected the curriculum writers' views of their own curricular assumptions and classification systems.

Today, curriculum theorists view teachers as having theoretical interests which encourage them to pursue knowing and understanding theories as well as pursuing practical interests in doing and making things. Curricular theory is also now considered mostly as a theoretical pursuit while painting, teaching and implementing curriculum have become practical pursuits. Moreover, education in schools is also considered to be education in something, be it art, science or history; to apply a theoretical stance in a practical field may therefore miss the point. The purpose of curriculum thinking today is, thus, not just for understanding but rather for improvement in the *practice* of curriculum.

Curricular Theory as a Guide to Practice

We also now know that curriculum theories can offer approaches to practice with which teachers can identify. Theories coinciding with the teacher's own perspective can become a springboard for the teacher to think more conceptually about the curriculum practiced in the classroom. Teachers can find helpful information in so-called curriculum criticism which provides a means for classifying different theories, conceptualizing them, and providing insights into their applications—all of which help practitioners decide whether theorists have any interests that practitioners can also identify with and use.

The Acceptance of Differing Curricular Viewpoints

One important index of our growing maturity as a profession is our willingness to view many different curricular policies, beliefs, or proposals as having value and being worthy of continuing study. When we think of a curriculum as practical matters, these are by their very nature diverse and do not lend themselves to theoretical thinking but rather to accepting a curriculum for what it is. Curriculum situations and circumstances vary, and as such, our conceptual understanding of the curriculum has only limited applicability. A diversity in curriculum policies today is, thus, essentially believed to be the true nature of the curriculum.

Needing to Know Whether the Curriculum is Working

Events over the past 30 years beginning with the launching of Sputnik have fueled many different initiatives to improve schooling through curricular reform. While most of these efforts have improved our knowledge and understanding of the curriculum, there is almost unequivocal evidence that the intended improvements were not accomplished. These failures have brought into being a curricular field of study known as curriculum implementation—a response to the fact that research, theory and new programs were not used by schools in the way they were intended. Implementation efforts are designed to discover what inhibits implementation and develop strategies for successful curriculum implementation.

PART II—DEVELOPING THE CURRICULUM PLAN

Understanding the Role of Stakeholders

While teachers are a key element in operationalizing curriculum, others frequently referred to as "stakeholders" also influence what occurs in classrooms. Stakeholders are those individuals and groups of individuals with a right to comment on and have input into the curriculum program of the schools. They include teachers, governments, students, public agencies, school administrators, parents, school resource people, the subject matter discipline, the business community, and school board members.

Stakeholders do have an influence on art curriculum practice. For example,

- Local school districts and state departments of public instruction publish mandated curricula or curriculum frameworks which seek to regulate the overall balance of the curriculum;

- Local law enforcement agencies conduct drug abuse programs in schools;

- Curriculum directors in school districts may promote whole language approaches in the general curriculum;

- Parents want to know what their children are learning and how well they are doing;

- School art supervisors may want the art teachers in the district to emphasize multiculturalism;

- The professional field may be pressuring its members to adopt a DBAE or other approaches to the curriculum;

- The business community wants students to have more effective communication skills;

- The school board wants to know what is going on generally in the classroom.

In dealing with stakeholders, Connelly and Clandinin (1988) suggest the teacher pursue this course:

1. Answer the following questions:

   A. What is the purpose of the curriculum situation?

   B. If there is a group, what is the makeup of the group? If you are planning with your students, remember to include them as part of your group.

   C. Who set up the project?

   D. How was the group's membership and purpose established? Even if your curriculum situation is classroom planning, think about the latter two questions. When we think about our classroom planning as a curriculum stakeholder situation we gain new insight into how we understand our classrooms. (p. 131)

2. Ask yourself the following questions:

   A. How accountable am I to this stakeholder?

   B. How much will this stakeholder be affected by my decision?

   C. How much risk is there in ignoring this stakeholder?

D. How much right has this stakeholder to direct my action?

3. Analyze the interests of the stakeholders by asking:

   A. What does the stakeholder see as the art teacher's role?

   B. What view of the students does the stakeholder have? What aspect of the learner in the art classroom is stressed by this stakeholder?

   C. What characteristics of art does the stakeholder stress?

   D. What does the stakeholder see as the appropriate art teaching environment for learning in this situation?

   E. What aim for society and/or educated persons in relation to art does the stakeholder have? (p. 132)

Before Developing the Curricular Plan

Many different curricular plans exist. Prior to embarking on the one outlined in the following pages, the reader may wish to consider some of the others to find the one most suited to his or her own philosophy and goals. Conceptual approaches can be found in the following writings:

- Peter Smith (1989) suggests using Mittler's theories of art, emotionalism, imitationalism, and formalism sequenced according to Piaget's stages of child development.

- Laura Chapman (1985) begins with ideas to improve practice, constructs a theoretical framework, and tests it with those who work in schools.

- Graeme Sullivan (1989) uses diverse social contexts and contents applied in contexts of uncertainty, unpredictability, serendipity and conjecture.

- Douglas Marschalek (1989) uses art facts reconstructed as conceptual statements and organized as groups of ideas or facts capable of being sequenced.

Contextual approaches the reader might like to consider include:

- Vincent Lanier's field trip approach (1986).

- Richard Ciganko's interactive model (1992).

- Jerry Hausman's (1974) mapping approach where teachers collect examples of ideas and themes, combine them with descriptions of art classroom activities, and order them according to grade levels and student interests.

All of these curriculum development models have something useful to offer the teacher in the art curriculum building process.

A Plan for Planning

The approach taken in this text is grounded on the belief that effective curriculum practice requires consideration of what teachers (1) believe about themselves, about art, and about education; (2) know about art teaching theories and believe will be useful; and (3) think will work in practice. The orientation is, therefore, to consider what both teachers and the art teaching profession value in deciding matters of art curriculum practice. The process used is therefore to: (1) decide what it is the teacher most values, (2) provide the means by which the teacher can identify the theories or paradigms that most closely reflect his or her values, and (3) assist in deciding how to structure a curricular conception before testing it in practice.

This process, furthermore, assumes that (1) priority should be given to what teachers do in classrooms, (2) differing conceptions of art and education exist, and (3) these conceptions can be demonstrated to have value in guiding curricular practice. While this approach may appear to be inductive, it is, rather, intended to be both practical and philosophically open except in believing that the school art curriculum begins with the teacher. I am, of course, not alone in this view and am especially indebted to the ideas of Michael Connelly and Jean Clandinin (1988) in their text, *Teachers as Curriculum Planners*.

The Teacher's Philosophy and Values

As with all individuals, teachers' values are shaped by the experiences they have had since birth. Their values are particularly influenced by the ideas of their parents, their peers, the schools they have attended and the communities in which they have lived and worked. As educators, teachers hold beliefs about the curriculum, about students, about art, and about art teaching. They value certain curricular priorities, certain needs and interests of children, the ideas and opinions of other teachers, and the connections that exist between content and the children they teach. Furthermore, teachers also care about what students want to know, what a curriculum requires, what an educational experience is intended to do, and what it is they feel they can or cannot do. To get in touch with these values, teachers can relive the experiences that have shaped them. This leads not only to self-understanding but also to an awareness of which experiences shape children's values.

Before beginning the process of curriculum implementation, the teacher first needs to know what his or her own personal philosophy is and subsequently how that personal philosophy shapes his or her philosophy of education. To discover one's own personal philosophy, the reader may wish to review the general philosophical constructs outlined in Chapter II dealing with the philosophical problems in metaphysics, epistemology, logic, and axiology or value. To start, the reader might also attempt to answer the following seven questions concerned with these philosophical domains:

1. What is the nature of man?

    a. The self is a soul, a spiritual being.
    b. The self is essentially the same as the body.
    c. The self is a social-vocal phenomenon.

2. What is freedom?

    a. A human being is not free; actions are determined by forces greater than he or she is.
    b. People have the power of choice and are capable of genuine initiative.
    c. A person is neither free nor determined, but can give new direction to subsequent activity.

3. To exist or to have being is:

    a. To be mind and spirit or dependent upon mind or spirit.
    b. To occupy time and space, to be matter or physical energy.
    c. Not valid as everything is flux and change.

4. Knowledge is obtained through:

    a. Reason.
    b. Sense-perceptual experience.
    c. Sense experience alone.

5. One arrives at valid thinking through:

    a. Reasoning from a general principle to particulars.
    b. Reasoning from particulars to a general conclusion.
    c. Reasoning through problem solving.

6. Things which have value are:

    a. Things people are interested in.

    b. Independent of the valuer and their interests.

    c. Things which yield the greatest sense of happiness.

7. The best guide to conduct is to:

    a. Act on the basis of principles.

    b. Act according to the needs of self preservation.

    c. Explore the probable consequences of an action.

Looking at your answers, if you selected "A" in all seven cases, you are likely to be a rationalist. If you chose "B", you are probably an empiricist, and if in all cases your answers were "C", you may be a neo-idealist. Referring back to Chapter II, you will note that rationalists tend to believe individual thought is of most value, empiricists, that group thinking is the most valuable; and neo-idealists, a bit of both toward the goal of making things work better.

Determining Your Educational Philosophy

Educational philosophers assume positions on a number of issues relating to the school, the teacher, the learner and the curriculum. Their philosophical systems include perennialism, essentialism, progressivism, reconstructionism, and/or existentialism.

- *Perennialism* supports the idea that certain knowledge persists in value over time.

- *Essentialism* places primary importance on knowing society's cultural and historical heritage.

- *Progressivism* sees the school as a democratic society in miniature.

- *Reconstructionism* views education as a means to change societal behavior.

- *Existentialism* advocates helping all students reach their fullest potential for self-fulfillment.

While these philosophies do cohere with the general philosophies of rationalism, empiricism and neo-idealism, they are also conceptually linked to the functions and rationales of schooling, thus concerned not only with the ends of education, but also with why certain ends are worthy of being pursued.

Using Existing Curricula

In deciding art curriculum practice, most teachers, fortunately, can choose to either use existing curricula that contains values similar to their own or to alter the curriculum in such a way as to make it fit their own classroom situation. Connelly and Clandinin refer to this process as using "curriculum potential" and offer a model as to how these choices might be implemented (Connelly & Clandinin, 1988, p. 149). They also point out that curriculum potential comes from both what one "reads out" of the curriculum and what one "reads into" it. Even poor standard materials in their view, can be used by the teacher to create vivid curriculum experiences. This happens they believe, when the teacher asks such questions as, what do these materials mean in my curriculum situation? And, what can I do with this material? The result of such questioning does in, their view, go beyond both the curriculum and the teacher, offering something even more because of the inter-action between the two (see Figure 5.1).

Figure 5.1–Choice on What to Do With a New Program

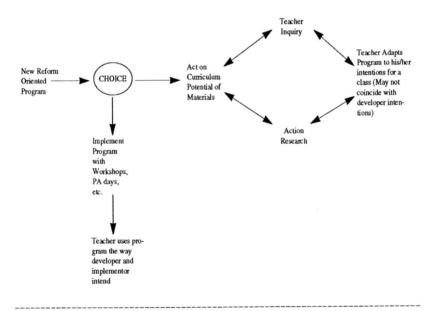

Note: From *Teachers as curriculum planners narratives of experience* (p. 149) by F. Connelly and D. Clandinin, 1988, New York: Teachers College Press. Copyright 1988 by Teachers College Press. Reprinted with permission.

In using existing curricula, first decide whether a given curriculum supports the teacher's values and reflects the teacher's philosophy of education and of art. To start the process the reader should review the philosophical positions described in Chapter II, the aesthetic paradigms outlined in Chapter IV, and the educational philosophies and forms of thought just discussed.

The reader can then attempt to identify what Connelly and Clandinin (1988) call "common places," that is, curricular arguments with a common focus. They note, for example, if "organized knowledge" is the focus of the curriculum, then the learner may be considered as a receptacle and the teacher a dispenser. Sometimes, they note, different foci are included, such as the learner as inquirer, as a social organism, and as a recording machine. This can lead to confusion about the real intent of the curriculum. More importantly they suggest that the reader look at how the curriculum deals with the subject matter, the classroom setting, the learner, and the teacher through raising the following questions:

> Which commonplace is the curriculum writer's argumentative starting point?
>
> Which commonplace is the curriculum writer's end in view?
>
> Which commonplace is emphasized in the text?

These authors also offer a set of questions which can be used by the teacher to analyze the curriculum literature. These questions cover (1) whether the curriculum is theoretical or practical, (2) what the curriculum's main topics are, (3) whether it is more about the general curriculum or about the subject matter discipline, (4) what the author's point of view is, (5) what it is the author wants you to do and (6) why the author wants you to do it.

Deciding Whether a Curriculum is Theoretical or Practical

Deciding whether a published art curriculum is either theoretical or practical can begin with determining the author's intended readership—teachers in training or teachers inservice. If intended for teachers in training, the curriculum is likely to be more theoretical. For teachers inservice, a more practical curriculum is likely, although it may range from cookbook-style lesson plans to a mixture of the theoretical and practical.

The information from the author on the procedures used in developing the content may also reveal whether it is a curriculum theory developed by a college professor, a theory a professor has tested with class-room teachers, or one developed jointly by teachers and children in an actual art classroom. Of course, a curriculum can be of interest whether it is theoretical or practical and even a college text may be just as reveal-ing about what teachers do in schools as the information found in some school-based curriculum series.

Deciding the Curriculum's Main Topics

The main topics used to organize the curriculum will reveal a good deal about which school practices the curriculum planner wants the teacher to develop. A curriculum writer whose main headings stress the elements and the formal qualities of art is probably more concerned about expres-sion than one who organizes a curriculum around the study of art con-tent, the production of art, the understanding of art and the importance of art judgment. While either one may suggest teachers introduce the ele-ments and principles and have children make art objects, in the first instance the end may be more toward the creation of expressive form and in the second more toward the teaching of art criticism.

A General Curriculum or an Art Curriculum

All art education curricula deal with the subject matter of art, but some may show more concern for the content of art and others more concern for general curriculum goals. The difference is found more in the cur-riculum writer's philosophical view in constructing the curriculum than in which activities the curriculum advocates the teacher undertake. For example, a writer who asks students to look at art through art occupa-tions, its effect on the physical environment, and its ability to increase understanding among peoples, has a different view of the value of art as general education than one who organizes the curriculum around obser-vational drawing, composition, action drawing, and talking and writing about drawing. While one author views the art curriculum in terms of what it can do in forwarding the social and environmental goals of the total school curriculum, another can view art as an intelligent activity that is valuable in and of itself.

Deciding the Author's Point of View

To decide the curriculum's general point of view, first determine the author's basic premises for constructing its concepts, especially whether they are argued psychologically, or sociologically. An author who builds a curriculum psychologically may see learning as a matter requiring readiness, cognitive response, psycho-cultural transactions, information handling and delineation of response. This is different from the planner who builds a curriculum on the sociological premise that in art a person acts as a moral agent, expressing identity and giving form to hopes and fears as a means for coping. Both may support art forming, but from the psychological stance, as a means to articulate aesthetic form and in the second sociological stance, as a means toward authenticating the self-identification of human beings.

What the Author Wants the Teacher to Do

To determine what the author wants the teacher to do, examine which practices the author objects to and which the author supports or wants the teacher to do differently. This may be easier to discern in an article or curriculum criticism than in a curriculum stressing which procedures to follow rather than why the reader needs to follow them. Often the practices advocated only imply what the curriculum intends to accomplish and what other practices will fail to accomplish. An author who proposes that children should search for cognitive solutions to art problems through investigation and study wants the teacher to do different things than one who advocates individual technical accomplishment. Someone who believes that aesthetic ends are best achieved in a studio context also may not want the teacher to emphasize disciplinary understandings. Put another way, the more prescriptive the curriculum, the more the author wants the reader to apply the intended meanings of the text rather than what practitioners may find from their own experience.

Why the Author Wants the Teacher to Do It

Finding out why the author wants the teacher to do it, or not do it, may be something better revealed where the author begins with a certain premise and then follows up with what the teacher needs to do. This will be evident in the emphases given to the subject matter, the learning situation, or the teacher. When the content of the curriculum focuses on how students can learn to make better art, the author may be more concerned about developing expressive abilities. Conversely, if the author wants the teacher to provide more group oriented inductive questioning about art, the author may be more concerned about educating future consumers of art. Once you determine why the curriculum writer wants you to undertake an activity, you must also decide if it is better than what you are now doing.

Another approach to analyzing a curriculum can be found in Eisner's idea that all schools have three curricula: the explicit, the implicit and the null curriculum. The explicit curriculum is the curriculum as stated, including the intentions of the developers, policy makers, and others. The implicit, or hidden, curriculum describes all the things to be taught even though they are not intended. The null curriculum refers to those things deliberately excluded, based on the premise that when something is taught it has been decided that something else will not be taught (Eisner, 1985).

While Eisner's description of the three curricula is intended for the general curriculum developer, it can also help the reader evaluate an existing art curriculum that he or she may wish to use in the classroom. A later part of this chapter examines several approaches to analyzing the explicit curricula, so the following paragraphs examine Eisner's implicit and null curricula.

The Implicit Curriculum

The implicit curriculum in schools can be seen as the ways in which, "the culture of both the classroom and the school socializes children to the values that are part of the structure of those places" (Eisner, 1985, p. 88). The most important school structures Eisner notes are (1) those that cause children to compete for the attention of the teacher, (2) which ideas covert text material persuades, (3) the reward systems emphasized, (4) the class differentiations used, and (5) the time constraints employed.

When evaluating an art curriculum, then it is important to know what is implicit in that curriculum. For example, does the curriculum:

- Require children to assume initiative or encourage compliant behavior?

- Offer a reward system?

- Encourage competitiveness?

- Differentiate students according to ability?

- Delineate how much time is to be given to some activities (and not to others)?

The implicit curriculum can, as Eisner notes, teach a host of intellectual and social virtues: punctuality, a willingness to work hard on tasks not immediately enjoyable, and the ability to defer immediate gratification to work for distant goals. All of these, in his view, are positive acts of schooling. To determine if an art curriculum encourages such behaviors, the reader needs to examine the social messages inspired by the written curriculum, such as whether it makes children dependent upon the teacher or encourages individual initiative or competitiveness; whether the rewards for good behavior are consistent with the ends of aesthetic valuing, and whether the time and attention given to certain activities are commensurate with the aims of the curriculum.

A curriculum that emphasizes cognitive forms of artistic activity, rewards group valuing, and expends the most time and effort on helping students to talk about and criticize art has a different implicit curriculum than one that emphasizes expressive behavior, and individual aesthetic valuing, and spends the most time and effort on creative problem solving. The means and ends of the curriculum become most related in the realm of the implicit curriculum. Therefore, the teacher needs to consider whether the means used in the curriculum inspire the ends desired in the art program. Any curriculum requiring a student to engage in art activities that conflict with the values the student is expected to achieve will prove truly counterproductive to the intended goals of the curriculum.

The Null Curriculum

The null curriculum is according to Eisner what schools do not teach. In art what the art curriculum does not teach could be as important as what it does teach. This can be discovered, according to Eisner, through: (1) what intellectual process the schools emphasize and (2) what subject or content is present or absent in the curriculum or, in the case of the art curriculum, what conceptual processes the curriculum emphasizes and what content is present or absent.

In examining the null curriculum effect, one needs to recognize as Eisner notes, that not all thinking is mediated by words or numbers and not all thinking is rule abiding. There are, as he notes, modes of thought that are nonverbal and illogical and that operate in visual, auditory, metaphoric and synesthetic ways, which may always not be developed in school programs. The art program he implies should be geared to meeting the forms of conception and expression greater than the logically determined criteria or discursive forms of thinking required in most schools. In doing this, the art curriculum would provide for what Eisner feels are the things students cannot consider, what they do not know, and which processes they are unable to use but which have implications for their lives—areas not addressed by most school curricula. When the art curriculum provides what the general curriculum does not, it makes its most significant contribution to schooling.

Constructing a Curriculum

Once the teacher has examined his or her own personal values and examined existing curricula to discover whether these values are evident in the implicit, explicit or null features of that curriculum, he or she is then ready to begin developing a curriculum. According to Eisner (1985), curriculum development is "the process of transforming images and aspirations about education into programs that will effectively realize the visions and images that initiated the process" (p. 85). Such a transformation may require a long systematic planning period. It may be decided on as a calendar of topics and activities to be pursued over a year or as a plan which emerges on a week-to-week basis. The plan selected is up to the teacher and the teacher's need for order or predictability in the program.

The Curriculum Plan

Not all approaches to planning are the same. Some, like Eisner, suggest a beginning at any point in the teaching/learning process; others, like Ralph Tyler (1950), suggest a more systematic linear approach. Such matters are not clearcut because the relationship between teaching and planning is not always distinct even though it is generally agreed that the curriculum is the content to be taught and the teaching is how it is taught. The difficulty comes in distinguishing between the two in practice because how content is taught also affects what is taught and vice versa.

In using Eisner's circular model, the process can either begin with intentions to plan which leads to content and structure in teaching which through courses of action leads back to intentions or, conversely, begin with planning which provides content and structure which leads to intention (see Figure 5.2).

In contrast to Eisner, Ralph Tyler (1950), provides an equally useful but much more linear and structured approach to curriculum planning. It begins with choosing objectives, selecting and organizing them, and then leads the reader to select classroom activities, conduct them, and lastly evaluate them through the originally prescribed objectives (see Figure 5.3).

More importantly, the Tyler model also identifies four questions which need to be answered in developing a curriculum:

1. What educational purpose should the school seek to attain?

Figure 5.2–Eisner's Circular Model for Curriculum Planning

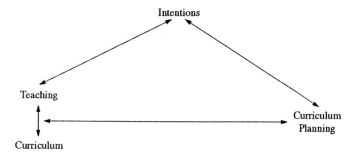

Note: Reprinted with the permission of Macmillan Publishing Company from The education imagination: On the design and evaluation of school programs, (p. 188), Second Edition by Elliot W. Eisner. Copyright © 1985 by Elliot W. Eisner.

Figure 5.3–Tyler's Classic Formulation Summarized

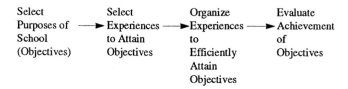

Note: From *Teachers as curriculum planners narratives of experience* (p. 140) by F. Connelly and D. Clandinin, 1988, New York: Teachers College Press. Copyright 1988 by Teachers College Press. Reprinted with permission.

2. What educational experiences are most likely to encourage attainment of these purposes?

3. How can these experiences be effectively organized?

4. How can we determine whether the purposes are being met? (Tyler, 1944, p. 1).

Barrett (1979), using Tyler's methods, offers a model of Tyler's objective curriculum where the aim is a general outcome that the teacher hopes to achieve, the objectives are formulated to achieve the general aim, the method is the organization or management of the learning experiences, the content is the body of knowledge to be taught and the evalu-

Figure 5.4–The objectives model

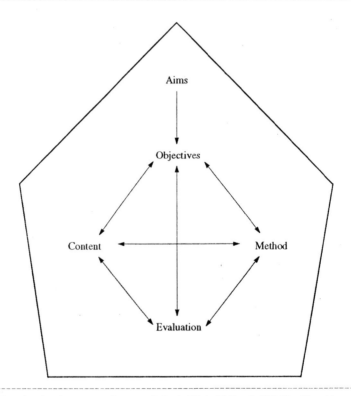

Note: From *Art education a strategy for course design* (p. 36), by M. Barrett, 1979, New Hampshire: Heinemann Educational Books. Copyright 1979 by M. Barrett. Reprinted with permission.

ation is the measurement of competencies or the ability of students to achieve actual or inferred outcomes (see Figure 5.4).

No matter which model is chosen, the reader needs to keep in mind that, more than anything else, curriculum planning is a way to think about what classroom events need to occur and what consequences these events will have on the lives of students. Thus a planning structure should begin with the school's aims as a reflection of community values, proceed to the naming of goals linking these aims to those objectives that define the purposes for the program, and then translate these into instructional objectives specifying what students should know and be able to do. This sequence is important especially because it requires the curriculum maker to relate the curricular means to the curricular ends he or she hopes to achieve. By using a process where goals provide the basis for content, content forms the basis for deciding objectives, and objectives helps the writer to formulate curriculum activities, the writer has to continuously keep in mind what it was he or she set out to achieve in the first place (see Figure 5.5).

Figure 5.5–Curricular Planning Structure

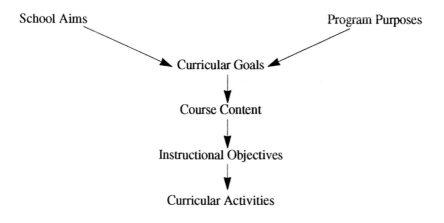

Some Sample Goals from Secondary Schools

The actual goals or objectives of an art program depend on whether those who write them value the study of motifs and themes, are committed to a form-Gestalt view, or to subscribe the metaphorical-linguistic values of art study. Where an art faculty is committed to a common view these emphases can be seen in the art program goal statements or be deduced from the statement using the paradigm models previously identified. Figures 5.6, 5.7, and 5.8 provide three program goal statements reflective of the kinds developed in different regions of the United States

---

Figure 5.6–School "A" Technical High School

Goal Statement

Program Goals

The art department's program goals as stated are to:

1) Provide experience in the use of tools for visual communication;

2) Recognize and understand the visual and physical laws of design technology;

3) Introduce socially acceptable concepts of good taste and respect for the work of others;

4) Develop an appreciation for art purely as a human endeavor or as an expression of diverse periods and cultures through many media;

5) Do research problems with references which stimulate imagination;

6) Provide an environment conducive to the creative intuition, and an incentive to pursue excellence in concept and craftsmanship; and

7) Enrich the students' leisure time pursuits through art.

Figure 5.7–School "B" High School

Goal Statement

We believe that art is a vital part of everyday living. High school students begin to realize their aesthetic potential by expressing themselves through art means. Students should be exposed to every possible media in high school art classes so that deliberate expression in one preferred medium does not limit the student's future art activities. Intensive use of drawing and sketching is the basis and stepping stone to a variety of facets of art expression. Students must study the contemporary trends of art as well as learn from its past accomplishments.

The teacher should stress the fact that expression in the Arts comes from sheer dedication and discipline of the mind and hand, relying upon a free-thinking, creative attitude. Teachers should plan lessons drawing from subjects reflecting the here and now, using themes appealing to the young adult.

"The art program drives to accomplish free-thinking, creative, problem-solving minds. Self-evaluation on the part of each student as well as the teacher should be ever constant. The solution of each problem should be approached differently by each student. The Art Department works in coordination with other subject areas in the development and improvement of the student's basic art experiences.

We believe in the concept approach to teaching, emphasizing two psychological factors. We recognize that there is a difference between spontaneous expression of feeling and artistic production. At the same time, we believe that the mind to be central to human behavior with the function of acquiring concepts which guide responses, activity, and expression. These concepts are acquired by means of the basic human sense organs, relating directly to sense perception in the gathering of information. Through the conceptual approach, the teacher encourages the student to organize the various stimuli collected by perceptual means. Such an approach relates directly to the thinking and problem-solving situations in

----

Figure 5.8–School "C" High School

Goal Statement

The visual arts are academic subjects like science, mathematics and philosophy, in that they are theoretical in nature and do not always have an immediate practical function. Visual works of art are a means of perceiving the historical world not accessible by other means. The visual arts are a process of thinking, as well as a process of manipulation, involved with the invention of visual images that represent the culture in time and space, reflecting the changes and growth of a civilization. The visual arts are ideas in plastic or conceptual form utilizing intellectual and expressive responses that emphasize the ability to think critically, analyze, synthesize, and reconstruct visual forms. By deepening personal experiences the visual arts help to humanize the environment and foster a greater appreciation of life and living in the sensory responses to one's environment. The visual arts are a major aspect of human culture—activities that reveal the development of civilization and a contemporary history of culture. The role of art education is to foster an understanding of that continuum and to insure the visual continuum for future generations.

----

and in different types of schools. School "A" is a technical high school with a selective admission policy which provides a curriculum in commercial art; School "B" is an academically focused general admission small-town high school. School "C" is a general admission, largely college preparatory high school in the suburbs of a large city.

School "A's" goal statement is brief and to the point listing a range of goals emphasizing the program's commitment to teaching art as a form of visual communication and design, but also with a general studies component that includes art appreciation and art for leisure-time pursuits. School "A's" statement makes no overt reference to creative or expressive activity.

The goals of School "B" are presented mostly as a statement of the program's philosophy with a number of direct references to the student engaging in exploratory, creative and disciplined artistic problem solving, using artistic exemplars. One can assume at School "B" students are judged to be individuals and expected to express themselves visually in a broad range of art materials in highly idiosyncratic ways.

At School "C" the staff offers a philosophically oriented goal state-ment, which defines art primarily as a disciplinary study to help students acquire the analytical higher order thinking skills needed for serving the art functions of the society. The School "C" statement stresses the ana-lytical over the individualistic and creative, and social obligations over expressive intents.

Art Curriculum Content

The subject matter content of the curriculum as previously noted should come from the school's objectives which may or may not prescribe the content to be used to achieve them. In deciding content, the curriculum designer needs to consider which modes of inquiry are necessary to understand art, the specific information or content to be explored, and which methods are most likely to achieve the instructional objectives. Content is usually defined in terms of a body of knowledge, information, events, processes, techniques or problems associated with particular seg-ments of human knowledge along with the media and the materials needed to pursue them. In art this means a synthesis of visual and tactile experience, integration, perception, thinking, doing and feeling. The par-ticular content to be explored, the modes of inquiry to be used, and the methods most likely to ensure that learning takes place will differ again according to which paradigm is embraced. However, some commonly agreed upon content will likely include art production, art history, art criticism and aesthetics.

Examples of School Curriculum Content

A program's art curriculum content is evident in its course descriptions and content emphases revealed through the distribution of the content across the curriculum. Sample course descriptions developed by Dennis and Tom Wolf for the College Board "red" book reveal how two courses with similar subject matter content may actually differ in what they aim to teach.

Course I

Introduction to the Visual Arts: Two- and Three-Dimensional Design

This is a full-year course. Its objective is to introduce stu-dents to all the elements of design: line, texture, value, shape, and color. Reflecting the concern for a balance of learning experiences, the course uses three approaches: students learn through creating their own work; they learn through class critiques of their work and that of their peers; and they learn through the study of historical models.

The course has been designed to accommodate the special demands of studio work. It has two double-period meetings a week. These longer periods allow students to work in a concentrated fashion, minimizing time spent in setup and cleanup. They are also encouraged to work on their projects after school or in free periods.

The course begins with a study of line through contour drawing. Using simple tools such as pencils, pens, or charcoal, students start by drawing figures. In order to learn eye-hand coordination, they are given exercises in which they are told to look only at the model they are drawing, not at the paper. A second project asks them to create illusions of space using only straight lines. A third asks them to vary the thickness of lines and, by use of the stroke and density of the line, create different textures.

After attempting to solve each of these problems, students display their work. The class discusses all the works and tries to understand why one is more successful in solving a design problem than another. This exercise is augmented by the study of significant works from art history—drawings by Leonardo da Vinci, Ingres, Picasso, and Matisse; medieval woodcuts; Chinese landscape paintings; African batiks; and the painting of Mondrian. From these models, students learn a variety of the ways that artists have worked with line.

The second segment of the course offers similar exercises for value and shape. Students learn to create volume by shading. They begin with geometric shapes drawn from familiar objects and move into simple still lifes. They use their hands to think about redesigning their own environments. The instructor integrates the development of historical knowledge and analytic-evaluative skills into this phase of the course by leading the students in discussions of drapery shading in early Renaissance paintings, shaded columns and spheres in works by David, and the illusion of light and shadow in Durer engravings. Later, they move on to elements of composition, learning how to select a point of view for a drawing.

They draw a still life from three different angles, framing it in different ways each time. They study the works of selected Cubist painters or Egyptian murals, learning what it means to have multiple points of view in the same composition.

Similar groups of exercises and learning activities center around studies of color and three-dimensionality. Students learn to mix colors, beginning with primary and complementary colors. They match color swatches from magazines, keeping a diary of how certain shades and tints were achieved. They compare works of Giotto, Caravaggio, Rembrandt, Monet, El Greco, Van Gogh, Gauguin, Albers, and Motherwell in order to learn concepts such as warmth, chiaroscuro, and vibrating color. Exercises in three-dimensionality center on additive and subtractive sculpture (using soft stone, fire brick, plaster, and wax), studies of local architecture, positive and negative space, and the relationship of light and three-dimensionality.

Students are evaluated on their studio work, written papers, and tests. They benefit from writing one paper during each segment of the course; in these papers they analyze artworks of various periods with respect to the specific design elements that are the focus of that segment's studio activities. The quizzes test the students' grasp of concept and vocabulary. Field trips to museums and visits by working artists also enrich the course. (College Entrance Examination Board, 1985, pp. 28-30)

This Wolf design course description reflects mostly a form-Gestalt paradigm through using problem-solving approach where

1. The content to be explored begins with the study of the elements of design, line, texture, value, shape and color.

2. The goal is to create a work by exploring a wide range of media.

3. Students solve problems in creating pictorial space.

While the students do study historical schema, they also draw from life using framing techniques for discovering pictorial organization. Although the course might appear to qualify as being disciplined based because it includes art history, art criticism and art production, it is study aimed mostly toward the students learning to express themselves through visually articulated form.

Course II

Introduction to the Visual Arts: Varied Media

This course introduces students to seven very different media: ceramics, weaving, architecture, drawing, painting, print making, and photography. Its intent is not only to familiarize students with the techniques and materials of these media but to help them understand the way that culture and historical variation shape the way a particular medium is used. The topical headings of the course are five human needs: food, clothing, shelter, communication and expression, and technology. In addition to examinations, students are assigned studio projects and papers involving out-of-class research. Field trips to museums in order to see original works of art are also extremely valuable.

The course begins with discussions of how the art of a culture allows us to understand that culture better. An initial assignment asks students to select two works of art from different periods and to speculate about their cultural contexts using **only** the works themselves as a guide. Students show photographs of their artworks to each other and offer their hypotheses. Their peers attempt to discover additional clues from close examination of the works.

The course then takes up its first major topic: food. Students examine various kinds of eating utensils from different periods. They analyze them from the point of view of function and decoration, discussing the difference between everyday uses and ritual uses. They learn about the living patterns and beliefs of specific cultures by analyzing these objects. Then working in clay, students make and decorate a pot, plate, or vessel, which they are to imagine that they have located in an archeological dig. Their peers attempt to describe the culture in which this utensil would have been appropriate.

A similar assignment centers around clothing. Looking at clothes worn by Eskimos, American prairie Indians, Puritans, and contemporary movie stars, they assess the influence of climate, religion, and culture on clothes. They are asked to keep a notebook of magazine clippings around a theme: ritual clothing, confining clothing, or functional clothing. Subsequently, students must design and execute a resist dye (batik). In each assignment, there is a discussion of how **aesthetical [sic]** aspects complement functional ones. This discussion is crucial in order to distinguish the course from a social science approach to food and clothing. It is during these discussions that students learn and practice, in a rudimentary way, the elements of aesthetic analysis, interpretation, and evaluation.

In the unit on architecture, students work together to draw a ground plan for a city after studying nomadic tent life, villages of mud huts, medieval churches as religious centers, Renaissance palaces glorifying individual families, and the modern skyscraper as a center for commerce. The unit on communication and expression deals with the themes of war, death, religion, and motherhood as treated in two-dimensional art (painting, drawing, print making) over the centuries. The students also execute their own examples in the medium of their choice and offer critiques of one another's work.

The final unit, technology, looks at the development of photography. Studying the photographs of Brassai, Lartigue, Stieglitz, Kasebier, Weston, Adams, Polk, and Van Der Zee, students learn about the medium from a technological point of view, trying simple photographic experiments of their own (with pin-hole or Polaroid cameras). They also learn how the medium has advanced technologically and how these advances have enabled it to become an art form expressive of specific eras, location, and cultural concerns. (College Entrance Examination Board, 1985, pp. 30-31)

Course II outlined by the Wolfs utilizes the basic modes of inquiry both as discovery learning and as discipline learning. In this course, students learn to think as scientists, reason inductively, and adopt behaviors specific to the subject matter domain in which the discovery takes place. Art is looked at from the linguistic-metaphorical paradigm point of view involving study of cultural objects in order to arrive at conceptions relating to the cultural functions of art and the meanings of artistic ritual, totem and taboo.

The course rather than truly focusing on the making of expressive objects, seeks to teach students to analyze, interpret and evaluate through discussions and critical discourse about these works of art. The course, therefore, represents a disciplined-based approach which, while familiarizing the student with various artistic media, actually focuses on the critical and analytical functions of art as a means for social understanding.

Developing Objectives

Before setting out to develop educational objectives for an art curriculum the writer should keep in mind that all objectives should be considered ideal behaviors and initially developed apart from the personal and situational events in which they are intended to be used. Not all objectives, for example, are possible or even desirable in some classroom contexts; they, nevertheless, all need to be carefully considered. This forces the planner to think about his or her goals and those activities most likely to achieve them prior to actually working them out in the classroom. Because art teachers, unlike those in the cognate fields, need to think about space, tools, materials, equipment and visuals in addition to content knowledge, advance planning becomes doubly important if only to avoid the potential of total chaos occurring in the art classroom.

Deciding on objectives requires determining the kinds of art studies to be provided, the forms of study to be emphasized and the methods of inquiry to offered to help students think about and create art. The answers to these questions will vary according to the concepts used in deciding what should be taught and how it should be taught. However, the objectives themselves require that their development include both objectivity and specificity. To objectively write objectives, the curriculum maker needs to write statements that prescribe both the behavior to be sought and the content to be learned, specifying what a student should be able to do with a certain content. In a formal curriculum plan, objectives can be organized into a unit or as course objectives specified on a two-dimensional grid listing all the content areas on one axis and all the behavioral objectives on the other, thus making each cell on the grid an objective which can then be used to describe an entire course of study (see Figure 5.9).

Methods of Instruction

The methods of instruction or the ways in which experiences are organized involve both (1) the organization of the art content to be learned and (2) its vertical and horizontal distribution across the curriculum. All forms of interaction between the learner, the teacher and the learning resources available should be considered as well as the

- Transmission of social, cultural and technical knowledge about art.

- The development of the skills and processes necessary for analytic, productive, and expressive thinking.

- The skills and processes concerned with emotion, motivation, values and personal relationships.

Figure 5.9–Approaches to Studying Art

	PERSONAL DEVELOPMENT	ARTISTIC HERITAGE	ART IN SOCIETY
E X P R E S S I O N	Discovering ideas for art in personal experiences	Learning how artists discover ideas in personal experiences	Learning how society expresses values and beliefs in visual forms
	Transforming ideas to create art	Learning how artists transform ideas to create art	Learning how society expresses changes in values and beliefs in visual forms
	Working with media to make art	Learning how artists work with media to make art	Learning how society works with its technologies to make visual forms
R E S P O N S E	Perceiving and describing works of art	Learning how critics and historians perceive and describe works of art	Learning how society perceives and recognizes visual images
	Interpreting works of art	Learning how critics and historians interpret works of art	Learning how society interprets visual images
	Judging works of art	Learning how critics and historians judge works of art	Learning how society judges visual images

Note: From *Planning art education in the middle/secondary schools of Ohio* (p. 129) by J. Tollifson, 1977, Ohio: State Department of Education, Jerry Tollifson. Reprinted with permission.

The Organization of Content

To organize the content of art instruction, the planner must first determine the major concepts of the art education field, its preminent valves, and the skills, abilities and habits basic to the field. These determinations like other curricular decisions will vary according to the conceptual categories or paradigms used in the decision-making process.

The mode of inquiry will, therefore, determine the content to be pursued and dictate whether the planner will organize the curriculum in terms of traditional content descriptions such as painting, drawing, and sculpting or in ways that foster the planner's desire to teach art as a form of communication, humanism, and social reconstruction or as popular culture. These organizational choices are described in the curriculum literature in terms of the relative closeness between contents—from totally separate to close—where the boundaries between disciplines is weak or extremely vague.

The Distribution of Content across the Curriculum

Learning opportunities occur in all curricula over time so the planner should decide the sequence of the content to be introduced and what degree of control needs to be exercised in the teaching/learning situation. Eisner describes approaches to sequence in two different ways: a "staircase" model that builds on a series of independent steps to arrive at the highest level and a "spiderweb" model that allows the designer to organize a set of heuristic projects, materials and activities leading to diverse outcomes (Eisner, 1985). In the "staircase" model, Eisner sees the route as well defined, mechanical in construction, and efficient; the "spiderweb" model is so ordered as to help students create ideas and develop the skills they most want to achieve.

Eisner's "staircase" model is similar to the curricular approach of Gagne who proposed that curriculum writers ask what the prerequisite behavior for any behavior to be learned might be (Gagne, 1964, p. 144). Gagne's approach results in a terminal objective reached by a sequence of finding out what one needs to know, first, second, third and so forth. Such a system of organization lends itself to more centralized educational systems which desire to know what every student in the system is studying on a particular day, week or month. This approach does, however, also appeal to objective logic and can later help the student build a reasonable and coherent learning structure useful in approaching other problem solving situations in school and community life.

The literature offers at least two "spiderweb" models worthy of consideration as alternatives to the "staircase" model. One is Maurice Barrett's process model and the other, Arthur Efland's Ohio curriculum planning approach. Barrett (1979) believes that art education is composed of worthwhile activities which have their own built-in concepts of excellence and can be appraised only by the standards inherent in them. He has outlined a studio process model involving a conceptual triangulation between: (1) student impulses, feelings and ideas, (2) media materials and techniques and (3) the perception of visual form (see Figure 5.10). In his model, Barrett conceptualizes art education as being engaged in the development of the senses wherein student impulses, feelings or sensory experience engage media, materials and techniques as the means for transmitting the impulses, feelings, and ideas that the student organizes perceptually through line, shape, color, tone, space and texture.

Barrett then relates the concept portion of the model with its other part entitled "procedure and criteria." This procedure involves the stu-

Figure 5.10–The Process Model

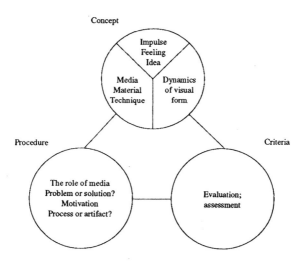

Note: From *Art education a strategy for course design* (p. 44), by M. Barrett, 1979, New Hampshire: Heinemann Educational Books. Copyright 1979 by M. Barrett. Reprinted with permission.

dent selecting a media, choosing an art problem based on one or more of the concepts, and being motivated enough to pursue a solution to the problem. The teacher can begin the activity at any point: with the idea, impulse or feeling; the material, media, and technique; or the perception of form. The model requires only that the student negotiate the activity with the teacher and identify and solve his or her own art problem .

Arthur Efland (1977) in *Planning Art Education in the Middle and Secondary Schools of Ohio* also offers a process model which, like the Barrett model, makes sequencing a matter of context. Arguing that there is no one place to begin planning the art curriculum, Efland recommends that the teacher first make a content analysis of an existing curriculum, decide what is missing and then design a new plan around specified themes or units of study through writing activities which combine into sequenced activities his recommended study approaches and the content areas. As to sequencing, Efland claims "that [in art] there is no inherently logical sequence that must occur if development is to proceed in an orderly or coherent way" (Efland, 1977, p. 124). His model allows the teacher to enter the curriculum process at any point. (Efland, 1977, p. 129). Conceivably, he notes, the teacher could begin planning a unit around a film or a book, or a particular reading which stimulates a worthwhile activity; some invented activity could even offer another starting place. The only requirement is that all four components—units, encounters, activities, resources—be included (see Figure 5.11).

Horizontal Organization

The horizontal organization of the curriculum, that is, the integration and balance of its parts, also needs to be addressed in planning. In a disciplinary curriculum, this integration and balance would primarily be focused on the components of production, art history, art criticism and aesthetics and in other programs on different organizational components including media and materials, social behaviors and the like. Curricular areas to check for integration and balance include age-grade levels, instructional time, matters of overlap, redundancy and curricular support. Achieving balance and relative emphases in content at a given level may be more under the control of a curriculum committee; however, the individual teacher may have more direct responsibility for integration which involves how common topics or themes are taught through different art content impacting on social skills and language development.

Figure 5.11–Efland's Process Model

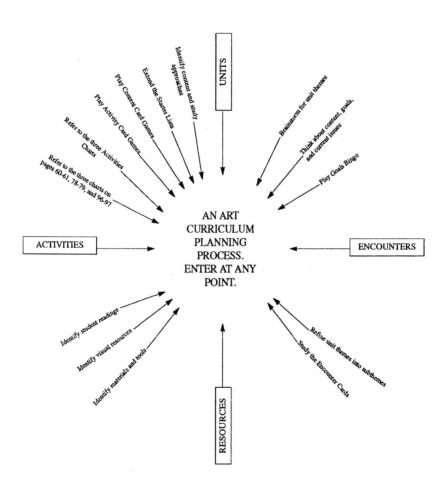

Note: From *Planning art education in the middle/secondary schools of Ohio* (p. 129) by J. Tollifson, 1977, Ohio: State Department of Education, Jerry Tollifson. Reprinted with permission.

Selecting Experiences

The curriculum specialist, Ralph Tyler, has contributed a good deal to the literature on the problem of selecting learning experiences or learning activities. Tyler's definition of experience is the interaction between the student and his or her environment, especially where the student is an active participant. Tyler's five principles for selecting learning experiences are

1. Selecting experiences that permit the student to deal with the content expressed in the objective.

2. Selecting experiences that the student will enjoy applying.

3. Selecting experiences appropriate to the age-grade level of the student.

4. Recognizing that different experiences can be used to reach the same objectives and

5. Knowing that a given learning experience will usually meet several different curriculum objectives (Tyler, 1950, pp. 65-68).

Tyler's principles are significant in what they reveal about students needing the opportunity to use what they have been taught, to enjoy using it, and to have what they are taught be something they can learn. Tyler's principles also should remind the curriculum planner that any activity can effect different kinds of learning so he or she must continuously examine the planning process to ensure that no hidden curriculum occurs antithetical to the implicit curricular goals.

School Course of Study Examples

The art curriculum content of the school program is evident in both the individual courses offered and the organization and distribution of course content across the curriculum. This can be observed in the courses of study developed by most U.S. secondary schools. The following paragraphs examine the three different curricular structures in schools "A," "B" and "C" that employ different patterns for organizing and distributing content through the various parts of the curriculum.

These are the same three schools whose goal statements were listed earlier in the chapter. It should be noted that while each school has a different philosophy about the total school art curriculum, all are equally successful in developing strong art programs. Their curricular conceptions, as previously noted, include a school with a four-year curriculum in commercial art, one offering a varied media expressive approach, and one with a linguistic or futuristic approach. While each school does not use the same approach to its curriculum, each school has a concept. The concept adopted by a school can be identified through what it claims in its published school curriculum and also through the activities the faculty undertake in the classroom.

Schools have differing concepts, values, and learning activities for various reasons including: (1) the historical mission of a school, (2) a faculty who works together toward achieving a common viewpoint or (3) a faculty unified by a common art education background. For example, because School "A," is a selective admission school, its curriculum is shaped by a 50-year-long technological mission. School "B" may on the other hand use a variety-of-media approach because all its faculty graduated from the same teacher training institution.

Schools with a common conceptual base usually reflect a curricular structure agreed upon and generally supported by the faculty. This is manifested in school situations where faculty are organized according to studio discipline or where team teaching or class rotation practices occur. When school art faculties have an agreed-upon curriculum plan, the students, teachers, and school administration know what is expected and where the program is going. In such schools students can pursue painting and drawing in a four-year commercial art curriculum, improve in their perceptual differentiation through in-depth studio concentrations in a variety-of-media approaches, or paint futuristically in deconstructionist studio contexts. When an art faculty agrees on the goals of a program, it also accepts certain common curricular strategies and program goals. Faculties can make a concept permeate the entire program through (1) agreeing on a program of foundational art learnings and (2) accepting a professional approach to designing the program's goals.

The curriculum in these three secondary schools while realistic about open enrollment as a means for filling classes, also requires that both majors and nonmajors begin their art studies with an art foundation. Foundation courses will vary according to the school's philosophy and emphasis, but all seem to stress learning based on the elements of art and the principles of design. Most require studio work to solve problems concerned with the use of line, shape, value, color and texture, with some programs centering on design, and others on traditional drawing and painting activities from still life and the human figure.

The content stressed in all three programs varies considerably: One school uses a college foundations design or drawing approach, and the others use a varied studio sampler approach. Whatever approach is used, however, most schools require a disciplined use of elements and principles as foundation for further study in art. Even in schools where beginning students are allowed entrance to art courses without a prerequisite, those courses usually provide some instruction in the basic elements and principles of design.

The sequence and scope of the foundation programs in these three schools also varies. In school "A's" four-year sequentially ordered curriculum, each year's course is the foundation for the next course; school "B's" foundation students rotate between instructors in different disciplines; and school "C's" students are exposed to even higher levels of cognitive understanding as they proceed up the curriculum ladder.

School "A" as noted in its goal statement is a professionally focused school with an education-as-discipline concept built into its four-year curriculum. Its course of study focuses on the discovery behaviors needed by potential designers or by scientists and engineers who need to understand design applications in the workplace. Each year's course builds on the previous year's course to achieve the higher and more sophisticated level of skills needed to achieve excellence in visual design. The content in the curriculum is specified mostly in terms of learning the principles, concepts, organizational skills and habits needed by the future designer (see Figure 5.12).

School "B's" curriculum like that of School "A" is ordered into single, year-long courses, but with a fine art emphasis. While it may appear to stress the disciplinary behaviors of artists, the courses emphasize the concept of education as problem solving. The education-as-problem-solving approach is evidenced in the course assignments in a variety of media, the faculty efforts to rotate students among studios in the Art I course, and the faculty's general agreement on the curricular approaches and language used in defining the process. The major concepts stressed are to learn the fundamentals of art making, be disciplined in acquiring new art skills and processes, and acquire good visual study habits (see Figure 5.13).

School "C's" course of study consists of five semester or year-long courses which, like those of Schools "A" and "B", increase in difficulty or sophistication, but only for a three-year period. School "C" views education as having a cognitive emphasis which can be seen in the course description thrust toward students developing higher level cognitive abilities, the development of thinking processes and the move toward self-impelled inquiry. In School "C's" program, art is considered a form of communication, and is a way to broaden mental and aesthetic processes. The artist in School "C's" program is considered to be someone with a clear purpose and with a specific cultural role to play in the society (see Figure 5.14).

Figure 5.12–School "A"

Course of Study

Commercial Art I (1 Unit). This course is an introduction to basic tools and processes with emphasis on individual development in their use for creative problem solving situations. Based on solid principles of design, this class provides an important foundation in drawing and painting.

Commercial Art II (1 Unit). This second course provides in depth drawing, painting, plus new experiences in printmaking, craftwork, ceramics, weaving, and interior decoration.

Commercial Art III (1 Unit). A training level course designed to provide the student an opportunity to develop job entry level knowledge and skills required for successful performance in the commercial art occupations. Course emphasis is on illustration and studio art procedures. Utilizing this concept, various commercial art media are introduced. Layout problems are utilized to prepare copy for 1-4 color reproductions.

Commercial Art IV (1 Unit). Emphasis here is on communication through layout and art as related to editorial and advertizing industries. Practical experiences in cropping, scaling, typefitting, screentints, cold type, paste-up, and photo considerations accomplished by printing the school yearbook. The students are also responsible for compiling a personal portfolio which illustrates the skills and knowledge attained in this series of courses and present a special report on job opportunities related to their educational preparation.

Design I (1 Unit). Practical design considerations and solid principles of concepts and organization pertinent to the fine and commercial arts are taught in this course. Areas or work include color theory, lettering, 2 and 3 dimensional space arrangement, fabric printing and drawing.

Design II (1 Unit). A self-directed course for the serious art student. Students demonstrate their technical skills in the areas of color, drawing, spatial illusion and 3D organization by means of a portfolio which is submitted for evaluation and possible job placement or for the continuation of training at a higher level.

Figure 5.13– School "B"

Course of Study

Art I. Art studio experiences with two and three dimensional exploration; fundamentals of drawing, color and design, pottery and ceramics. Art history and appreciation related to studio work. Homework and student sketchbook required.

Art II. Advanced problems in printmaking, etching, woodcuts and silkscreen; painting in acrylics, oils and watercolor; ceramic sculpture, jewelry and metal casting. Art aesthetics and philosophy included, elements of photography introduced. Sketchbook and homework assigned.

Art III. Advanced problems in all media. Portfolio preparation (admission to art college or school). Drawing from models and advanced printmaking and lithography. Photography on advanced problems, darkroom technique. Art history and philosophy expanded. Sketchbook and homework.

Art Appreciation (1/2 year). History of painting, sculpture and architecture from past to present. Emphasis on American Art and today's culture. Reports, text study and outside work required. Field trips to museums and exhibits.

Figure 5.14– School "C"

Course of Study

Art Appreciation, *Semester course open to grades 10, 11, and 12,* Pre-requisite: None—A course planned for those students who seek to obtain a visual awareness and appreciation for the fine arts. It offers study through the use of slides, films, filmstrips, and a textbook.

Art I, *Semester or year course open to grades 10, 11, and 12,* Pre-requisite: None—Art I is a lab course in which the use of art elements and design principles are explored through some or all of the following media: pencil, charcoal, water color, tempera paint and india ink. Good craftsmanship in using art materials will be pursued. Emphasis will be placed on individual self expression and communication through the art process.

Art II, *Semester or year course open to grades 10, 11, & 12,* Pre-requisite: One full year of Art I with grade of *C* or better, or teacher recommendation.—Art II is a continuation and expansion of the basic design principles explored in Art I. This class is for the more seriously oriented art student. Emphasis will be placed on a broadening of mental and aesthetic processes involved in the communication of expressions in art.

Art III, *Semester or year course open to grades 11 & 12,* Pre-requisite: One full year of Art II with a grade of *C* or better, or teacher recommendation.—Art III is a course designed to allow the individual student the maximum freedom to explore various art media which interest him. Emphasis will be placed on the students understanding of the artists purpose and role in their society in relationship to past cultures. Introduction of more sophisticated art media will also be introduced.

Art IV, *Semester or year course open to grade 12*, Pre-requisite: One full year of Art III with a grade of *C* or better—Art IV is a lab course in which the student studies, evaluates, and creates, using art concepts and art materials in many areas. The emphasis will be on the individual exploration, growth, planning, and craftsmanship and preparing a portfolio.

Many other schools, of course, distribute content differently throughout a curricular course of study. Some, for example, provide sequenced instruction in two different tracks, that is in a fine art painting, drawing and sculpture track or in a design, crafts or applied art track. Others are organized around studios where students "major" in either painting, ceramics, or textiles, and still others focus on perceptual learning for the general studies student. Any one course of study can lead to an effective school art program regardless of emphasis, and all have a concept which can be readily identified in the school's curriculum plan.

Evaluating the Plan

This chapter has so far focused on ensuring the viability of the parts of the curriculum plan, including the delineation of the school's goals; the program objectives; and the content, activities, and horizontal and vertical organization of the curriculum. Once the parts of the plan exist, it is then time to focus on whether the curriculum proposal shows promise of developing into an adequate curriculum or, in other words, how well will the proposal work in practice? In defining objectives, the designer specifies an intentional, directional, future orientation. Next is needed an evaluation process to aid in the continuous move back and forth from the future to the present in a never ending cycle to adjust and fine tune the curriculum in actual practice. Using evaluation as a tool in this process, however, should be more for feedback and diagnosis than for achievement and promotion.

Eisner (1985) defines five functions of evaluation: (1) to diagnose, (2) to revise curricula, (3) to compare programs, (4) to identify educational needs and (5) to determine if objectives have been met. A brief look at Eisner's descriptions of these function follows:

1. To diagnose is to locate the sources of difficulties the student faces in learning.

2. To revise curricula is to determine educational consequences.

3. To compare programs is to decide educational policy.

4. To identify educational needs is to justify change.

5. To determine if objectives have been achieved is to receive feedback for revising curricula.

The most important function of evaluation, at this point, is for the purposes of curriculum revision.

In beginning the evaluation of a modified curriculum plan, the planner should be aware that he or she has, at various stages in developing the curriculum, already been engaged in an evaluation process. This includes evaluating the content and the aims of the curriculum through appraising the content selected and the aims formulated. This necessary part of the curriculum process lays the groundwork for translating content and goals into learning activities with the potential for leading to the consequences anticipated in the curricular objectives.

Moreover, by finding fault with an existing curriculum and seeking to construct new material which must be evaluated as to whether it is better than what was already there, curriculum designers have again engaged in a formative evaluation process. If the curriculum plan is field-tested while being developed the designer is, in addition, getting feedback from the learner and from other educators. Such feedback if fairly elaborate will also involve summative evaluation in the early testing of the plan in practice. In the feedback process the teacher is usually involved with colleagues who comment on the material as they see it.

A curriculum planner engaged in the process of evaluating the curriculum in terms of goals, objective tests, standards, and research is involved in what Robert Stake (1981) calls pre-ordinate evaluation. For Stake, this is a preliminary step to responsive evaluation which people do naturally in evaluating things, that is, they observe and react (Stake, 1981, p. 284). In Stake's opinion, educational evaluation is a responsive evaluation because it: (1) orients more to program activities than to program intents, (2) responds to audience requirements for information, and (3) offers a different evaluative prospective in reporting the results of an evaluation. Stake suggests teachers doing responsive evaluation should use observers to look at what is occurring, encourage observer comments, find out what the observers value, and use their ideas to gain a different point of view. The teacher also should get other teachers and school personnel to look at what is going on and provide them with relevant findings to help in their evaluations.

Stake views responsive evaluation as requiring both planning and structure, but with little emphasis on formal statements, charts and test scores and greater reliance on statements of objectives, hypothesis, and teaching syllabi. These become, in his view, not the basis for an evaluation plan but, rather, the components of an instructional plan. He suggests that the teacher begin with a study of issues, and then organize responses to the issues into a functional structure around twelve prominent events (see Figure 5.15).

Stake advocates, that the evaluator first discuss issues with program staff and other stakeholders in the school curriculum and then check the program's scope, activities, purposes and issues against the views of the stakeholders while sharing what information has been already gathered on the curriculum in practice. Reactions to these inputs will, according to Stake, enhance the teacher's communication skills and provide useful information for both responsive and pre-ordinate evaluation efforts.

Figure 5.15–Prominent events in a responsive evaluation

Talk with
clients, pro-
gram staff,
audiences

Assemble
formal reports,
if any

Identify
program
scope

Format for
audience use

Overview
program
activities

Winnow,
match issues
to audience

Discover
purposes,
concerns

Thematize;
prepare por-
trayals, case
studies

Conceptualize
issues,
problems

Observe
designated
antecedents
transactions
and outcomes

Select
observers,
judges, instru-
ments, if any

Identify
data needs,
re. issues

Note: From To evaluate an art program by R. Stake in *Foundations for curriculum development and evaluation in art education* (p. 288), G. Hardiman and T. Zernich, 1981, Illinois: Stipes Publishing. Copyright 1981. Reprinted with permission.

To interpret the inputs from these sources the planner also needs to
have some criteria for judging the group's responses to the curriculum in
practice. Ralph Thompson's six criteria (1981) are both useful and time-
tested. These criteria check the curriculum for its psychological validity,
social validity, philosophical validity, subject validity, political feasibility and technical adequacy.

Psychological Validity

Psychological validity according to Thompson asks whether the curriculum proposal accounts for human growth and development, learning, individual differences and the like. It raises the questions of *what* can be taught, *when* and *how* it can be taught and to *whom*. For example, in testing an art-as-general-education curriculum for its psychological validity, the most important question concerns whether the curricular design can effectively achieve the general education goals it supports. For an art-as-general-education curriculum that requires children to analyze, describe, interpret, judge, justify, evaluate, account and explain art, questions about whether such strategies do actually contribute to the child's intellectual growth need to be addressed.

Social Validity

Social validity in Thompson's view relates to whether a curricular proposal accounts for (a) the school as a social institution existing in a particular society and (b) the pupil as an inheritor of mores, social class roles, socialization patterns, technological shifts and the like. He notes many curricular proposals do not recognize the social factors necessary to motivate teachers, administrators and patrons to accept curricular change. The sociological factors to be met include technological change, pressure group power, and the philosophical and pedagogical differences among teachers. An art curriculum may lack social validity because the art teachers do not support it. They may feel that it does not evolve from art or from what they commonly accept as school art practice but, rather, from the minds of professional theorists. To be socially valid, a curriculum must come, if not directly from practice itself, at least through the advice and counsel of those who are actively and successfully involved in teaching art in the schools. Though such a curriculum may not always be logically consistent, it would at least contain the basic elements that art teachers themselves support in their own teaching-learning situations.

Philosophical Validity

Philosophical validity, according to Thompson, concerns whether a curricular proposal possesses internal consistency so that the ends and means relate to the fundamental premises inspiring the curriculum, and whether these premises support a reasonable conception of the good life. In his view, programs which emphasize the producer or the consumer's view of knowledge or insist on general studies or vocational studies may not be philosophically valid.

For an art curriculum to be philosophically valid, the means and ends of education need to be consistent with the means and ends of art. Art teachers who believe that art can never refer to anything outside of itself and does not come from reasoned argument, generally do not support statements of fact or scientific proof external to the work. Nor do they usually recognize purposes of art that include to display verisimilitude, argue political truths or speak for the public good.

Art teachers with a Gestalt point of view, tend to prefer a curriculum where the student is engaged in art making rather than in using words, statements, metaphors or other analogic means. From this viewpoint, the most effective approach would be to engage the student in describing, evaluating and making art as a single experience. This is similar to Dewey's (1934) belief that sensory satisfaction in a work of art cannot stand by itself but is, rather, linked to the processes used in its making.

Subject Validity

Subject validity in Thompson's view, asks whether the curriculum proposal in a given field provides for accurate and significant representation of the products of inquiry as well as the means of inquiry, to the end of serving truth. Here, Thompson notes that curriculum makers recommend toughness in lieu of thoroughness by selecting content and skills within the disciplines, rather than studying the products of the disciplines alone. In an art curriculum where the teacher is concerned with developing social skills and values rather than the skills and values necessary for art making, the answer to whether social skill development relates to the discipline of art or whether it is merely a study of the product or function of the discipline is not at issue. For those who view art as means toward developing personal identity, a socially centered curriculum is central to the art discipline, for those more concerned with art production it is not.

Political Feasibility

Thompson views political feasibility as being similar to social validity but more specifically answering questions about whether the curricular proposal satisfies the expectations of the various communities it must represent—local, regional and national—as well as the community of educated people of all time. He points out, however, that satisfying one of these communities may, at the same time, conflict with another and in this regard he notes the curriculum designer runs a narrow course between when to agree with popular opinion and when to run counter to it.

When the expectations of teachers, administrators, students and parents are focused mostly on art production, art class outcomes are seen to be the production of art objects and the acquisition of factual art knowledge. In such a program the school's stakeholders do not view the art class as a debating society or a mechanism for teaching values clarification but rather as a place where students learn about art and art making rather than about Science, English, Social Studies and the like. Moreover, these stakeholders expect students to show progress in their creative self-expression and perhaps, even later, an improvement in their abilities to go on to advanced study and performance in the discipline.

Technical Adequacy

Technical adequacy, Thompson's last criteria, asks whether the curricular proposal adequately provides for instructional materials and techniques, preparation of teachers, and the like. It is not enough in Thompson's view to suggest newer techniques or approaches to instruction and not at the same time prepare teachers, to use newer materials and resources. Teachers, he notes, can rarely, if ever, extrapolate from nothing, and unless more up to date means and media are available, the curriculum birthing bed can, in his view, become its death bed.

To plan a new curriculum where the majority of instructional time will be spent on the teaching of art history and criticism and where the past emphasis had been almost exclusively on studio instruction requires that consideration be given to the retraining of teachers and to the acquiring of funds for new teaching materials, equipment and visual resources. Art teachers generally know and are most thoroughly trained to use a studio approach as the principal mode of art instruction. To change to a curriculum that emphasizes teaching art history and criticism most assuredly will require the re-education of the teachers and a thorough evaluation of the instructional materials and equipment needed to support such teaching. Concerns about whether the school can afford to build a new slide library, hire slide librarians, and obtain the projectors, television monitors, screens and darkening equipment needed are all relevant and important to establishing such a curriculum.

Summary

This chapter suggests some approaches the reader might consider to: (1) clarify or discover his or her own personal philosophy and educational values, (2) analyze existing curricula to see if it shares some of these values, and (3) develop a newer curriculum and begin to test it in a classroom. However, if in the process the reader ends up being disappointed to find that the ball has been left in his or her court, this is as it should be, that is, in the hands of the curriculum player rather than in the mind of the theorist.

Much more could be said about any and all of the matters touched on in this chapter. Readers wanting to know more (the majority I hope) can consult, in greater depth, a number of the sources already cited, including Elliot Eisner's *The Education Imagination* (1985), Maurice Barrett's *Art Education: A Strategy for Course Design* (1979), Connelly and Clandinin's *Teachers as Curriculum Planners* (1988), and Arthur Efland's Planning Art Education in the Middle/Secondary Schools of Ohio (1977). These and other sources referred to in this Chapter should offer many more helpful ideas teachers can use in the art curriculum planning process.

Conclusion

In ending this examination of how various scholars have thought about the nature of both life and art, I am hopeful there is also a new beginning for the reader. This new beginning can take the form of a second look at some of the more heady stuff presented in the sections on philosophy or aesthetics and at the critical analysis of existing art theory in conjunction with the reader's thinking about art, education and schooling. Hopefully, this new beginning will lead to a never ending search for greater understanding of the matters only briefly touched on here—matters and ideas which can effectively consume a lifetime of study and thought.

Put more simply, if through this discourse, the reader ends up knowing something more than what they started out with in the beginning, the effort was worthwhile and particularly so if the reader now feels he or she does know something more about their own personal beliefs, about the beliefs of others in their profession and about the need for their personal involvement in the art curriculum planning process.

Art in education is intelligent activity; that is what this book was about. Thinking about and making art has more to do with aesthetic conception than with the so-called art disciplines, and such conceptions are useful in defining the school art curriculum as a unified concept. Most of all, this text was also about the value of teachers having values and about using these values to decide what to do in the art classroom. Art education is then not about slogans and movements, but about art teachers themselves assuming their rightful responsibilities as school art curriculum developers.

References

Barrett, M. (1979). *Art education: A strategy for course design*. London: Heinemann Educational Books.

Bloom, B. (Ed.), Englehart, M., Furst, E., Hill W., Krathwohl, D. Taxonomy of Educational objectives: Handbook. Cognitive domain. New York: David McKay.

Bruner, J. (1960). *The process of education*. Cambridge, MA: Harvard University Press.

Chapman, L. (1985). Curriculum development as process and product. *Studies in Art Education, 24*(4), 206-211.

Ciganko, R. (1992). Creating realities: Curriculum and the teacher. *Art Education, 45*(3), 54-60.

College Entrance Examination Board. (1985). *Academic preparation for college: What students need to know and be able to do*. New York: Author.

Connelly, F., & Clandinin, D. (1988). *Teachers as curriculum planners*, New York: Teachers College Press.

Dewey, J. (1910). *How we think*. Lexington, MA: Heath.

Dewey, J. (1934). *Art as experience*. New York: G.P. Putnam's Sons.

Efland, A. *(1977)*. Planning Art Education in the Middle/Secondary Schools of Ohio. Columbus: Ohio Department of Education.

Eisner, E. (1985). *The education imagination on the design and evaluation of school programs*. New York: MacMillan Publishing Co.

Foshay, A.W. (1969). Curriculum. In R.I. Edel (Ed.), *Encyclopedia of Educational Research Association* (4th ed, pp. 5-119). New York: MacMillan.

Gagne, R. (1964). The acquisition of knowledge. In J. P. DeCecco (Ed.), *Educational Technology* (pp. 115-1 31). New York: Holt, Rinehart and Winston.

Hausman, J. (1974). Mapping as an approach to curriculum planning. *Curriculum Theory Network, 4*(2), 192-203.

Lanier, V. (1986). The fourth domain: Building a new art curriculum. *Studies in Art Education, 28*(1), 5-10.

Marschalek, D. (1989). A new approach to curriculum development in environmental design. *Art Education, 42*(4), 8-17.

Smith, P. (1989). A modest proposal for using ingredients at hand to make an art curriculum. *Art Education, 42*(6), 9-15.

Stake, R. (1981). To evaluate an art program. In G. Hardiman, & T. Zernich, (Eds.), *Foundations for curriculum development and evaluation in art education*. Champaign, IL: Stipes Publishing Co.

Sullivan, G. (1989). Curriculum in art education: The uncertainty principle. *Studies in Art Education, 30*(4), 225-235.

Taba, H. (1962). *Curriculum development: Theory and practice*. New York: Harcourt Brace and World.

Thompson, R. (1981). *General Criteria for Curriculum Analysis*. In G. Hardiman, & T. Zernich (Eds.), *Foundations for curriculum development and evaluation in art education*. Champaign, IL: Stipes Publishing Co.

Tyler, R. (1950). *Basic principles of curriculum instruction*. Chicago: University of Chicago Press.